THE COLLECTED PLAYS OF HARLEY GRANVILLE-BARKER

VOLUME I

The Marrying of Ann Leete
The Voysey Inheritance
Rococo

Other plays in this series by

HARLEY GRANVILLE-BARKER

VOLUME II

Waste
The Madras House
Vote by Ballot

VOLUME III

Secret Life
His Majesty
Farewell to the Theatre

The Collected Plays of
Harley Granville-Barker

VOLUME I

The Marrying of Ann Leete
The Voysey Inheritance
Rococo

FOREWORD BY J. B. PRIESTLEY

INTRODUCTIONS BY IVOR BROWN

SIDGWICK & JACKSON
LONDON

This edition published 1967

"The Marrying of Ann Leete" was first
published in 1909
by Sidgwick and Jackson Ltd
"The Voysey Inheritance" was first published
in 1909
Revised in 1913 and again in 1934
by Sidgwick and Jackson Ltd
"Rococo" was first published in 1917
by Sidgwick and Jackson Ltd

Printed in the Republic of Ireland by
Hely Thom Ltd., Dublin
for Sidgwick and Jackson Ltd
1 Tavistock Chambers
Bloomsbury Way
London, W.C.1

CONTENTS

FOREWORD   9
    by J. B. Priestley

HARLEY GRANVILLE-BARKER   11
    by Ivor Brown

INTRODUCTION TO THE PLAYS   23
    by Ivor Brown

The Marrying of Ann Leete   27

The Voysey Inheritance   89

Rococo   181

NOTE

FOREWORD

First, I must congratulate the publishers on their decision to give us a collected edition of Granville-Barker's plays and to ask Ivor Brown to write the various Introductions. Granville-Barker has always seemed to me one of the oddest figures in that gallery of odd figures, the English Theatre. Consider his history. Before he was thirty he had succeeded brilliantly as an actor, a producer, and, if less obviously, as a dramatist. (His most successful and perhaps his strongest play, *The Voysey Inheritance*, was the work of his middle twenties.) Yet this dazzling theatrical prodigy spent the latter part of his life almost entirely outside the Theatre, translating Spanish plays that were not as good as his own, and apparently content to turn himself—or so it seemed to me when I met him—into a disappointingly dull and rather donnish figure. There is something equally odd about him as a dramatist.

He came to writing through acting and producing, and so we might reasonably expect from him plays easy and economical to stage. But not a bit of it. All his more ambitious plays share the same weakness, one usually associated with poets and novelists trying to write for the stage—they ask for too many sets and too many players, so that they are expensive both to produce and to keep running. (Even his stage directions often suggest a novelist and not a former actor and producer.) And quite apart from costs—and here I write as a dramatist—his most interesting plays might have been improved by some pruning of scenes and characters. Yet he is undoubtedly one of the most original, intelligent and sensitive English dramatists of this century, who often takes Shavian themes but scores them for an orchestra and not for Shaw's military band. And now that we have generously subsidized theatrical companies, which can afford his elaborate sets and long cast lists, there is no longer any excuse for neglecting him. I hope this collected edition will help to give Granville-Barker the place he deserves to occupy in our Theatre.

J. B. PRIESTLEY

HARLEY GRANVILLE-BARKER
by Ivor Brown

Harley Granville Barker was born in London on 25th November, 1877. He was known as Granville Barker during his most active years in the theatre. The hyphen came after his second marriage.

His father was an architect whose income was never large. His mother, from whose side of the family came a strain of Italian blood, was a professional entertainer, sometimes acting in plays, sometimes reciting and displaying her skill as a bird-mimic. Her son, though not featured as an Infant Phenomenon, was very early on the stage. Dressed in a sailor suit, he recited "The Boy Stood on the Burning Deck", and similar pieces; he was promoted to delivering Shakespearian extracts.

The amount and locality of his education are uncertain. But he soon became an eager reader and his later and fully realized ambition was to be a scholar of the theatre and a writer of distinction. His aims were achieved. He was awarded an Honorary Doctorate of Edinburgh University. He was President of the Royal Literary Society in 1928. When speaking on public platforms and to academic audiences in British and American Universities he brought a brilliance of method and freshness of matter. If he resented his lack of orthodox schooling he had his compensation when he withdrew from popular theatrical practice to his desk in Devonshire and to his warmly welcomed appearances on the dais.

Unlike Bernard Shaw, at one time his close friend and colleague in the creation of the New Drama, he was an early starter. Until he was nearly forty Bernard Shaw's name was little known outside some small Socialist groups: at thirty Barker had established himself as a fine actor in a certain range of parts, as a producer who put new and vivid life into any play he directed, and as a playwright of unusual quality.

The best of his work in the performance and production of plays had been done before the outbreak of the European war in August, 1914, when he was not yet thirty-seven. The war devastated the English theatre as well as Europe. The urgent, disturbing, socially committed type of play in which Shaw and

Barker were the joint masters of writing and presentation had never been widely popular. That kind of drama became completely unwanted. When London was a lodging-house for soldiers on leave, moving between life and death, only the escape provided by Show Business with the lightest and gayest entertainment was required and that prospered richly.

For Barker it had so far been a restless, quick-moving career. At thirteen he was a member of a troupe of juvenile actors. At fourteen he was a pupil of Sarah Thorne's dramatic academy at the Theatre Royal, Margate, a seed-bed of many talents. He went on tour as Paris in *Romeo and Juliet* with the Thorne Company in which the Juliet was the beautiful Evelyn Millard whom he was subsequently to cast as Olivia in a notable production of *Twelfth Night* in 1912. He played small parts on various tours and in London. As he read, thought, and matured he found the ordinary type of popular play distasteful and the English theatre wretchedly inadequate in its use of its talents and lack of social purpose. He was happier amid the activities of Ben Greet, in whose far-wandering company he first met his future wife, Lillah McCarthy, and of William Poel who defied the conventions of the time, staged Shakespeare without scenery, and had strong personal opinions about the speaking of verse. Neither of these men had money to spend and then there were no State endowments for such enterprise. It was a hard and needy life which demanded the devotion of those who faced it. But there were good training and good chances to follow.

Poel gave Barker the opportunity to play the title-part in *Richard II* when he was not yet eighteen. This took place in the Lecture Room at Burlington House, where there was no warmth of a theatre atmosphere. A. B. Walkley, the critic of *The Times*, saw him and praised "the pathos that seemed to touch every section of his rather difficult audience." He later shone in the parts of distressed, neurotic men, such as Marlowe's Edward II and Eugene Marchbanks in Shaw's *Candida*. Shaw said that this was the best Eugene in his experience.

He was as eager to write as to act. In 1895 he collaborated in two plays with an actor called Berte Thomas, but in neither case could they find a manager to stage them. Their third piece, *The Weather-Hen*, after a trial matinée in June, 1899, was given the chance of a run at the Comedy Theatre in July. It was not a success, but two critics, once more A. B. Walkley and also St. John Hankin, praised it as fresh and stimulating. It was never

printed. Barker was not discouraged and he took a place in "the
intellectual theatre" when *The Marrying of Ann Leete*, all his own
work, was given by the Stage Society in January, 1902. His usual
champion, Walkley, was disappointed and found it weak in
construction, incoherent, and confused.

Amid the worries and privations of finding work as an actor
Barker was determined to be an innovator. He wanted to produce
plays. (Now plays are spoken of as directed, but during most of
his life the director had been a producer and will be so called in
this brief biography.) In the theatre of the nineteen-hundreds the
actor-manager was sovereign and usually produced his plays to
suit himself with the aid of a competent stage-manager. But in
Europe the producer had arrived as a third party to the play,
interpreting the dramatist, supervising the staging, and schooling
the players. Barker established the status and proved the value of
the producer in this country.

His great opportunity came at the small Court Theatre in
Sloane Square where, with the favouring interest of a manager,
J. H. Leigh, and with the ability in administration of J. E.
Vedrenne, a series of mid-week matinées was introduced in 1904.
The capital investment was tiny; the dividend in the vitality
brought to the English theatre was incalculable.

A start came with Gilbert Murray's translation of Euripides'
Hippolytus which attracted some attention. Box-office success and
wider repute came with Shaw's *John Bull's Other Island* which
drew good houses, was much talked about in high places, and
was seen with great approval by the Prime Minister, A. J. Balfour,
and two leaders of the Liberal Opposition, Sir Henry Campbell-
Bannerman and Mr. Asquith. The Barker-Vedrenne seasons
were now on the playgoer's map and stayed there for three years.

Barker had been meeting influential people of congenial tastes.
Acquaintance ripened into friendship. Chief among his advisers
and colleagues were William Archer, the dramatic critic and
Ibsenite, and Gilbert Murray, a Greek scholar in particular, a
humanist in general, and an inspiring personality. Closest to him
was Shaw, now nearly fifty, abounding in vigour, and at last
accepted as a playwright by more than a small minority. G.B.S.
knew the value of Barker's handling and casting of his plays and
also of his performance in them. Among the famous Shavian
parts played by Barker at the Court Theatre were Keegan in
John Bull's Other Island, Valentine in *You Never Can Tell*, John
Tanner in *Man and Superman*, Adolphus Cusins in *Major Barbara*

and Dubedat in *The Doctors' Dilemma*. He did not produce the
pieces in which he appeared, but no doubt he had much to do
with the general presentation.

New dramatists were naturally eager to enjoy the privilege of
a Barker production and there were several important discoveries.
Among them was the novelist John Galsworthy, not previously
a playwright. His poignant treatment of legal injustice in *The
Silver Box*, produced in 1906, immediately attracted attention.
John Masefield was another of the new playwrights devoted to
Barker. The Court, where evening runs of several weeks became
possible while the experimental matinées continued, was a fertile
centre of the New Drama with its mixture of social realism,
poetry, and almost everything not to be found in the routine of
West End entertainment. Barker also fascinated ambitious young
actors who were not thinking of their salaries because they knew
that he could bring out the best in them. He communicated the
light in his own eyes; his instruction was technically skilful as
well as an inspiration. As a trainer he worked them hard and
could be firm with courtesy. To be rehearsed by him was a
quickening experience, a "lift" as well as a lesson.

Despite the burden and strain of these busy years he found time
to continue as a playwright himself. He took his time. He dated
the writing of *The Voysey Inheritance* as 1903–5 and of *Waste* as
1906–7. He had collaborated in 1904 with Laurence Housman
in the delightful fantasy *Prunella, or Love in a Dutch Garden*. It was
produced at the Court as a Christmas entertainment but
disappointingly drew most unrewarding audiences. That
theatre's public evidently wanted sterner stuff.

Among the actresses who made a name during Court seasons
was the dark and handsome Lillah McCarthy who was partic-
ularly effective in strong dynamic roles and in the Gilbert
Murray versions of Greek Tragedy. She and Barker married in
April, 1906. They spent their honeymoon in Germany and the
Tyrol. It was a marriage of true minds. Their thoughts and
talents went together. When he over-worked, which was often,
she was a devoted warden of his welfare. During the ten years of
their union they were the best of companions and joined cordially
in any company of colleagues or of friends outside the theatre who
shared their zest for life and crusading spirit.

A new phase was opened in 1906 with the ending of the work
at the Court. Barker, his methods, his authors, and his most
trusted players were promoted to West End ranking. The Savoy

was the playhouse rented with Shaw's financial backing. (It cost him three thousand pounds in the end, a fact which contradicts some later unjust complaint that he never put his winnings back into nourishing theatrical enterprise.) The policy was one of short runs and experimental mid-week matinées. It did not appeal. Galsworthy's poor play *Joy* was a total loss and the season petered out.

Meanwhile Barker was devoting himself to theatrical campaigns and also working with the Socialist Fabian Society in which Shaw was the leading public figure helping to make it intellectually fashionable. Both men advocated the creation and endowment of a National Theatre whose repertory would have a quality and dignity well above the general level of the Edwardian stage and its commercially viable entertainments. He also joined the battle for the ending or mending of the Stage Censorship. Owing to the banning of his own play *Waste* he had a personal grievance as well as a general argument for challenging the dominion of the Lord Chamberlain and his officials whose vetoes were then of a most absurd and frustrating kind.

In 1909 J. M. Barrie helped to persuade the American manager, Charles Frohman, to back a repertory season in London with Barker in charge. The experiment was made at the Duke of York's Theatre in February of the following year. It began with John Galsworthy's *Justice*, a tragedy of modern English life, a play with a purpose powerfully demonstrating the cruelty of solitary confinement in prisons. Barker's production was masterly and Galsworthy was at his best. It drew the attention of the Home Office, as intended. But the effect on the expectant public was dispiriting. Was this to be a theatre only of high purpose and deep gloom?

Audiences were not re-assured by Shaw's contribution, *Misalliance*, which had its Shavian liveliness of wit but lacked the interest of a plot. The author himself described it as "a debate in one sitting". Some critics were severe and there was resentment that a cast of gifted players should be turned into a Discussion Group. Another important item was Barker's production of his own play *The Madras House*. It was also conversational, brilliantly so, but not dramatic as drama was then understood. Despite some lighter contributions to the repertory, the financial losses were mounting. On the death of King Edward VII in June all theatrical business in London fell away and Frohman, who could be justly proud of his association with the leading producer of the time, called a halt.

2

It was a blow, but the Barkers had a happy move in the following year to the gracious Little Theatre in the Adelphi, which was "blitzed" in the 1940–45 war and not replaced. They had a flat above it and made it a charming niche of civilized theatre, always a pleasure to enter. Barker first directed some of the "Anatol" short plays by Arthur Schnitzler which he had adapted and in which he acted. Next came Ibsen's *The Master Builder* with Lillah as Hilda Wangel and then Shaw's light and lively *Fanny's First Play*. This proved immensely popular, gave G.B.S. his first long run in the West End, and evoked his comment that "The New Drama has found its 'Charley's Aunt' ".

While this was running on there was time for two productions at the Kingsway Theatre. Then came an opportunity which the Barkers, especially Lillah, had long coveted. They could play Shakespeare as they wanted. With the generous backing of Lord Lucas they were in command at the Savoy Theatre in September, 1912, with a complete freedom to plan and practise as they chose. The policy was to play a full text, to cut down scenery, scene changes, and frequent intervals, to cut out traditional "comic business", and to have the lines spoken rapidly with no loss of clarity. An apron stage was used and the décor of an uncluttered stage was simple in form, striking in colour, and brilliantly lit. There was no thought of novelty to attract attention and display cleverness, that fatal temptation to young producers of familiar classics. Barker rejected the bare boards favoured by his old master, William Poel. He would not be a nudist since that was neither good theatre nor good history. The Elizabethan teams had spent lavishly on costumes. So at the Savoy eye and ear were both well served. The achievement might be called "Shakespeare set free".

People accustomed to the massed canvas and crowds of Beerbohm Tree's Shakespearian "spectaculars" found this liberation to be something of a shock. Norman Wilkinson's settings for *The Winter's Tale*, the opening piece, and *Twelfth Night* appealed intensely to those ready for a new vision of Shakespeare. So did Barker's productions. But those unready for the new look complained of disconcerting as well as novel aspects and of diction much speedier than was usual. Unqualified praise came from the devotees of Barker. *The Winter's Tale* was admired by the passionate few and not visited by many, but *Twelfth Night* was well supported.

At the end of 1912 and in the following year he had several

productions at the Kingsway Theatre, including Galsworthy's *The Eldest Son* and Arnold Bennett's *The Great Adventure*. The latter turned out to be a Marathon runner. Bennett had become established as author and journalist. In his casting and coaching Barker had used and disciplined Henry Ainley's theatrical bravura and magnificence of voice and looks for Shakespeare at the Savoy. Now he taught that romantic actor to bring a quietly fascinating realism to the character of a shy and famous painter who pretended to be dead in order to escape the pressures of fame. During his productive years there were many players who were raised to a higher power by his animating influence and were diminished by his absence.

Before returning to Shakespeare Barker produced Shaw's new classical-comical piece *Androcles and the Lion* with Lillah in the part of Lavinia which the author had written with her in mind. Here was another success, carrying Barker to the summit of his reputation. In 1914 he came back to the Savoy to present *A Midsummer Night's Dream*. Again there was further liberation from tradition. Old English music replaced Mendelssohn and the clowns won their laughter in new ways. A great fuss was made about the golden faces of the fairies in the Athenian woods. It was a detail. There were more important changes and beauties to remember.

The war came in August. Only levity was wanted to relieve the strain of waiting for news of battle and the appalling casualty lists. *A Little Bit of Fluff* was a typical title and early playhouse victory. Barker could not compete in that market. He offered a stage version of Thomas Hardy's *The Dynasts* at the Kingsway. It was relevant to the atmosphere of conflict but it could not largely please. In January and February of 1915 Lillah accompanied him to New York where he initiated a repertory season at the Wallack Theatre with two Shavian and one Shakespearian production. The American audiences were unused to repertory and preferred one play at a time.

Barker felt a call to the war. He went to France with the Red Cross and in 1916, although nearly forty, entered a Royal Artillery Cadet School. When commissioned he was intelligently assigned to Intelligence and his duties took him back to America, where he had already met Mrs. Helen Huntington, his future second wife. He became deeply attached to her during his second visit while Lillah was in England. After a divorce they were married in London in July, 1918. This did not entirely end his work in the London theatres. He produced a version of *The Romantic Young Lady* by the Spanish dramatist Sierra in 1920 and Maeterlinck's *The Betrothal* in 1921. Thenceforward authorship, translation, and lecturing were to be his occupation. He was now the mentor of the English theatre, wise in counsel but no longer the dynamic conductor of rehearsals.

The breach of the marriage had been heart-breaking for Lillah who continued to hope that her husband would return to her. Shaw and Barrie were reluctantly involved as her counsellors. The embarrassments and sufferings which these negotiations caused are well described and documented in C. B. Purdom's biography *Harley Granville-Barker*. Archer Huntington, a lover of Spanish art and inheritor of a fortune, was Helen's second husband. He did not want the separation for which she asked, but magnanimously allowed her to obtain a divorce for desertion. Lillah demanded restitution of conjugal rights according to the legal formula. There was no response and she was granted a divorce. She soon left the stage and married Professor Keeble, later knighted, a prominent biologist at Oxford.

"Do'ant thou marry for munny, but goa where munny is" was the advice of Tennyson's Northern Farmer. Barker did not re-marry with a financial motive: he was genuinely attracted by Helen who genuinely but too possessively adored him. She could not endure Shaw and caused a complete and deplorable break in the old and happy alliance. She was a minor poetess and novelist who knew Spanish and admired the arts of Spain. Although several years his senior she charmed and held him. She could take pride in her new role, wife to a genius, rescuing him from the wearing theatrical routine of a producer, and bringing him all the comforts of an English country-house and a flat in Paris. Thus he would be able to relax, write plays and books, and win academic regard. There was no lack of money. (Huntington had treated Helen with generosity.)

The prospect was congenial to Barker, who is said to have mapped out his life some time before; he was to spend ten years as an actor, ten years as a producer, and ten years as a writer. The last ten did in fact become more than twenty. But his kind of writing would not provide a substantial income. With his new marriage he would have time and room for unworried reflection and composition. He did not marry for "munny" but he went where "munny" was.

There were inevitably those who regarded him as a lost leader of the English stage and resented what they deemed to be a desertion. But when he left his theatre work-shop for the study he worked with great application at the desk. His series of Prefaces to Shakespeare, illuminating guides to producers as well as readers, are unique in their mingling of scholarship with stage-experience. It is a pity that he covered only ten plays, but they are covered in detail, and remain a constant source of light and leading to producers who have the sense to study them.

He wrote two full-length plays of his own, *The Secret Life* and *His Majesty*. With Helen he made numerous translations or adaptations of Spanish plays by Gregorio Martinez Sierra and by Sérafin and Joaquin Alvarez Quintero. He himself made versions from the French, *Debureau* by Sacha Guitry, and *Doctor Knock* and *Six Gentlemen in a Row* by Jules Romains. When, as London dramatic critic of the *Manchester Guardian*, I added to a favourable notice of one of the Spanish comedies a mild complaint that this was not good enough for the greatest producer and an important dramatist of the English theatre at the time, he protested to the Editor, C. P. Scott, that it was not a critic's business to arrange his career. That was fair enough, but he was obviously sensitive to any suggestion of misdirected labour. Possibly Helen prompted his letter. She wanted him to remain above the playhouse battle and not to rejoin the stress of preparation and production.

Certainly he was determined to be a good citizen. Taking chairs and presiding over committees is no idle form of session. Barker was the first and very active Chairman of the Council of the British Drama League founded in 1919. He was President of the Shakespeare Association in 1930 and with G. B. Harrison edited *A Companion to Shakespeare Studies* to which he contributed an essay of his own on "Shakespeare's Dramatic Art". His colleague found him "a perfectionist", carefully suggesting amendments to the work of other hands and constantly polishing and revising his own. He was a frequent contributor to academic and theatrical publications. Welcome in the Universities, he lectured in England and America on many platforms. He was abundantly busy in the kind of work which he had chosen for his years of middle age.

He did make occasional, rather furtive, returns to the rehearsal and staging of plays. He would not have his name on the programme, but he took great pains to assist the production by Michael Macowan of the re-written text of *Waste* at the Westminster Theatre in 1936. He zealously co-operated in a

presentation of *King Lear* at the Old Vic Theatre in April,
stipulating that Lewis Casson's name, not his, should be cr
on the programme. When he returned to Helen in Pari
soon found that France was in peril, defeat, and chaos.
made their way to Spain, Portugal, and the U.S.A. wh
worked with the British Information Service and was v
lecturer at Harvard and Princeton Universities.

They returned to England in May, 1945. He was now
seven and his health was failing. They were in Paris wh
died suddenly on 31st August, 1946. The fatal illness was
nosed as arterio-sclerosis. Helen lived till February, 195
was buried beside him in the cemetery of Père Lachaise.

He had kept the proposed pattern of his life. This dist
those who would have had him always in the harness
producer, but he could claim to have done what he inte
The legacy of his early seasons at the Court and later w
central playhouses was a quickening and expansion of the E
theatre. In his ideas and their execution he was a radical re
and not one of those "far-out" revolutionaries who mal
headlines with reckless and sometimes fatuous experimen
lived before the time of the press-agent who speciali
"promotion" and getting names into the papers. Barke
determined to do sensible new things in a sensibly new wa
did not seek to be "news".

He was incapable of doing or writing anything dull. M
experience of his vivacity was that of a school boy attenc
meeting of an Ethical Society whose members tempered
rationalism by singing secular hymns. I saw a notice that I
would be the lecturing attraction. That, I thought, woulc
the strain of agnostic uplift. He came to speak about !
quoting and reciting some Shavian speeches. I was alre
Shavian, but this was double value. On the platform he be
a theatre in himself. For this he may have got five guinea
nothing. For me it was an unforgettable hour, beyond pri

While working in the theatre as actor, author, and pro
his industry was unquenchable but he did not let routine
him rusty. In conducting rehearsals he was never a drill-ser
He was strict without severity and was liked, even love
those whom he enlivened while he schooled them. They re
how richly he could create the background of a play wh
drove into the heart of it. My wife, who had a small part wh
produced Galsworthy's *The Eldest Son*, spoke to me much la

a scene in the home of the girl whom she played. I pointed
at there was no such scene. Barker had created the home
imagination with such vividness that she believed it must
re in the text.

:n the National Theatre, whose future he had helped to
nd to promote, is at last built there should be a tablet to
emory of Granville-Barker. All drama was his province.
s a supreme interpreter of Shakespeare in practice and on
while he injected a new life into the plays and players of
te.

INTRODUCTION TO
PLAYS IN VOLUME I
by Ivor Brown

1. THE MARRYING OF ANN LEETE

The Marrying of Ann Leete was produced by Barker for the Stage Society on 26th January, 1902, when he was twenty-four. That was a private performance limited to members. The play never had a London run: the text was not published until 1907 and then it was five times reprinted within five years. The author's name was established and obviously attractive to the advanced amateur groups and play-readers.

The events occur in a country house in late Georgian England. The speech is modern; there is no attempt at a period style. Barker was evidently so eager to avoid the obvious that the talk is sometimes confusing, even puzzling. There are twenty characters and one must read or listen closely to distinguish their relationships and functions in the play. It was the work of a clever young man who was not afraid of being difficult in his desire to be different.

Ann Leete anticipates Shaw's Ann Whitefield of *Man and Superman*, first published in 1903, by firmly deciding on the man whom she means to marry and marching him to the altar. He is quite poor, a simple and humble young gardener, obedient to all orders, including the command to wed. The Leetes, wealthy, sophisticated Georgian types with a foot in politics, are shocked, but Ann, who brings no dowry with her, is ready to be a floor-scrubbing wife, sharing labour as well as love in a cottage.

Here was a change indeed. At that time "costume plays" were usually of the romantic kind. Barker would have none of that. He rejected "tushery" in his crisp, colloquial dialogue. He substituted a "New Woman" who knows her mind for the conventional heroines who were wooed and won by an attractive gallant of their own class. He was original in his ideas but he had not yet the technical ability to give his play effective form. But it is fascinating to follow his attempt to present an almost Ibsenite woman in the Georgian world.

2. THE VOYSEY INHERITANCE

The Voysey Inheritance was written between 1903 and 1905 and produced by Barker himself at the Court Theatre in November of the latter year. It was enthusiastically received and in the next sixty years was six times revived in various London theatres with various lengths of run. "Let there be nothing but praise", wrote Max Beerbohm, Shaw's successor as dramatic critic of *The Saturday Review*. No other play of Barker's has had such critical acclaim and such a popular appeal.

The theme remains urgent and relevant to family and business life. The problem facing its central figure, Edward Voysey, is one which the passing of time does not affect. The trusted family solicitor who gambles with family estates committed to his care is still occasionally exposed and brought into court. The well-established Voysey firm seem to be the essence of solid respectability, but when Edward's father dies he learns the bitter facts of fraudulent practice. He is the heir to dishonesty and possibly to imminent disaster. He is a man of high principle. Is he to go on covering up the deceit and replacing the losses with his own honourable labour?

Edward's brothers, one a successful barrister, one an Army officer, one a wayward artist, the mother, and the stay-at-home sister are vividly drawn. Old George Booth, a crusty, close-fisted friend of the family whose funds are in danger is another excellent character. So is Peacey, the lawyer's clerk who has known and kept the ugly secret—at a price.

The dialogue is natural, keen in humour when the opportunity occurs and has none of the strain to provide unnaturally clever conversation which sometimes appeared in Barker's later plays. When he wrote of Ann Leete he seemed eager to be elusive. In this case he was making no intellectual gesture; he wrote for the ordinary play-goer who wanted a story well told and was given an inside view of one of those seemingly substantial and happy English homes whose foundations were by no means what they seemed.

3. Rococo

Apart from his translations and co-operations, Barker wrote three one-act plays, first published in 1917. The earliest of these, *Rococo*, was dated 1912. That an English clergyman's home should be his battle-field is unusual and here is Barker in unusually high spirits as he conducts in comical-farcical style a family squabble about a hideous vase through domestic rough-and-tumble.

THE MARRYING OF ANN LEETE

A comedy in four acts

E MARRYING OF ANN LEETE

THE FIRST ACT

three acts of the comedy pass in the garden at Markswayde, MR.
ARNABY LEETE's house near Reading, during a summer day
wards the close of the eighteenth century: the first act at four in
he morning, the second shortly after mid-day, the third near to
unset. The fourth act takes place one day in the following winter;
he first scene in the hall at Markswayde, the second scene in a
ottage some ten miles off.

of the Markswayde garden looks to have been laid out during the
eventeenth century. In the middle a fountain; the centrepiece the
gure of a nymph, now somewhat cracked, and pouring nothing
rom the amphora; the rim of the fountain is high enough and
road enough to be a comfortable seat.

turf around is in parts worn bare. This plot of ground is sur-
ounded by a terrace three feet higher. Three sides of it are seen.
rom two corners broad steps lead down; stone urns stand at the
ottom and top of the stone balustrades. The other two corners are
ounded convexly into broad stone seats.

edges of the terrace are growing rose trees, close together; behind
hese, paths; behind those, shrubs and trees. No landscape is to be
en. A big copper beech overshadows the seat on the left. A silver
irch droops over the seat on the right. The trees far to the left
dicate an orchard, the few to the right are more of the garden sort.
is the height of summer, and after a long drought the rose trees
re dilapidated.

dark in the garden. Though there may be by now a faint morning
ght in the sky it has not penetrated yet among these trees. It is
ery still, too. Now and then the leaves of a tree are stirred, as if
its sleep; that is all. Suddenly a shrill, frightened, but not tragical
ream is heard. After a moment ANN LEETE runs quickly down
e steps and on to the fountain, where she stops, panting. LORD
HN CARP follows her, but only to the top of the steps, evidently
t knowing his way. ANN is a girl of twenty; he an English
ntleman, nearer forty than thirty.

29

LORD JOHN. I apologise.

ANN. Why is it so dark?

LORD JOHN. Can you hear what I'm saying?

ANN. Yes.

LORD JOHN. I apologise for having kissed you . . . almost unintentionally.

ANN. Thank you. Mind the steps down.

LORD JOHN. I hope I'm sober, but the air . . .

ANN. Shall we sit for a minute? There are several seats to sit on somewhere.

LORD JOHN. This is a very dark garden.

> *There is a slight pause.*

ANN. You've won your bet.

LORD JOHN. So you did scream!

ANN. But it wasn't fair.

LORD JOHN. Don't reproach me.

ANN. Somebody's coming.

LORD JOHN. How d'you know?

ANN. I can hear somebody coming.

LORD JOHN. We're not sitting down.

> ANN's *brother,* GEORGE LEETE *comes to the top of the steps, and afterwards down them. Rather an old young man.*

GEORGE. Ann!

ANN. Yes.

GEORGE. My lord!

LORD JOHN. Here.

GEORGE. I can't see you. I'm sent to say we're all anxious to know what ghost or other bird of night or beast has frightened Ann to screaming point, and won you . . . the best in Tatton's stables—so he says now. He's quite annoyed.

LORD JOHN. The mare is a very good mare.

ANN. He betted it because he wanted to bet it; I didn't want him to bet it.

GEORGE. What frightened her?

ANN. I had rather, my lord, that you did not tell my brother why I screamed.

LORD JOHN. I kissed her.

GEORGE. Did you?

ANN. I had rather, Lord John, that you had not told my brother why I screamed.

LORD JOHN. I misunderstood you.

GEORGE. I've broke up the whist party. Ann, shall we return?

LORD JOHN. She's not here.

GEORGE. Ann.

> LADY COTTESHAM, ANN'S *sister and ten years older, and* MR.
> DANIEL TATTON, *a well-living, middle-aged country gentleman,*
> *arrive together.* TATTON *carries a double candlestick. . . the lights*
> *out.*

MR. TATTON. Three steps?

SARAH. No . . . four.

LORD JOHN. Miss Leete.

> TATTON *in the darkness finds himself close to* GEORGE.

MR. TATTON. I am in a rage with you, my lord.

GEORGE. He lives next door.

MR. TATTON. My mistake. [*He passes on*]. Confess that she did
it to please you.

LORD JOHN. Screamed!

MR. TATTON. Lost my bet. We'll say . . . won your bet . . . to
please you. Was skeered at the dark . . . oh, fie!

LORD JOHN. Miss Leete trod on a toad.

MR. TATTON. I barred toads . . . here.

LORD JOHN. I don't think it.

MR. TATTON. I barred toads. Did I forget to? Well . . . it's better
to be a sportsman.

SARAH. And whereabout is she?

ANN [*from the corner she has slunk to*]. Here I am, Sally.

MR. TATTON. Miss Ann, I forgive you. I'm smiling, I assure
you, I'm smiling.

SARAH. We all laughed when we heard you.

MR. TATTON. Which reminds me, young George Leete, had you
the ace?

GEORGE. King . . . knave . . . here are the cards, but I can't
see.

MR. TATTON. I had the king.

ANN [*quietly to her sister*]. He kissed me.

SARAH. A man would.

GEORGE. What were trumps?

MR. TATTON. What were we playing . . . cricket?

ANN [*as quietly again*]. D'you think I'm blushing?

SARAH. It's probable.

ANN. I am by the feel of me.

SARAH. George, we left Papa sitting quite still.

LORD JOHN. Didn't he approve of the bet?

MR. TATTON. He said nothing.

3

SARAH. Why, who doesn't love sport!

MR. TATTON. I'm the man to grumble. Back a woman's pluck again . . . never. My Lord . . . you weren't the one to go with her as umpire.

GEORGE. No . . . to be sure.

MR. TATTON. How was it I let that pass? Playing two games at once. Haven't I cause of complaint? But a man must give and take.

The master of the house, father of GEORGE *and* SARAH COTTESHAM *and* ANN, MR. CARNABY LEETE, *comes slowly down the steps, unnoticed by the others. A man over fifty—à la Lord Chesterfield.*

GEORGE [*to Lord John*]. Are you sure you're quite comfortable there?

LORD JOHN. Whatever I'm sitting on hasn't given way yet.

MR. TATTON. Don't forget that you're riding to Brighton with me.

LORD JOHN. Tomorrow.

GEORGE. Today. Well . . . the hour before sunrise is no time at all.

MR. TATTON. Sixty-five miles.

LORD JOHN. What are we all sitting here for?

MR. TATTON. I say people ought to be in bed and asleep.

CARNABY. But the morning air is delightful.

MR. TATTON [*jumping at the new voice*]. Leete! Now, had you the ace?

CARNABY. Of course.

MR. TATTON. We should have lost that too, Lady Charlie.

SARAH. Bear up, Mr. Tat.

MR. TATTON. Come, a game of whist is a game of whist.

CARNABY. And so I strolled out after you all.

MR. TATTON. She trod on a toad.

CARNABY [*carelessly*]. Does she say so?

MR. TATTON [*with mock roguishness*]. Ah!

GEORGE *is on the terrace, looking to the left through the trees.* TATTON *is sitting on the edge of the fountain.*

GEORGE. Here's the sun . . . to show us ourselves.

MR. TATTON. Leete, this pond is full of water!

CARNABY. Ann, if you are there . . .

ANN. Yes, Papa.

CARNABY. Apologise profusely; it's your garden.

ANN. Oh . . .

CARNABY. Coat-tails, Tatton . . . or worse?

MR. TATTON [*ruefully discovering damp spots about him*]. Nothing vastly to matter.

LORD JOHN. Hardy, well-preserved, country gentleman!

MR. TATTON. I bet I'm a younger man than you, my lord.

ANN [*suddenly to the company generally*]. I didn't tread upon any toad . . . I was kissed.

There is a pause of some discomfort.

SARAH. Ann, come here to me.

LORD JOHN. I apologised.

GEORGE [*from the terrace*]. Are we to be insulted?

CARNABY. My dear Carp, say no more.

There is another short pause. By this it is twilight, faces can be plainly seen.

SARAH. Listen . . . the first bird.

MR. TATTON. Oh, dear no, they begin to sing long before this.

CARNABY. What is it now . . . a lark?

MR. TATTON. I don't know.

ANN [*quietly to* SARAH]. That's a thrush.

SARAH [*capping her*]. A thrush.

CARNABY. Charming!

MR. TATTON [*to* LORD JOHN]. I don't see why you couldn't have told me how it was that she screamed.

CARNABY. Our dear Tatton! [*Sotto voce to his son.*] Hold your tongue, George.

MR. TATTON. I did bar toads and you said I didn't, and anyway I had a sort of right to know.

LORD JOHN. You know now.

SARAH. I wonder if this seat is dry.

LORD JOHN. There's been no rain for weeks.

SARAH. The roads will be dusty for you, Mr. Tat.

MR. TATTON. Just one moment. You don't mind me, Miss Ann do you?

ANN. I don't mind much.

MR. TATTON. We said distinctly . . . To the orchard end of the garden and back and if frightened—that's the word—so much as to scream . . . ! Now, what I want to know is. . .

LORD JOHN. Consider the bet off.

MR. TATTON. Certainly not. And we should have added. . . Alone.

CARNABY. Tatton has persistence.

SARAH. Mr. Tat, do you know where people go who take things seriously?

MR. TATTON. Miss Leete, were you frightened when Lord John kissed you?

GEORGE. Damnation!

CARNABY. My excellent Tatton, much as I admire your searchings after truth I must here parentally intervene, regretting, my dear Tatton, that my own carelessness of duennahood has permitted this—this . . . to occur.

After this, there is silence for a minute.

LORD JOHN. Can I borrow a horse of you, Mr. Leete?

CARNABY. My entire stable; and your Ronald shall be physicked.

SARAH. Spartans that you are to be riding!

LORD JOHN. I prefer it to a jolting chaise.

MR. TATTON. You will have my mare.

LORD JOHN [*ignoring him*]. This has been a most enjoyable three weeks.

CARNABY. Four.

LORD JOHN. Is it four?

CARNABY. We bow to the compliment. Our duty to his grace.

LORD JOHN. When I see him.

GEORGE. To our dear cousin.

MR. TATTON [*to* LADY COTTESHAM]. Sir Charles at Brighton?

SARAH [*not answering*]. To be sure . . . we did discover . . . our mother was second cousin . . . once removed to you.

CARNABY. If the prince will be there . . . he is in waiting.

LORD JOHN. Any message, Lady Cottesham? . . . since we speak out of session.

SARAH. I won't trust you.

CARNABY. Or trouble you while I still may frank a letter. But my son-in-law is a wretched correspondent. Do you admire men of small vices? They make admirable husbands though their wives will be grumbling—Silence, Sarah—but that's a good sign.

SARAH. Papa is a connoisseur of humanity.

ANN [*to the company as before*]. No, Mr. Tatton, I wasn't frightened when Lord John . . . kissed me. I screamed because I was surprised, and I'm sorry I screamed.

SARAH [*quietly to* ANN]. My dear Ann, you're a fool.

ANN [*quietly to* SARAH]. I will speak sometimes.

SARAH. Sit down again.

Again an uncomfortable silence, a ludicrous air about it this time.

TATTON. Now, we'll say no more about that bet, but I was right.

LORD JOHN. Do you know, Mr. Tatton, that I have a temper to lose?

MR. TATTON. What the devil does that matter, to me sir . . . my lord?

LORD JOHN. I owe you a saddle and bridle.

MR. TATTON. You'll oblige me by taking the mare.

LORD JOHN. We'll discuss it to-morrow.

MR. TATTON. I've said all I have to say.

GEORGE. The whole matter's ridiculous!

MR. TATTON. I see the joke. Goodnight, Lady Cottesham, and I kiss your hand.

SARAH. Good morning, Mr. Tat.

MR. TATTON. Good morning, Miss Ann, I . . .

SARAH [shielding her sister]. Good morrow is appropriate.

MR. TATTON. I'll go by the fields. [To CARNABY.] Thank you for a pleasant evening. Good morrow, George. Do we start at mid-day, my lord?

LORD JOHN. Any time you please.

MR. TATTON. Not at all. [he hands the candlestick—of which he has never before left go—to GEORGE]. I brought this for a link. Thank you.

CARNABY. Mid-day will be midnight if you sleep at all now; make it two or later.

MR. TATTON. We put up at Guildford. I've done so before. I haven't my hat. It's a day and a half's ride.

> TATTON goes quickly up the other steps and away. It is now quite light. GEORGE stands by the steps, LORD JOHN is on one of the seats, CARNABY strolls round, now and then touching the rose trees, SARAH and ANN are on the other seat.

GEORGE. Morning! These candles still smell.

SARAH. How lively one feels and isn't.

CARNABY. The flowers are opening.

ANN [in a whisper]. Couldn't we go in?

SARAH. Never run away.

ANN. Everything looks so odd.

SARAH. What's o'clock . . . my lord?

LORD JOHN. Half after four.

ANN [to SARAH]. My eyes are hot behind.

GEORGE. What ghosts we seem!

SARAH. What has made us spend such a night?

CARNABY. Ann incited me to it. [He takes snuff.]

SARAH. In a spirit of rebellion against good country habits. . .

ANN [*to her sister again*]. Don't talk about me.

SARAH. They can see that you're whispering.

CARNABY. . . . Informing me now she was a woman and wanted excitement.

GEORGE. There's a curse.

CARNABY. How else d'ye conceive life for women?

SARAH. George is naturally cruel. Excitement's our education. Please vary it, though.

CARNABY. I have always held that to colour in the world-picture is the greatest privilege of the husband, Sarah.

SARAH [*not leaving* ANN's *side*]. Yes, Papa.

CARNABY. Sarah, when Sir Charles leaves Brighton . . .

SARAH *rises but will not move further.*

CARNABY [*sweetly threatening*]. Shall I come to you?

But she goes to him now.

CARNABY. By a gossip letter from town . . .

SARAH [*tensely*]. What is it?

CARNABY. You mentioned to me something of his visiting Naples.

SARAH. Very well. I detest Italy.

CARNABY. Let's have George's opinion.

He leads her towards GEORGE.

GEORGE. Yes?

CARNABY. Upon Naples.

GEORGE. I remember Naples.

CARNABY. Sarah, admire those roses.

SARAH [*cynically echoing her father*]. Let's have George's opinion.

Now CARNABY *has drawn them both away, upon the terrace, and, the coast being clear,* LORD JOHN *walks towards* ANN, *who looks at him very scaredly.*

CARNABY. Emblem of secrecy among the ancients.

SARAH. Look at this heavy head, won't it snap off?

The three move out of sight.

LORD JOHN. I'm sober now.

ANN. I'm not.

LORD JOHN. Uncompromising young lady.

ANN. And excuse me I don't want to . . . play.

LORD JOHN. Don't you wish me to apologise quietly to you?

ANN. Good manners are all mockery, I'm sure.

LORD JOHN. I'm very much afraid you're a cynic.

ANN. I'm not trying to be clever.

LORD JOHN. Do I tease you?

ANN. Do I amuse you?

LORD JOHN. How dare I say so!

ANN [*after a moment*]. I was not frightened.

LORD JOHN. You kissed me back.

ANN. Not on purpose. What do two people mean by behaving so . . . in the dark?

LORD JOHN. I am exceedingly sorry that I hurt your feelings.

ANN. Thank you, I like to feel.

LORD JOHN. And you must forgive me.

ANN. Tell me, why did you do it?

LORD JOHN. Honestly I don't know. I should do it again.

ANN. That's not quite true, is it?

LORD JOHN. I think so.

ANN. What does it matter at all!

LORD JOHN. Nothing.

> GEORGE, SARAH *and then* CARNABY *move into sight and along the terrace,* LORD JOHN *turns to them.*

LORD JOHN. Has this place been long in your family, Mr. Leete?

CARNABY. Markswayde my wife brought us, through the Peters's . . . old Chiltern people . . . connections of yours, of course. There is no entail.

> LORD JOHN *walks back to* ANN.

SARAH. George you assume this republicanism as you would—no, would not—a coat of latest cut.

CARNABY. Never argue with him . . . persist.

SARAH. So does he.

> *The three pass along the terrace.*

ANN [*to* LORD JOHN]. Will you sit down?

LORD JOHN. It's not worth while. Do you know I must be quite twice your age?

ANN. A doubled responsibility, my lord.

LORD JOHN. I suppose it is.

ANN. I don't say so. That's a phrase from a book . . . sounded well.

LORD JOHN. My dear Miss Ann . . . [*He stops*].

ANN. Go on being polite.

LORD JOHN. If you'll keep your head turned away.

ANN. Why must I?

LORD JOHN. There's lightning in the glances of your eye.

ANN. Do use vulgar words to me.

LORD JOHN [*with a sudden fatherly kindness*]. Go to bed . . . you're dead tired. And good-bye . . . . I'll be gone before you wake.

ANN. Good-bye.

> *She shakes hands with him, then walks towards her father who is coming down the steps.*

ANN. Papa, don't my roses want looking to?

CARNABY [*pats her cheek*]. These?

ANN. Those.

CARNABY. Abud is under your thumb, horticulturally speaking.

ANN. Where's Sally?

> *She goes on to* SARAH, *who is standing with* GEORGE *at the top of the steps.* CARNABY *looks* LORD JOHN *up and down.*

LORD JOHN [*dusting his shoulder*]. This cursed powder!

CARNABY. Do we respect innocence enough . . . any of us?

> GEORGE *comes down the steps and joins them.*

GEORGE. Respectable politics will henceforth be useless to me.

CARNABY. My lord, was his grace satisfied with the young man's work abroad or was he not?

LORD JOHN. My father used to curse everyone.

CARNABY. That's a mere Downing Street custom.

LORD JOHN. And I seem to remember that a letter of yours from . . . where were you in those days?

GEORGE. Paris . . . Naples . . . Vienna.

LORD JOHN. One place . . . once lightened a fit of gout.

CARNABY. George, you have in you the makings of a minister.

GEORGE. No.

CARNABY. Remember the Age tends to the disreputable.

> GEORGE *moves away,* SARAH *moves towards them.*

CARNABY. George is something of a genius, stuffed with theories and possessed of a curious conscience. But I am fortunate in my children.

LORD JOHN. All the world knows it.

CARNABY [*to* SARAH]. It's lucky that yours was a love match, too. I admire you. Ann is 'to come', so to speak.

SARAH [*to* LORD JOHN]. Were you discussing affairs?

LORD JOHN. Not I.

GEORGE. Ann.

ANN. Yes, George.

> *She goes to him; they stroll together up the steps and along the terrace.*

SARAH. I'm desperately fagged.

LORD JOHN [*politely*]. A seat.

SARAH. Also tired of sitting.

CARNABY. Let's have the Brighton news, Carp.

LORD JOHN. If there's any.

CARNABY. Probably I still command abuse. Even my son-in-law must, by courtesy, join in the cry . . . ah, poor duty-torn Sarah! You can spread abroad that I am as a green bay tree.

> CARNABY *paces slowly away from them.*

LORD JOHN. Your father's making a mistake.

SARAH. D'you think so?

LORD JOHN. He's played the game once.

SARAH. I was not then in the knowledge of things when he left you.

LORD JOHN. We remember it.

SARAH. I should like to hear it.

LORD JOHN. I have avoided this subject.

SARAH. With him, yes.

LORD JOHN. Oh! . . . why did I desert the army for politics?

SARAH. Better fighting.

LORD JOHN. It sat so nobly upon him . . . the leaving us for conscience sake when we were strongly in power. Strange that six months later we should be turned out.

SARAH. Papa was lucky.

LORD JOHN. But this second time . . . ?

SARAH. Listen. This is very much a private quarrel with Mr. Pitt, who hates Papa . . . gets rid of him.

LORD JOHN. Shall I betray a confidence?

SARAH. Better not.

LORD JOHN. My father advised me to this visit.

SARAH. Your useful visit. More than kind of his Grace.

LORD JOHN. Yes . . . there's been a paragraph in the *Morning Chronicle*, 'The Whigs woo Mr. Carnaby Leete.'

SARAH. We saw to it.

LORD JOHN. My poor father seems anxious to discover whether the Leete episode will repeat itself entirely. He is chronically unhappy in opposition. Are your husband and his colleagues trembling in their seats?

SARAH. I can't say.

LORD JOHN. Politics is a game for clever children, and women, and fools. Will you take a word of warning from a soldier? Your father is past his prime.

> CARNABY *paces back towards them.*

CARNABY. I'm getting to be old for these all-night sittings. I must be writing to your busy brother.

LORD JOHN. Arthur? . . . is at his home.

SARAH. Pleasantly sounding phrase.

CARNABY. His grace deserted?

SARAH. Quite secretaryless!

LORD JOHN. Lady Arthur lately has been brought to bed. I heard yesterday.

SARAH. The seventh, is it not? Children require living up to. My congratulations.

LORD JOHN. Won't you write them?

SARAH. We are not intimate.

LORD JOHN. A good woman.

SARAH. Evidently. Where's Ann? We'll go in.

LORD JOHN. You're a mother to your sister.

SARAH. Not I.

CARNABY. My wife went her ways into the next world; Sarah hers into this; and our little Ann was left with a most admirable governess. One must never reproach circumstances. Man educates woman in his own good time.

LORD JOHN. I suppose she, or any young girl, is all heart.

CARNABY. What is it that you call heart . . . sentimentally speaking?

SARAH. Any bud in the morning.

LORD JOHN. That man Tatton's jokes are in shocking taste.

CARNABY. Tatton is honest.

LORD JOHN. I'm much to blame for having won that bet.

CARNABY. Say no more.

LORD JOHN. What can Miss Ann think of me?

SARAH. Don't ask her.

CARNABY. Innocency's opinions are invariably entertaining.

LORD JOHN. Am I the first . . . ? I really beg your pardon.

GEORGE *and* ANN *come down the steps together.*

CARNABY. Ann, what do you think . . . that is to say—and answer me truthfully . . . what at this moment is your inclination of mind towards my lord here?

ANN. I suppose I love him.

LORD JOHN. I hope not.

ANN. I suppose I love you.

CARNABY. No . . no . . no . . no . . no . . no . . no.

SARAH. Hush, dear.

ANN. I'm afraid papa, there's something very ill-bred in me.
Down the steps and into the midst of them comes JOHN ABUD, *carrying his tools, among other things a twist of bass. A young gardener, honest, clean and common.*

ABUD [*to* CARNABY]. I ask pardon, sir.

CARNABY. So early, Abud! . . . this is your territory. So late . . .
Bed.

ANN starts away up the steps, SARAH *is following her.*

LORD JOHN. Good-bye, Lady Cottesham.

At this ANN *stops for a moment, but then goes straight on.*

SARAH. A pleasant journey.

SARAH departs too.

GEORGE [*stretching himself*]. I'm roused.

CARNABY. [*To* ABUD.] Leave your tools here for a few moments.

ABUD. I will, sir.

ABUD leaves them, going along the terrace and out of sight.

CARNABY. My head is hot. Pardon me.

*CARNABY is sitting on the fountain rim; he dips his handkerchief
in the water, and wrings it; then takes off his wig and binds the
damp handkerchief round his head.*

CARNABY. Wigs are most comfortable and old fashioned . . .
unless you choose to be a cropped republican like my son.

GEORGE. Nature!

CARNABY. Nature grows a beard, sir.

LORD JOHN. I've seen Turks.

CARNABY. Horrible . . . horrible! Sit down, Carp.

LORD JOHN sits on the fountain rim, GEORGE *begins to pace
restlessly; he has been nursing the candlestick ever since* TATTON
handed it to him.

CARNABY. George, you look damned ridiculous strutting arm-
in-arm with that candlestick.

GEORGE. I am ridiculous.

CARNABY. If you're cogitating over your wife and her
expectations . . .

GEORGE *paces up the steps and away. There is a pause.*

CARNABY. D'ye tell stories . . . good ones?

LORD JOHN. Sometimes.

CARNABY. There'll be this.

LORD JOHN. I shan't.

CARNABY. Say no more. If I may so express myself, Carp, you
have been taking us for granted.

LORD JOHN. How wide awake you are! I'm not.

CARNABY. My head's cool. Shall I describe your conduct as
an unpremeditated insult?

LORD JOHN. Don't think anything of the sort.

CARNABY. There speaks your kind heart.

LORD JOHN. Are you trying to pick a quarrel with me?

CARNABY. As may be.

LORD JOHN. Why?

CARNABY. For the sake of appearances.

LORD JOHN. Damn all appearances.

CARNABY. Now I'll lose my temper. Sir, you have compromised my daughter.

LORD JOHN. Nonsense!

CARNABY. Villain! What's your next move?

For a moment LORD JOHN *sits with knit brows.*

LORD JOHN [*brutally*]. Mr. Leete, your name stinks.

CARNABY. My point of dis-ad-vantage!

LORD JOHN [*apologising*]. Please say what you like. I might have put my remark better.

CARNABY. I think not; the homely Saxon phrase is our literary dagger. Princelike, you ride away from Markswayde. Can I trust you not to stab a socially sick man? Why it's a duty you owe to society . . . to weed out . . . us.

LORD JOHN. I'm not a coward. How?

CARNABY. A little laughter . . . in your exuberance of health.

LORD JOHN. You may trust me not to tell tales.

CARNABY. Of what . . . of whom?

LORD JOHN. Of here.

CARNABY. And what is there to tell of here?

LORD JOHN. Nothing.

CARNABY. But how your promise betrays a capacity for good-natured invention!

LORD JOHN. If I lie call me out.

CARNABY. I don't deal in sentiment. I can't afford to be talked about otherwise than as I choose to be. Already the Aunt Sally of the hour; having under pressure of circumstances resigned my office; dating my letters from the borders of the Chiltern Hundreds . . . I am a poor politician, sir, and I must live.

LORD JOHN. I can't see that your family's infected . . . affected.

CARNABY. With a penniless girl you really should have been more circumspect.

LORD JOHN. I might ask to marry her.

CARNABY. My lord!

In the pause that ensues he takes up the twist of bass to play with.

LORD JOHN. What should you say to that?

CARNABY. The silly child supposed she loved you.

LORD JOHN. Yes.

CARNABY. Is it a match?

LORD JOHN [*full in the other's face*]. What about the appearances of blackmail?

CARNABY [*compressing his thin lips*]. Do you care for my daughter?

LORD JOHN. I could . . . at a pinch.

CARNABY. Now, my lord, you are insolent.

LORD JOHN. Is this when we quarrel?

CARNABY. I think I'll challenge you.

LORD JOHN. That will look well.

CARNABY. You'll value that kiss when you've paid for it. Kindly choose Tatton as your second. I want his tongue to wag both ways.

LORD JOHN. I was forgetting how it all began.

CARNABY. George will serve me . . . protesting. His principles are vile, but he has the education of a gentleman. Swords or . . .? Swords. And at noon shall we say? There's shade behind a certain barn, midway between this and Tatton's.

LORD JOHN [*not taking him seriously yet*]. What if we both die horridly?

CARNABY. You are at liberty to make me a written apology.

LORD JOHN. A joke's a joke.

CARNABY *deliberately strikes him in the face with the twist of bass.*

LORD JOHN. That's enough.

CARNABY [*in explanatory apology*]. My friend, you are so obtuse. Abud!

LORD JOHN. Mr. Leete, are you serious?

CARNABY. Perfectly serious. Let's go to bed. Abud, you can get to your work.

Wig in hand, MR. LEETE *courteously conducts his guest towards the house.* ABUD *returns to his tools and his morning's work.*

THE SECOND ACT

Shortly after mid-day, while the sun beats strongly upon the terrace, ABUD *is working dexterously at the rose trees.* DR. REMNANT *comes down the steps, hatted, and carrying a stick and a book. He is an elderly man with a kind manner; type of the eighteenth century casuistical parson. On his way he stops to say a word to the gardener.*

DR. REMNANT. Will it rain before nightfall?

ABUD. About then, sir, I should say.

Down the other steps comes MRS. OPIE, *a prim, decorous, but well bred and unobjectionable woman. She is followed by* ANN.

MRS. OPIE. A good morning to you, Parson.

DR. REMNANT. And to you, Mrs. Opie, and to Miss Ann.

ANN. Good morning, Dr. Remnant. [*To* ABUD.] Have you been here ever since . . . ?

ABUD. I've had dinner, Miss.

ABUD's *work takes him gradually out of sight.*

MRS. OPIE. We are but just breakfasted.

DR. REMNANT. I surmise dissipation.

ANN [*to* MRS. OPIE]. Thank you for waiting five hours.

MRS. OPIE. It is my rule to breakfast with you.

DR. REMNANT [*exhibiting the book*]. I am come to return, and to borrow.

ANN. Show me.

DR. REMNANT. Ballads by Robert Burns.

ANN [*taking it*]. I'll put it back.

MRS. OPIE [*taking it from her*]. I've never heard of him.

DR. REMNANT. Oh, ma'am, a very vulgar poet!

GEORGE LEETE *comes quickly down the steps.*

GEORGE [*to* REMNANT]. How are you?

DR. REMNANT. Yours, sir.

GEORGE. Ann.

ANN. Good morning, George.

GEORGE. Did you sleep well?

ANN. I always do . . . but I dreamt.

44

GEORGE. I must sit down for a minute. [*Nodding.*] Mrs. Opie.

MRS. OPIE. I wish you a good morning, sir.

GEORGE [*to* ANN]. Don't look so solemn.

LADY COTTESHAM *comes quickly to the top of the steps.*

SARAH. Is Papa badly hurt?

ANN [*jumping up*]. Oh, what has happened?

GEORGE. Not badly.

SARAH. He won't see me.

His three children look at each other.

DR. REMNANT [*tactfully*]. May I go my ways to the library?

SARAH. Please do, Doctor Remnant.

DR. REMNANT. I flatly contradicted all that was being said in the village.

SARAH. Thoughtful of you.

DR. REMNANT. But tell me nothing.

DR. REMNANT *bows formally and goes.* GEORGE *is about to speak when* SARAH *with a look at* MRS. OPIE *says. . .*

SARAH. George, hold your tongue.

MRS. OPIE [*with much hauteur*]. I am in the way.

At this moment DIMMUCK, *an old but unbenevolent-looking butler, comes to the top of the steps.*

DIMMUCK. The master wants Mrs. Opie.

MRS. OPIE. Thank you.

GEORGE. Your triumph!

MRS. OPIE *is departing radiant.*

DIMMUCK. How was I to know you was in the garden?

MRS. OPIE. I am sorry to have put you to the trouble of a search, Mr. Dimmuck.

DIMMUCK. He's in his room.

And he follows her towards the house.

GEORGE. Carp fought with him at twelve o'clock.

The other two cannot speak from amazement.

SARAH. No!

GEORGE. Why, they didn't tell me and I didn't ask. Carp was laughing. Tatton chuckled . . . afterwards.

SARAH. What had he to do?

GEORGE. Carp's second.

SARAH. Unaccountable children!

GEORGE. Feather parade . . . throw in . . . parry quarte: over the arm . . . put by: feint . . . flanconade and through his arm . . . damned easy. The father didn't wince or say a word. I bound it up . . . the sight of blood makes me sick.

After a moment, SARAH *turns to* ANN.

SARAH. Yes, and you've been a silly child.

GEORGE. Ah, give me a woman's guess and the most unlikely reason to account for anything!

ANN. I hate that man. I'm glad Papa's not hurt. What about a surgeon?

GEORGE. No, you shall kiss the place well, and there'll be poetic justice done.

SARAH. How did you all part?

GEORGE. With bows and without a word.

SARAH. Coming home with him?

GEORGE. Not a word.

SARAH. Papa's very clever; but I'm puzzled.

GEORGE. Something will happen next, no doubt.

ANN. Isn't this done with?

SARAH. So it seems.

ANN. I should like to be told just what the game has been.

GEORGE. Bravo, Ann.

ANN. Tell me the rules . . . for next time.

SARAH. It would have been most advantageous for us to have formed an alliance with Lord John Carp, who stood here for his father and his father's party . . . now in opposition.

GEORGE. Look upon yourself—not too seriously—Ann, as the instrument of political destiny.

ANN. I'm afraid I take in fresh ideas very slowly. Why has Papa given up the Stamp Office?

SARAH. His colleagues wouldn't support him.

ANN. Why was that?

SARAH. They disapproved of what he did.

ANN. Did he do right . . . giving it up?

SARAH. Yes.

GEORGE. We hope so. Time will tell. An irreverent quipster once named him Carnaby Leech.

SARAH. I know.

GEORGE. I wonder if his true enemies think him wise to have dropped off the Stamp Office?

ANN. Has he quarrelled with Sir Charles?

SARAH. Politically.

ANN. Isn't that awkward for you?

SARAH. Not a bit.

GEORGE. Hear a statement that includes our lives. Markswayde goes at his death . . . see reversionary mortgage. The income's an annuity now. The cash in the house will be ours. The debts are paid . . . at last.

ANN. And there remains me.

GEORGE. Bad grammar. Meanwhile our father is a tongue, which is worth buying; but I don't think he ought to go over to the enemy . . . for the second time.

SARAH. One party is as good as another; each works for the same end, I should hope.

GEORGE. I won't argue about it.

ANN. I suppose that a woman's profession is marriage.

GEORGE. My lord has departed.

ANN. There'll be others to come. I'm not afraid of being married.

SARAH. What did Papa want Mrs. Opie for?

ANN. There'll be a great many things I shall want to know about men now.

GEORGE. Wisdom cometh with sorrow . . . oh, my sister.

SARAH. I believe you two are both about as selfish as you can be.

GEORGE. I am an egotist . . . with attachments.

ANN. Make use of me.

GEORGE. Ann, you marry—when you marry—to please yourself.

ANN. There's much in life that I don't like, Sally.

SARAH. There's much more that you will.

GEORGE. I think we three have never talked together before.

> ABUD, *who has been in sight on the terrace for a few moments, now comes down the steps.*

ABUD. May I make so bold, sir, as to ask how is Mrs. George Leete?

GEORGE. She was well when I last heard.

ABUD. Thank you, sir.

> *And he returns to his work.*

ANN. I wonder will it be a boy or a girl.

GEORGE. Poor weak woman.

SARAH. Be grateful to her.

ANN. A baby is a wonderful thing.

SARAH. Babyhood in the abstract . . . beautiful.

ANN. Even kittens . . .

> *She stops, and then in rather childish embarrassment, moves away from them.*

SARAH. Don't shudder, George.

GEORGE. I have no wish to be a father. Why?

4

SARAH. It's a vulgar responsibility.

GEORGE. My wayside flower!

SARAH. Why pick it?

GEORGE. Sarah, I love my wife.

SARAH. That's easily said.

GEORGE. She should be here.

SARAH. George, you married to please yourself.

GEORGE. By custom her rank is my own.

SARAH. Does she still drop her aitches?

GEORGE. Dolly . . .

SARAH. Pretty name.

GEORGE. Dolly aspires to be one of us.

SARAH. Child-bearing makes these women blowzy.

GEORGE. Oh heaven!

ANN [*calling to* ABUD *on the terrace*]. Finish to-day, Abud. If it rains . . .

> *She stops, seeing* MR. TETGEEN *standing at the top of the steps leading from the house. This is an intensely respectable, self-contained-looking lawyer, but a man of the world too.*

MR. TETGEEN. Lady Cottesham.

SARAH. Sir?

MR. TETGEEN. My name is Tetgeen.

SARAH. Mr. Tetgeen. How do you do?

MR. TETGEEN. The household appeared to be in some confusion and I took the liberty to be my own messenger. I am anxious to speak with you.

SARAH. Ann, dear, ask if Papa will see you now.

> DIMMUCK *appears.*

DIMMUCK. The master wants you, Miss Ann.

SARAH. Ask papa if he'll see me soon.

> ANN *goes towards the house.*

SARAH. Dimmuck, Mr. Tetgeen has been left to find his own way here.

DIMMUCK. I couldn't help it, my lady.

> *And he follows* ANN.

SARAH. Our father is confined to his room.

GEORGE. By your leave.

> *Then* GEORGE *takes himself off up the steps, and out of sight. The old lawyer bows to* LADY COTTESHAM, *who regards him steadily.*

MR. TETGEEN. From Sir Charles . . . a talking machine.

SARAH. Please sit.

He sits carefully upon the rim of the fountain, she upon the seat opposite.

SARAH [*glancing over her shoulder*]. Will you talk nonsense until the gardener is out of hearing? He is on his way away. You have had a tiring journey?

MR. TETGEEN. Thank you, no . . . by the night coach to Reading and thence I have walked.

SARAH. The country is pretty, is it not?

MR. TETGEEN. It compares favourably with other parts.

SARAH. Do you travel much, Mr. Tetgeen? He has gone.

MR. TETGEEN [*deliberately and sharpening his tone ever so little*]. Sir Charles does not wish to petition for a divorce.

SARAH [*controlling even her sense of humour*]. I have no desire to jump over the moon.

MR. TETGEEN. His scruples are religious. The case would be weak upon some important points, and there has been no public scandal . . . at the worst, very little.

SARAH. My good manners are, I trust, irreproachable, and you may tell Sir Charles that my conscience is my own.

MR. TETGEEN. Your husband's in the matter of . . .

SARAH. Please say the word.

MR. TETGEEN. Pardon me . . . not upon mere suspicion.

SARAH. Now, is it good policy to suspect what is incapable of proof?

MR. TETGEEN. I advise Sir Charles, that, should you come to an open fight, he can afford to lose.

SARAH. And have I no right to suspicions?

MR. TETGEEN. Certainly. Are they of use to you?

SARAH. I have been a tolerant wife, expecting toleration.

MR. TETGEEN. Sir Charles is anxious to take into consideration any complaints you may have to make against him.

SARAH. I complain if he complains of me.

MR. TETGEEN. For the first time, I think . . . formally.

SARAH. Why not have come to me?

MR. TETGEEN. Sir Charles is busy.

SARAH [*disguising a little spasm of pain*]. Shall we get to business?

MR. TETGEEN *now takes a moment to find his phrase.*

MR. TETGEEN. I don't know the man's name.

SARAH. This, surely, is how you might address a seduced housemaid.

MR. TETGEEN. But Sir Charles and he, I understand, have talked the matter over.

The shock of this brings SARAH *to her feet, white with anger.*

SARAH. Divorce me.

MR. TETGEEN [*sharply*]. Is there ground for it?

SARAH [*with a magnificent recovery of self control*]. I won't tell you that.

MR. TETGEEN. I have said we have no case . . . that is to say, we don't want one; but any information is a weapon in store.

SARAH. You did quite right to insult me.

MR. TETGEEN. As a rule I despise such methods.

SARAH. It's a lie that they met . . . those two men?

MR. TETGEEN. It may be.

SARAH. It must be.

MR. TETGEEN. I have Sir Charles's word.

Now he takes from his pocket some notes, putting on his spectacles to read them.

SARAH. What's this . . . a written lecture?

MR. TETGEEN. We propose . . . first: that the present complete severence of conjugal relations shall continue. Secondly: that Lady Cottesham shall be at liberty to remove from South Audley Street and Ringham Castle all personal and private effects, excepting those family jewels which have merely been considered her property. Thirdly: Lady Cottesham shall undertake, formally and in writing not to molest—a legal term—Sir Charles Cottesham. [*Her handkerchief has dropped, here he picks it up and restores it to her.*] Allow me, my lady.

SARAH. I thank you.

MR. TETGEEN [*continuing*]. Fourthly: Lady Cottesham shall undertake . . . etc. . . . not to inhabit or frequent the city and towns of London, Brighthelmstone, Bath, The Tunbridge Wells, and York. Fifthly: Sir Charles Cottesham will, in acknowledgement of the maintenance of this agreement, allow Lady C. the sum of two hundred and fifty pounds per annum, which sum he considers sufficient for the upkeep of a small genteel establishment; use of the house known as Pater House, situate some seventeen miles from the Manor of Barton-le-Street, Yorkshire; coals from the mine adjoining; and from the home farm, milk, butter and eggs. [*Then he finds a further note.*] Lady Cottesham is not to play cards.

SARAH. I am a little fond of play.

MR. TETGEEN. There is no question of jointure.

SARAH. None. Mr. Tetgeen . . . I love my husband.

MR. TETGEEN. My lady . . . I will mention it.

SARAH. Such a humorous answer to this. No . . . don't. What is important? Bread and butter . . . and eggs. Do I take this?

MR. TETGEEN [*handing her the paper*]. Please.

SARAH [*with the ghost of a smile*]. I take it badly.

MR. TETGEEN [*courteously capping her jest*]. I take my leave.

SARAH. This doesn't call for serious notice? I've done nothing legal by accepting it?

MR. TETGEEN. There's no law in the matter; it's one of policy.

SARAH. I might bargain for a bigger income. [MR. TETGEEN *bows*.] On the whole I'd rather be divorced.

MR. TETGEEN. Sir Charles detests scandal.

SARAH. Besides there's no case . . . is there?

MR. TETGEEN. Sir Charles congratulates himself.

SARAH. Sir Charles had best not bully me so politely . . . tell him.

MR. TETGEEN. My lady!

SARAH. I will not discuss this impertinence. Did those two men meet and talk . . . chat together? What d'you think of that?

MR. TETGEEN. 'Twas very practical. I know that the woman is somehow the outcast.

SARAH. A bad woman . . . an idle woman! But I've tried to do so much that lay to my hands without ever questioning . . . ! Thank you, I don't want this retailed to my husband. You'll take a glass of wine before you go?

MR. TETGEEN. Port is grateful.

She takes from her dress two sealed letters.

SARAH. Will you give that to Sir Charles . . . a letter he wrote me which I did not open. This, my answer, which I did not send.

He takes the one letter courteously, the other she puts back.

SARAH. I'm such a coward, Mr. Tetgeen.

MR. TETGEEN. May I say how sorry . . . ?

SARAH. Thank you.

MR. TETGEEN. And let me apologise for having expressed one opinion of my own.

SARAH. He wants to get rid of me. He's a bit afraid of me, you know, because I fight . . . and my weapons are all my own. This'll blow over.

MR. TETGEEN [*with a shake of the head*]. You are to take this offer as final.

SARAH. Beyond this?

MR. TETGEEN. As I hinted, I am prepared to advise legal measures.

SARAH. I could blow it over . . . but I won't perhaps. I must smile at my husband's consideration in suppressing even to you . . . the man's name. Butter and eggs . . . and milk. I should grow fat.

ANN appears suddenly.

ANN. We go to Brighton to-morrow! [*And she comes excitedly to her sister.*]

SARAH. Was that duel a stroke of genius?

ANN. All sorts of things are to happen.

SARAH [*turning from her to* MR. TETGEEN]. And you'll walk as far as Reading?

MR. TETGEEN. Dear me, yes.

SARAH [*to* ANN]. I'll come back.

SARAH takes MR. TETGEEN *towards the house.* ANN *seats herself. After a moment* LORD JOHN CARP, *his clothes dusty with some riding appears from the other quarter. She looks up to find him gazing at her.*

LORD JOHN. Ann, I've ridden back to see you.

ANN [*after a moment*]. We're coming to Brighton tomorrow.

LORD JOHN. Good.

ANN. Papa's not dead.

LORD JOHN [*with equal cheerfulness*]. That's good.

ANN. And he said we should be seeing more of you.

LORD JOHN. Here I am. I love you, Ann. [*He goes on his knees.*]

ANN. D'you want to marry me?

LORD JOHN. Yes.

ANN. Thank you very much; it'll be very convenient for us all. Won't you get up?

LORD JOHN. At your feet.

ANN. I like it.

LORD JOHN. Give me your hand.

ANN. No.

LORD JOHN. You're beautiful.

ANN. I don't think so. You don't think so.

LORD JOHN. I do think so.

ANN. I should like to say I don't love you.

LORD JOHN. Last night you kissed me.

ANN. Do get up, please.

LORD JOHN. As you wish.

Now he sits by her.

ANN. Last night you were nobody in particular . . . to me.

LORD JOHN. I love you.

ANN. Please don't; I can't think clearly.

LORD JOHN. Look at me.

ANN. I'm sure I don't love you because you're making me feel very uncomfortable and that wouldn't be so.

LORD JOHN. Then we'll think.

ANN. Papa . . . perhaps you'd rather not talk about Papa.

LORD JOHN. Give yourself to me.

ANN [drawing away from him]. Four words! There ought to be more in such a sentence . . . it's ridiculous. I want a year to think about its meaning. Don't speak.

LORD JOHN. Papa joins our party.

ANN. That's what we're after . . . thank you.

LORD JOHN. I loathe politics.

ANN. Tell me something against them.

LORD JOHN. In my opinion your father's not a much bigger blackguard—I beg your pardon—than the rest of us.

ANN. . . . Miserable sinners.

LORD JOHN. Your father turns his coat. Well . . . ?

ANN. I see nothing at all in that.

LORD JOHN. What's right and what's wrong?

ANN. Papa's right . . . for the present . . . When shall we be married?

LORD JOHN. Tomorrow?

ANN [startled]. If you knew that it isn't easy for me to be practical you wouldn't make fun.

LORD JOHN. Why not tomorrow?

ANN. Papa—

LORD JOHN. Papa says yes . . suppose.

ANN. I'm very young . . not to speak of clothes. I must have lots of new dresses.

LORD JOHN. Ask me for them.

ANN. Why do you want to marry me?

LORD JOHN. I love you.

ANN. It suddenly occurs to me that sounds unpleasant.

LORD JOHN. I love you.

ANN. Out of place.

LORD JOHN. I love you.

ANN. What if Papa were to die?

LORD JOHN. I want y o u .

ANN. I'm nothing . . I'm nobody . . I'm part of my family.

LORD JOHN. I want you.

ANN. Won't you please forget last night?

LORD JOHN. I want you. Look straight at me.

She looks, and stays fascinated.

LORD JOHN. If I say now that I love you—

ANN. I know it.

LORD JOHN. And love me?

ANN. I suppose so.

LORD JOHN. Make sure.

ANN. But I hate you too . . I know that.

LORD JOHN. Shall I kiss you?

ANN [*helplessly*]. Yes.

He kisses her full on the lips.

ANN. I can't hate you enough.

LORD JOHN [*triumphantly*]. Speak the truth now.

ANN. I feel very degraded.

LORD JOHN. Nonsense.

ANN [*wretchedly*]. This is one of the things which don't matter.

LORD JOHN. Ain't you to be mine?

ANN. You want the right to behave like that as well as the power.

LORD JOHN. You shall command me.

ANN [*with a poor laugh*]. I rather like this in a way.

LORD JOHN. Little coquette!

ANN. It does tickle my vanity.

For a moment he sits looking at her, then shakes himself to his feet.

LORD JOHN. Now I must go.

ANN. Yes . . I want to think.

LORD JOHN. For Heaven's sake . . no!

ANN. I came this morning straight to where we were last night.

LORD JOHN. As I hung about the garden my heart was beating.

ANN. I shall like you better when you're not here.

LORD JOHN. We're to meet in Brighton?

ANN. I'm afraid so.

LORD JOHN. Good-bye.

ANN. There's just a silly sort of attraction between certain people, I believe.

LORD JOHN. Can you look me in the eyes and say you don't love me?

ANN. If I looked you in the eyes you'd frighten me again. I can say anything.

LORD JOHN. You're a deep child.

GEORGE LEETE *appears on the terrace.*

GEORGE. My lord!

LORD JOHN [*cordially*]. My dear Leete.

GEORGE. No . . I am not surprised to see you.

ANN. George, things are happening.

LORD JOHN. Shake hands.

GEORGE. I will not.

ANN. Lord John asks me to be married to him. Shake hands.

GEORGE. Why did you fight?

ANN. Why d i d you fight?

LORD JOHN [*shrugging*]. Your father struck me.

ANN. Now you've hurt him . . that's fair.

Then the two men do shake hands, not heartily.

GEORGE. We've trapped you, my lord.

LORD JOHN. I know what I want. I love your sister.

ANN. I don't like you . . but if you're good and I'm good we shall get on.

GEORGE. Why shouldn't one marry politically?

LORD JOHN [*in* ANN's *ear*]. I love you.

ANN. No . . no . . no . . no . . no . . [*discovering in this an echo of her father, she stops short*].

GEORGE. We're a cold-blooded family.

LORD JOHN. I don't think so.

GEORGE. I married for love.

LORD JOHN. Who doesn't? But, of course there should be other reasons.

GEORGE. You won't receive my wife.

LORD JOHN. Here's your sister.

LADY COTTESHAM *comes from the direction of the house.*

SARAH. Back again?

LORD JOHN. You see.

From the other side appears MR. TATTON.

MR. TATTON. As you all seem to be here I don't mind interrupting.

GEORGE [*hailing him*]. Well . . neighbour?

MR. TATTON. Come . . come . . what's a little fighting more or less!

GEORGE. Bravo, English sentiment . . relieves a deal of awkwardness.

The two shake hands.

SARAH [*who by this has reached* LORD JOHN]. . . . And back so soon?

ANN. Lord John asks to marry me.

LORD JOHN. Yes.

MR. TATTON. I guessed so . . give me a bit of romance!

SARAH [*suavely*]. This is perhaps a little sudden, my dear Lord John. Papa may naturally be a little shocked.

GEORGE. Not at all, Sarah.

MR. TATTON. How's the wound?

GEORGE. Not serious . . nothing's serious.

SARAH. You are very masterful, wooing sword in hand.

ANN. George and I have explained to Lord John that we are all most anxious to marry me to him and he doesn't mind—

LORD JOHN. Being made a fool of. I love—

ANN. I will like you.

GEORGE. Charming cynicism, my dear Sarah.

MR. TATTON. Oh, Lord!

ANN [*to her affianced*]. Good-bye now.

LORD JOHN. When do I see you?

ANN. Papa says soon.

LORD JOHN. Very soon, please. Tatton, my friend, Brighton's no nearer.

MR. TATTON. Lady Cottesham . . Miss Leete . . I kiss your hands.

LORD JOHN [*ebulliently clapping* GEORGE *on the back*]. Look more pleased. [*Then he bends over* LADY COTTESHAM's *hand.*] Lady Charlie . . my service to you . . all. Ann. [*And he takes* ANN's *hand to kiss.*]

ANN. If I can think better of all this, I shall. Good-bye.

> *She turns away from him. He stands for a moment considering her, but follows* TATTON *away through the orchard.* GEORGE *and* SARAH *are watching their sister, who then comments on her little affair with life.*

ANN. I'm growing up. [*Then with a sudden tremor.*] Sally, don't let me be forced to marry.

GEORGE. Force of circumstances, my dear Ann.

ANN. Outside things. Why couldn't I run away from this garden and over the hills . . I suppose there's something on the other side of the hills.

SARAH. You'd find yourself there . . and circumstances.

ANN. So I'm trapped as well as that Lord John.

SARAH. What's the injury?

ANN. I'm taken by surprise and I know I'm ignorant and I think I'm learning things backwards.

GEORGE. You must cheer up and say: John's not a bad sort.

SARAH. A man of his age is a young man.

ANN. I wish you wouldn't recommend him to me.

SARAH. Let's think of Brighton. What about your gowns?

ANN. I've nothing to wear.

SARAH. We'll talk to Papa.

GEORGE. The war-purse is always a long one.

SARAH. George . . be one of us for a minute.

GEORGE. But I want to look on too, and laugh.

SARAH [caustically]. Yes . . that's your privilege . . except occasionally. [Then to her sister.] I wish you all the happiness of courtship days.

GEORGE. Arcadian expression!

ANN. I believe it means being kissed . . often.

SARAH. Have you not a touch of romance in you, little girl?

ANN. Am I not like Mr. Dan Tatton? He kisses dairy-maids and servants and all the farmers' daughters . . I beg your pardon, George.

GEORGE [nettled]. I'll say to you, Ann, that—in all essentials—one woman is as good as another.

SARAH. That is not so in the polite world.

GEORGE. When you consider it no one l i v e s in the polite world.

ANN. Do they come outside for air sooner or later?

SARAH [briskly]. Three best dresses you must have and something very gay if you're to go near the Pavilion.

ANN. You're coming to Brighton, Sally?

SARAH. No.

ANN. Why not?

SARAH. I don't wish to meet my husband.

GEORGE. That man was his lawyer.

ANN. The political difference, Sally?

SARAH. Just that. [Then with a deft turn of the subject.] I don't say that yours is a pretty face, but I should think you would have charm.

GEORGE. For fashion's sake cultivate sweetness.

SARAH. You dance as well as they know how in Reading.

ANN. Yes . . I can twiddle my feet.

SARAH. Do you like dancing?

ANN. I'd sooner walk.

GEORGE. What . . . and get somewhere!

ANN. Here's George laughing.

SARAH. He's out of it.

ANN. Are you happy, George?

GEORGE. Alas . . Dolly's disgraceful ignorance of etiquette damns us both from the beautiful drawing-room.

SARAH. That laugh is forced. But how can you . . . look on?

There is a slight pause in their talk. Then . . .

ANN. He'll bully me with love.

SARAH. Your husband will give you just what you ask for.

ANN. I hate myself too. I want to take people mentally.

GEORGE. You want a new world . . you new woman.

ANN. And I'm a good bit frightened of myself.

SARAH. We have our places to fill in this. My dear child, leave futile questions alone.

GEORGE. Neither have I any good advice to give you.

ANN. I think happiness is a thing one talks too much about.

DIMMUCK *appears. And by now* ABUD'S *work has brought him back to the terrace.*

DIMMUCK. The master would like to see your Ladyship now.

SARAH. I'll say we've had a visitor . . Guess.

GEORGE. And you've had a visitor, Sarah.

ANN. Papa will know.

SARAH. Is he in a questioning mood?

ANN. I always tell everything.

SARAH. It saves time.

She departs towards the house.

DIMMUCK. Mr. George.

GEORGE. What is it?

DIMMUCK. He said No to a doctor when I haven't even mentioned the matter. Had I better send . . ?

GEORGE. Do . . if you care to waste the doctor's time.

DIMMUCK *gives an offended sniff and follows* LADY COTTESHAM.

ANN. I could sit here for days. George, I don't think I quite believe in anything I've been told yet.

GEORGE. What's that man's name?

ANN. John—John is a common name—John Abud.

GEORGE. Abud!

ABUD. Sir?

GEORGE. Come here.

ABUD *obediently walks towards his young master and stands before him.*

GEORGE. Why did you ask after the health of Mrs. George Leete?

ABUD. We courted once.

GEORGE [*after a moment*]. Listen, Ann. Do you hate me, John Abud?

ABUD. No, sir.

GEORGE. You're a fine looking fellow. How old are you?

ABUD. Twenty-seven, sir.

GEORGE. Is Once long ago?

ABUD. Two years gone.

GEORGE. Did Mrs. Leete quarrel with you?

ABUD. No, sir.

GEORGE. Pray tell me more.

ABUD. I was beneath her.

GEORGE. But you're a fine-looking fellow.

ABUD. Farmer Crowe wouldn't risk his daughter being unhappy.

GEORGE. But she was beneath me.

ABUD. That was another matter, sir.

GEORGE. I don't think you intend to be sarcastic.

ABUD. And . . being near her time for the first time, sir . . I wanted to know if she is in danger of dying yet.

GEORGE. Every precaution has been taken . . a nurse . . there is a physician near. I need not tell you . . but I do tell you.

ABUD. Thank you, sir.

GEORGE. I take great interest in my wife.

ABUD. We all do, sir.

GEORGE. Was it ambition that you courted her?

ABUD. I thought to start housekeeping.

GEORGE. Did you aspire to rise socially?

ABUD. I wanted a wife to keep house, sir.

GEORGE. Are you content?

ABUD. I think so, sir.

GEORGE. With your humble position?

ABUD. I'm a gardener, and there'll always be gardens.

GEORGE. Frustrated affections . . I beg your pardon . . . To have been crossed in love should make you bitter and ambitious.

ABUD. My father was a gardener and my son will be a gardener if he's no worse a man than I and no better.

GEORGE. Are you married?

ABUD. No, sir.

GEORGE. Are you going to be married?

ABUD. Not especially, sir.

GEORGE. Yes . . you must marry . . some decent woman; we want gardeners.

ABUD. Do you want me any more now, sir?

GEORGE. You have interested me. You can go back to your work.

    ABUD *obeys.*

GEORGE [*almost to himself*]. I am hardly human.

    He slowly moves away and out of sight.

ANN. John Abud.

    He comes back and stands before her too.

ANN. I am very sorry for you.

ABUD. I am very much obliged to you, Miss.

ANN. Both those sayings are quite meaningless. Say something true about yourself.

ABUD. I'm not sorry for myself.

ANN. I won't tell. It's very clear you ought to be in a despairing state. Don't stand in the sun with your hat off.

ABUD [*putting on his hat*]. Thank you, Miss.

ANN. Have you nearly finished the rose trees?

ABUD. I must work till late this evening.

ANN. Weren't you ambitious for Dolly's sake?

ABUD. She thought me good enough.

ANN. I'd have married her.

ABUD. She was ambitious for me.

ANN. And are you frightened of the big world?

ABUD. Fine things dazzle me sometimes.

ANN. But gardening is all that you're fit for?

ABUD. I'm afraid so, Miss.

ANN. But it's great to be a gardener . . to sow seeds and to watch flowers grow and to cut away dead things.

ABUD. Yes, Miss.

ANN. And you're in the fresh air all day.

ABUD. That's very healthy.

ANN. Are you very poor?

ABUD. I get my meals in the house.

ANN. Rough clothes last a long time.

ABUD. I've saved money.

ANN. Where do you sleep?

ABUD. At Mrs. Hart's . . at a cottage . . it's a mile off.

ANN. And you want no more than food and clothes and a bed and you earn all that with your hands.

ABUD. The less a man wants, Miss, the better.

ANN. But you mean to marry?

ABUD. Yes . . I've saved money.

ANN. Whom will you marry? Would you rather not say? Perhaps you don't know yet?

ABUD. It's all luck what sort of a maid a man gets fond of. It won't be a widow.

ANN. Be careful, John Abud.

ABUD. No . . I shan't be careful.

ANN. You'll do very wrong to be made a fool of.

ABUD. I'm safe, Miss; I've no eye for a pretty face.

DIMMUCK arrives asthmatically at the top of the steps.

DIMMUCK. Where's Mr. George? Here's a messenger come post.

ANN. Find him, Abud.

ABUD [*to* DIMMUCK]. From Dolly?

DIMMUCK. Speak respectful.

ABUD. Is it from his wife?

DIMMUCK. Go find him.

ANN [*as* ABUD *is immovable*]. Dimmuck . . . tell me about Mrs. George.

DIMMUCK. She's doing well, Miss.

ABUD [*shouting joyfully now*]. Mr. George! Mr. George!

ANN. A boy or a girl, Dimmuck?

DIMMUCK. Yes, Miss.

ABUD. Mr. George! Mr. George!

DIMMUCK. Ecod . . is he somewhere else?

DIMMUCK, somewhat excited himself, returns to the house.

ANN. George!

ABUD. Mr. George! Mr. George!

GEORGE comes slowly along the terrace, in his hand an open book, which some people might suppose he was reading. He speaks with studied calm.

GEORGE. You are very excited, my good man.

ABUD. She's brought you a child, sir.

ANN. Your child!

GEORGE. Certainly.

ABUD. Thank God, Sir!

GEORGE. I will if I please.

ANN. And she's doing well.

ABUD. There's a messenger come post.

GEORGE. To be sure . . it might have been bad news.

And slowly he crosses the garden towards the house.

ABUD [*suddenly, beyond all patience*]. Run . . damn you!

GEORGE makes one supreme effort to maintain his dignity, but fails utterly. He gasps out . . .

GEORGE. Yes, I will. [*And runs off as hard as he can.*]

ABUD [*in an ecstasy*]. This is good. Oh, Dolly and God . . this is good!

ANN [*round eyed*]. I wonder that you can be pleased.

ABUD [*apologising . . without apology*]. It's life.

ANN [*struck*]. Yes, it is.

And she goes towards the house, thinking this over.

THE THIRD ACT

It is near to sunset. The garden is shadier than before.
ABUD *is still working.* CARNABY LEETE *comes from the house followed by* DR. REMNANT. *He wears his right arm in a sling. His face is flushed, his speech rapid.*

CARNABY. Parson, you didn't drink enough wine . . . damme, the wine was good.

DR. REMNANT. I am very grateful for an excellent dinner.

CARNABY. A good dinner, sir, is the crown to a good day's work.

DR. REMNANT. It may also be a comfort in affliction. Our philosophy does ill, Mr. Leete, when it despises the more simple means of contentment.

CARNABY. And which will be the better lover of a woman, a hungry or a well-fed man?

DR. REMNANT. A good meal digests love with it; for what is love but a food to live by . . but a hungry love will ofttimes devour its owner.

CARNABY. Admirable! Give me a man in love to deal with. Vous l'avez vu?

DR. REMNANT. Speak Latin, Greek or Hebrew to me, Mr. Leete.

CARNABY. French is the language of little things. My poor France! Ours is a little world, Parson . . . a man may hold it here. [*His open hand.*] Lord John Carp's a fine fellow.

DR. REMNANT. Son of a Duke.

CARNABY. And I commend to you the originality of his return. At twelve we fight . . . at one-thirty he proposes marriage to my daughter. D'ye see him humbly on his knees? Will there be rain, I wonder?

DR. REMNANT. We need rain . . Abud?

ABUD. Badly, sir.

CARNABY. Do we want a wet journey tomorrow! Where's Sarah?

DR. REMNANT. Lady Cottesham's taking tea.

CARNABY [*to* ABUD *with a sudden start*]. And why the devil didn't you marry my daughter-in-law . . my own gardener?

63

5

GEORGE *appears dressed for riding*.

GEORGE. Good-bye, sir, for the present.

CARNABY. Boots and breeches!

GEORGE. You shouldn't be about in the evening air with a green wound in your arm. You drank wine at dinner. Be careful, sir.

CARNABY. Off to your wife and the expected?

GEORGE. Yes, sir.

CARNABY. Riding to Watford?

GEORGE. From there alongside the North Coach, if I'm in time.

CARNABY. Don't founder my horse. Will ye leave the glorious news with your grandfather at Wycombe?

GEORGE. I won't fail to. [*Then to* ABUD.] We've been speaking of you.

ABUD. It was never any secret, sir.

GEORGE. Don't apologise.

Soon after this ABUD *passes out of sight*.

CARNABY. Nature's an encumbrance to us, Parson.

DR. REMNANT. One disapproves of flesh uninspired.

CARNABY. She allows you no amusing hobbies . . always takes you seriously.

GEORGE. Good-bye, Parson.

DR. REMNANT [*as he bows*]. Your most obedient.

CARNABY. And you trifle with damnable democracy, with pretty theories of the respect due to womanhood and now the result . . . hark to it squalling.

DR. REMNANT. Being fifty miles off might not one say: The cry of the new-born?

CARNABY. Ill-bred babies squall. There's no poetic glamour in the world will beautify an undesired infant . . George says so.

GEORGE. I did say so.

CARNABY. I feel the whole matter deeply.

GEORGE *half laughs*.

CARNABY. George, after days of irritability, brought to bed of a smile. That's a home thrust of a metaphor.

GEORGE *laughs again*.

CARNABY. Twins!

GEORGE. Yes, a boy and a girl . . . I'm the father of a boy and a girl.

CARNABY [*in dignified, indignant horror*]. No one of you dared tell me that much!

SARAH *and* ANN *come from the house*.

GEORGE. You could have asked me for news of your grand-children.

CARNABY. Twins is an insult.

SARAH. But you look very cheerful, George.

GEORGE. I am content.

SARAH. I'm surprised.

GEORGE. I am surprised.

SARAH. Now what names for them?

CARNABY. No family names, please.

GEORGE. We'll wait for a dozen years or so and let them choose their own.

DR. REMNANT. But, sir, christening will demand—

CARNABY. Your son should have had my name, sir.

GEORGE. I know the rule . . as I have my grandfather's which I take no pride in.

SARAH. George!

GEORGE. Not to say that it sounds his, not mine.

CARNABY. Our hopes of you were high once.

GEORGE. Sarah, may I kiss you? [*He kisses her cheek.*] Let me hear what you decide to do.

CARNABY. The begetting you, sir, was a waste of time.

GEORGE [*quite pleasantly*]. Don't say that.

At the top of the steps ANN *is waiting for him.*

ANN. I'll see you into the saddle.

GEORGE. Thank you sister Ann.

ANN. Why didn't you leave us weeks ago?

GEORGE. Why!

They pace away, arm-in-arm.

CARNABY [*bitterly*]. Glad to go! Brighton, Sarah.

SARAH. No, I shall not come, Papa.

CARNABY. Coward. [*Then to* REMNANT.] Good-night.

DR. REMNANT [*covering the insolent dismissal*]. With your kind permission I will take my leave. [*Then he bows to* SARAH.] Lady Cottesham.

SARAH [*curtseying*]. Doctor Remnant, I am yours.

CARNABY [*sitting by the fountain, stamping his foot*]. Oh, this cracked earth! Will it rain . . will it rain?

DR. REMNANT. I doubt now. That cloud has passed.

CARNABY. Soft, pellucid rain! There's a good word and I'm not at all sure what it means.

DR. REMNANT. Per . . lucere . . . letting light through.

REMNANT *leaves them.*

CARNABY. Soft, pellucid rain! . . thank you. Brighton, Sarah.

SARAH. Ann needs new clothes.

CARNABY. See to it.

SARAH. I shall not be there.

She turns from him.

CARNABY. Pretty climax to a quarrel!

SARAH. Not a quarrel.

CARNABY. A political difference.

SARAH. Don't look so ferocious.

CARNABY. My arm is in great pain and the wine's in my head.

SARAH. Won't you go to bed?

CARNABY. I'm well enough . . to travel. This marriage makes us safe, Sarah . . an anchor in each camp . . There's a mixed metaphor.

SARAH. If you'll have my advice, Papa, you'll keep those plans clear from Ann's mind.

CARNABY. John Carp is so much clay . . a man of forty ignorant of himself.

SARAH. But if the Duke will not . .

CARNABY. The Duke hates a scandal.

SARAH. Does he detest scandal!

CARNABY. The girl is well-bred and harmless . . why publicly quarrel with John and incense her old brute of a father? There's the Duke in a score of words. He'll take a little time to think it out so.

SARAH. And I say: Do you get on the right side of the Duke once again—that's what we've worked for—and leave these two alone.

CARNABY. Am I to lose my daughter?

SARAH. Papa . . your food's intrigue.

CARNABY. Scold at Society . . and what's the use?

SARAH. We're over-civilized.

ANN *rejoins them now. The twilight is gathering.*

CARNABY. My mother's very old . . . your grandfather's younger and seventy-nine . . he swears I'll never come into the title. There's little else.

SARAH. You're feverish . . why are you saying this?

CARNABY. Ann . . George . . George via Wycombe . . Wycombe Court . . Sir George Leete baronet, Justice of the Peace, Deputy Lieutenant . . the thought's tumbled. Ann, I first saw your mother in this garden . . there.

ANN. Was she like me?

SARAH. My age when she married.

CARNABY. She was not beautiful . . then she died.

ANN. Mr. Tatton thinks it a romantic garden.

CARNABY [*pause*]. D'ye hear the wind sighing through that tree?

ANN. The air's quite still.

CARNABY. I hear myself sighing . . when I first saw your mother in this garden . . . that's how it was done.

SARAH. For a woman must marry.

CARNABY [*rises*]. You all take to it as ducks to water . . but apple sauce is quite correct . . I must not mix metaphors.

MRS. OPIE comes from the house.

SARAH. Your supper done, Mrs. Opie?

MRS. OPIE. I eat little in the evening.

SARAH. I believe that saves digestion.

MRS. OPIE. Ann, do you need me more to-night?

ANN. Not any more.

MRS. OPIE. Ann, there is gossip among the servants about a wager . . .

ANN. Mrs. Opie, that was . . . yesterday.

MRS. OPIE. Ann, I should be glad to be able to contradict a reported . . embrace.

ANN. I was kissed.

MRS. OPIE. I am shocked.

CARNABY. Mrs. Opie, is it possible that all these years I have been nourishing a prude in my . . back drawing-room?

MRS. OPIE. I presume I am discharged of Ann's education; but as the salaried mistress of your household, Mr. Leete, I am grieved not to be able to deny such a rumour to your servants.

She sails back, righteously indignant.

CARNABY. Call out that you're marrying the wicked man . . comfort her.

SARAH. Mrs. Opie!

CARNABY. Consider that existence. An old maid . . so far as we know. Brevet rank . . missis. Not pleasant.

ANN. She wants nothing better . . at her age.

SARAH. How forgetful!

CARNABY [*the force of the phrase growing*]. Brighton, Sarah.

SARAH. Now you've both read the love-letter which Tetgeen brought me.

CARNABY. Come to Brighton.

ANN. Come to Brighton, Sally.

SARAH. No. I have been thinking. I think I will accept the income, the house, coals, butter and eggs.

CARNABY. I give you a fortnight to bring your husband to his knees . . to your feet.

SARAH. I'm not sure that I could. My marriage has come naturally to an end.

CARNABY. Sarah, don't annoy me.

SARAH. Papa, you joined my bridegroom's political party . . now you see fit to leave it.

She glances at ANN, *who gives no sign, however.*

CARNABY. What have you been doing in ten years?

SARAH. Waiting for this to happen . . now I come to think.

CARNABY. Have ye the impudence to tell me that ye've never cared for your husband?

SARAH. I was caught by the first few kisses; but he . . .

CARNABY. Has he ever been unkind to you?

SARAH. Never. He's a gentleman through and through . . . quite charming to live with.

CARNABY. I see what more you expect. And he neither drinks nor . . nor . . no one even could suppose your leaving him.

SARAH. No. I'm disgraced.

CARNABY. Fight for your honour.

SARAH. You surprise me sometimes by breaking out into cant phrases.

CARNABY. What is more useful in the world than honour?

SARAH. I think we never had any . . we!

CARNABY. Give me more details. Tell me, who is this man?

SARAH. I'm innocent . . if that were all.

ANN. Sally, what do they say you've done?

SARAH. I cry out like any poor girl.

CARNABY. There must be no doubt that you're innocent. Why not go for to force Charles into court?

SARAH. My innocence is not of the sort which shows up well.

CARNABY. Hold publicity in reserve. No fear of the two men arranging to meet, is there?

SARAH. They've met . . and they chatted about me.

CARNABY [*after a moment*]. There's sound humour in that.

SARAH. I shall feel able to laugh at them both from Yorkshire.

CARNABY. God forbid! Come to Brighton . . we'll rally Charles no end.

SARAH. Papa, I know there's nothing to be done.

CARNABY. Coward!

SARAH. Besides I don't think I want to go back to my happiness.
They are silent for a little.

CARNABY. How still! Look . . leaves falling already. Can that
man hear what we're saying?

SARAH [*to* ANN]. Can Abud overhear?

ANN. I've never talked secrets in the garden before to-day.
[*Raising her voice but a very little.*] Can you hear me, Abud?
No reply comes.

CARNABY. Evidently not. There's brains shown in a trifle.

SARAH. Does your arm pain you so much?

ANN. Sarah, this man that you're fond of and that's not your
husband is not by any chance Lord John Carp?

SARAH. No.

ANN. Nothing would surprise me.

SARAH. You are witty . . but a little young to be so hard.

CARNABY. Keep to your innocent thoughts.

ANN. I must study politics.

SARAH. We'll stop talking of this.

ANN. No . . let me listen . . quite quietly.

CARNABY. Let her listen . . she's going to be married.

SARAH. Good luck, Ann.

CARNABY. I have great hopes of Ann.

SARAH. I hope she may be heartless. To be heartless is to be
quite safe.

CARNABY. Now we detect a taste of sour grapes in your mouth.

SARAH. Butter and eggs.

CARNABY. We must all start early in the morning. Sarah will
take you, Ann, round the Brighton shops . . fine shops. You shall
have the money. . .

SARAH. I will not come with you.

CARNABY [*vexedly*]. How absurd . . how ridiculous . . to persist
in your silly sentiment.

SARAH [*her voice rising*]. I'm tired of that world . . which goes
on and on, and there's no dying . . . one grows into a ghost . .
visible . . then invisible. I'm glad paint has gone out of fashion
. . . the painted ghosts were very ill to see.

CARNABY. D'ye scoff at civilization?

SARAH. Look ahead for me.

CARNABY. Banished to a hole in the damned provinces! But
you're young yet, you're charming . . you're the wife . . and the
honest wife of one of the country's best men. My head aches.
D'ye despise good fortune's gifts? Keep as straight in your place

in the world as you can. A monthly packet of books to Yorkshire
.. no .. you never were fond of reading. Ye'd play patience ..
cultivate chess problems .. kill yourself!

SARAH. When one world fails take another.

CARNABY. You have no more right to commit suicide than to
desert the society you were born into. My head aches.

SARAH. George is happy.

CARNABY. D'ye dare to think so?

SARAH. No .. it's a horrible marriage.

CARNABY. He's losing refinement .. mark me .. he no longer
polishes his nails.

SARAH. But there are the children now.

CARNABY. You never have wanted children.

SARAH. I don't want a little child.

CARNABY. She to be Lady Leete .. some day .. soon! What
has he done for his family?

SARAH. I'll come with you. You are clever, Papa. And I know
just what to say to Charles.

CARNABY [with a curious change of tone]. If you study anatomy
you'll find that the brain, as it works, pressing forward the eyes
... thought is painful. Never be defeated. Chapter the latest ..
the tickling of the Carp. And my throat is dry .. shall I drink
that water?

SARAH. No, I wouldn't.

CARNABY. Not out of my hand?

ANN [speaking in a strange quiet voice, after her long silence]. I will
not come to Brighton with you.

CARNABY. Very dry!

ANN. You must go back, Sally.

CARNABY [as he looks at her, standing stiffly]. Now what is Ann's
height .. five feet .. ?

ANN. Sally must go back, for she belongs to it .. but I'll stay
here where I belong.

CARNABY. You've spoken three times and the words are
jumbling in at my ears meaninglessly. I certainly took too much
wine at dinner .. or else... Yes .. Sally goes back .. and you'll
go forward. Who stays here? Don't burlesque your sister. What's
in the air .. what disease is this?

ANN. I mean to disobey you.. to stay here.. never to be unhappy.

CARNABY. So pleased!

ANN. I want to be an ordinary woman .. not clever .. not
fortunate.

CARNABY. I can't hear.

ANN. Not clever. I don't believe in you, Papa.

CARNABY. I exist . . I'm very sorry.

ANN. I won't be married to any man. I refuse to be tempted . . I won't see him again.

CARNABY. Yes. It's raining.

SARAH. Raining!

CARNABY. Don't you stop it raining.

ANN [*in the same level tones, to her sister now, who otherwise would turn, alarmed, to their father*]. And I curse you . . because, we being sisters, I suppose I am much what you were, about to be married; and I think, Sally, you'd have cursed your present self. I could become all that you are and more . . but I don't choose.

SARAH. Ann, what is to become of you?

CARNABY. Big drops . . big drops!

At this moment ABUD *is passing towards the house, his work finished.*

ANN. John Abud . . you mean to marry. When you marry . . will you marry me?

A blank silence, into which breaks CARNABY'S *sick voice.*

CARNABY. Take me indoors. I heard you ask the gardener to marry you.

ANN. I asked him.

CARNABY. I heard you say that you asked him. Take me in . . but not out of the rain.

ANN. Look . . he's straight-limbed and clear-eyed . . and I'm a woman.

SARAH. Ann, are you mad?

ANN. If we two were alone here in this garden and everyone else in the world were dead . . what would you answer?

ABUD [*still amazed*]. Why . . yes.

CARNABY. Then that's settled . . pellucid.

He attempts to rise, but staggers backwards and forwards.
SARAH goes to him alarmed.

SARAH. Papa! . . there's no rain yet.

CARNABY. Hush, I'm dead.

ANN [*her nerves failing her*]. Oh . . oh . . oh . . !

SARAH. Abud, don't ever speak of this.

ABUD. No, my lady.

ANN [*with a final effort*]. I mean it all. Wait three months.

CARNABY. Help me up steps . . son-in-law.

CARNABY *has started to grope his way indoors. But he reels and falls helpless.*

ABUD. I'll carry him.

> *Throwing down his tools* ABUD *lifts the frail sick man and carries him towards the house.* SARAH *follows.*

ANN [*sobbing a little, and weary*]. Such a long day it has been . . now ending.

> *She follows too.*

THE FOURTH ACT

The hall at Markswayde is square; in decoration strictly eighteenth century. The floor polished. Then comes six feet of soberly painted wainscot and above the greenish blue and yellowish green wall painted into panels. At intervals are low relief pilasters; the capitals of these are gilded. The ceiling is white and in the centre of it there is a frosted glass dome through which a dull light struggles. Two sides only of the hall are seen.

In the corner is a hat stand and on it are many cloaks and hats and beneath it several pairs of very muddy boots.

In the middle of the left hand wall are the double doors of the dining-room led up to by three or four stairs with balusters, and on either side standing against the wall long, formal, straight backed sofas.

In the middle of the right hand wall is the front door; glass double doors can be seen and there is evidently a porch beyond. On the left of the front door a small window. On the right a large fireplace, in which a large fire is roaring. Over the front door, a clock (the hands pointing to half-past one). Over the fireplace a family portrait (temp. Queen Anne), below this a blunderbuss and several horse-pistols. Above the sofa full-length family portraits (temp. George I). Before the front door a wooden screen, of lighter wood than the wainscot, and in the middle of it a small glass panel. Before this a heavy square table on which are whips and sticks, a hat or two and brushes; by the table a wooden chair. On either side the fire stand tall closed-in armchairs, and between the fireplace and the door a smaller red-baize screen.

When the dining-room doors are thrown open another wooden screen is to be seen.

There are a few rugs on the floor, formally arranged.

MRS. OPIE *stands in the middle of the hall, holding out a woman's brown cloak: she drops one side to fetch out her handkerchief and apply it to her eye.* DIMMUCK *comes in by the front door, which he carefully closes behind him. He is wrapped in a hooded cloak and carries a pair of boots and a newspaper. The boots he arranges to warm before the fire. Then he spreads the* Chronicle *newspaper*

*upon the arm of a chair, then takes off his cloak and hangs it upon
a peg close to the door.*

DIMMUCK. Mrs. Opie . . will you look to its not scorching?

> MRS. OPIE *still mops her eyes.* DIMMUCK *goes towards the dining-
> room door, but turns.*

DIMMUCK. Will you kindly see that the *Chronicle* newspaper does
not burn?

MRS. OPIE. I was crying.

DIMMUCK. I leave this tomorrow sennight . . thankful, ma'am,
to have given notice in a dignified manner.

MRS. OPIE. I understand . . Those persons at table . .

DIMMUCK. You give notice.

MRS. OPIE. Mr. Dimmuck, this is my home.

> LORD ARTHUR CARP *comes out of the dining-room. He is a
> thinner and more earnest-looking edition of his brother.* MRS. OPIE
> *turns a chair and hangs the cloak to warm before the fire, and then
> goes into the dining-room.*

LORD ARTHUR. My chaise round?

DIMMUCK. I've but just ordered it, my lord. Your lordship's
man has given me your boots.

LORD ARTHUR. Does it snow?

DIMMUCK. Rather rain than snow.

> LORD ARTHUR *takes up the newspaper.*

DIMMUCK. Yesterday's, my lord.

LORD ARTHUR. I've seen it. The mails don't hurry hereabouts.
Can I be in London by the morning?

DIMMUCK. I should say you might be, my lord.

> LORD ARTHUR *sits by the fire, while* DIMMUCK *takes off his
> pumps and starts to put on his boots.*

LORD ARTHUR. Is this a horse called "Ronald"?

DIMMUCK. Which horse, my lord?

LORD ARTHUR. Which I'm to take back with me . . my brother
left here. I brought the mare he borrowed.

DIMMUCK. I remember, my lord. I'll enquire.

LORD ARTHUR. Tell Parker . .

DIMMUCK. Your lordship's man?

LORD ARTHUR. . . he'd better ride the beast.

> SARAH *comes out of the dining-room. He stands up; one boot,
> one shoe.*

SARAH. Please put on the other.

LORD ARTHUR. Thank you . . I am in haste.

SARAH. To depart before the bride's departure.

LORD ARTHUR. Does the bride go with the bridegroom?

SARAH. She goes away.

LORD ARTHUR. I shall never see such a thing again.

SARAH. I think this entertainment is unique.

LORD ARTHUR. Any commissions in town?

SARAH. Why can't you stay to travel with us tomorrow and talk business to Papa by the way?

> DIMMUCK *carrying the pumps and after putting on his cloak goes out through the front door. When it is closed, her voice changes.*

SARAH. Why . . Arthur?

> *He does not answer. Then* MRS. OPIE *comes out of the dining-room to fetch the cloak. The two, with an effort, reconstruct their casual disjointed conversation.*

SARAH. . . Before the bride's departure?

LORD ARTHUR. Does the bride go away with the bridegroom?

SARAH. She goes.

LORD ARTHUR. I shall never see such an entertainment again.

SARAH. We are quite unique.

LORD ARTHUR. Any commissions in town?

SARAH. Is she to go soon too, Mrs. Opie?

MRS. OPIE. It is arranged they are to walk . . in this weather . . ten miles . . to the house.

SARAH. Cottage.

MRS. OPIE. Hut.

> MRS. OPIE *takes the cloak into the dining-room. Then* SARAH *comes a little towards* LORD ARTHUR, *but waits for him to speak.*

LORD ARTHUR [*a little awkwardly*]. You are not looking well.

SARAH. To our memory . . and beyond your little chat with my husband about me . . I want to speak an epitaph.

LORD ARTHUR. Charlie Cottesham behaved most honourably.

SARAH. And I think you did. Why have you not let me tell you so in your ear till now, to-day?

LORD ARTHUR. Sarah . . we had a narrow escape from. . .

SARAH. How's your wife?

LORD ARTHUR. Well . . thank you.

SARAH. Nervous, surely, at your travelling in winter?

LORD ARTHUR. I was so glad to receive a casual invitation from you and to come . . casually.

SARAH. Fifty miles.

LORD ARTHUR. Your father has been ill?

SARAH. Very ill through the autumn.

LORD ARTHUR. Do you think he suspects us?

SARAH. I shouldn't care to peep into Papa's innermost mind. You are to be very useful to him.

LORD ARTHUR. No.

SARAH. Then he'll go back to the government.

LORD ARTHUR. If he pleases . . if they please . . if you please.

SARAH. I am not going back to my husband. Arthur . . be useful to him.

LORD ARTHUR. No . . you are not coming to me. Always your father! [*After a moment.*] It was my little home in the country somehow said aloud you didn't care for me.

SARAH. I fooled you to small purpose.

LORD ARTHUR. I wish you had once made friends with my wife.

SARAH. If we . . this house I'm speaking of . . had made friends where we've only made tools and fools we shouldn't now be cursed as we are . . all. George, who is a cork, trying to sink socially. Ann is mad . . and a runaway.

LORD ARTHUR. Sarah, I've been devilish fond of you.

SARAH. Be useful to Papa. [*He shakes his head, obstinately.*] Praise me a little. Haven't I worked my best for my family?

LORD ARTHUR. Suppose I could be useful to him now, would you, in spite of all, come to me . . no half measures?

SARAH. Arthur . . [*He makes a little passionate movement towards her, but she is cold.*] It's time for me to vanish from this world, because I've nothing left to sell.

LORD ARTHUR. I can't help him. I don't want you.

He turns away.

SARAH. I feel I've done my best.

LORD ARTHUR. Keep your father quiet.

SARAH. I mean to leave him.

LORD ARTHUR. What does he say to that?

SARAH. I've not yet told him.

LORD ARTHUR. What happens?

SARAH. To sell my jewels . . spoils of a ten years' war. Three thousand pound . . how much a year?

LORD ARTHUR. I'll buy them.

SARAH. And return them? You have almost the right to make such a suggestion.

LORD ARTHUR. Stick to your father. He'll care for you?

SARAH. No . . we all pride ourselves on our lack of sentiment.

LORD ARTHUR. You must take money from your husband.

SARAH. I have earned that and spent it.

LORD ARTHUR [*yielding once again to temptation*]. I'm devilish fond of you . . .

> At that moment ABUD *comes out of the dining-room. He is dressed in his best.* SARAH *responds readily to the interruption.*

SARAH. And you must give my kindest compliments to Lady Arthur and my . . affectionately . . to the children and I'll let Papa know that you're going.

LORD ARTHUR. Letters under cover to your father?

SARAH. Papa will stay in town through the session of course . . but they all tell me that seventy-five pounds a year is a comfortable income in . . Timbuctoo.

> *She goes into the dining-room.* ABUD *has selected his boots from the corner and now stands with them in his hand looking rather helpless. After a moment—*

LORD ARTHUR. I congratulate you, Mr. Abud.

ABUD. My lord . . I can't speak of myself.

> CARNABY *comes out of the dining-room. He is evidently by no means recovered from his illness. He stands for a moment with an ironical eye on* JOHN ABUD.

CARNABY. Son-in-law.

ABUD. I'm told to get on my boots, sir.

CARNABY. Allow me to assist you?

ABUD. I couldn't, sir.

CARNABY. Désolé!

> *Then he passes on.* ABUD *sits on the sofa, furtively puts on his boots and afterwards puts his shoes in his pockets.*

LORD ARTHUR. You were so busy drinking health to the two fat farmers that I wouldn't interrupt you.

CARNABY. Good-bye. Describe all this to your brother John.

LORD ARTHUR. So confirmed a bachelor!

CARNABY. Please say that we missed him.

> LORD ARTHUR *hands him the newspaper.*

LORD ARTHUR. I've out-raced your *Chronicle* from London by some hours. There's a paragraph . . second column . . near the bottom.

CARNABY [*looking at it blindly*]. They print villainously now-a-days.

LORD ARTHUR. Inspired.

CARNABY. I trust his Grace is well?

LORD ARTHUR. Gouty.

CARNABY. Now doesn't the social aspect of this case interest you?

LORD ARTHUR. I object to feeding with the lower classes.

CARNABY. There's pride! How useful to note their simple manners! From the meeting of extremes new ideas spring . . new life.

LORD ARTHUR. Take that for a new social-political creed, Mr. Leete.

CARNABY. Do I lack one?

LORD ARTHUR. Please make my adieux to the bride.

CARNABY. Appropriate . . . 'à Dieu' . . . she enters Nature's cloister. My epigram.

LORD ARTHUR. But . . good heavens . . are we to choose to be toiling animals?

CARNABY. To be such is my daughter's ambition.

LORD ARTHUR. You have not read that.

CARNABY [*giving back the paper, vexedly*]. I can't see.

LORD ARTHUR. "The Right Honourable Carnaby Leete is, we are glad to hear, completely recovered and will return to town for the opening of Session."

CARNABY. I mentioned it.

LORD ARTHUR. "We understand that although there has been no reconciliation with the Government it is quite untrue that this gentleman will in any way resume his connection with the Opposition."

CARNABY. Inspired?

LORD ARTHUR. I am here from my father to answer any questions.

CARNABY [*with some dignity and the touch of a threat*]. Not now, my lord.

> DIMMUCK *comes in at the front door.*

DIMMUCK. The chaise, my lord.

CARNABY. I will conduct you.

LORD ARTHUR. Please don't risk exposure.

CARNABY. Nay, I insist.

LORD ARTHUR. Health and happiness to you both, Mr. Abud.

> LORD ARTHUR *goes out, followed by* CARNABY, *followed by* DIMMUCK. *At that moment* MR. SMALLPEICE *skips excitedly out of the dining-room. A ferret-like little lawyer.*

MR. SMALLPEICE. Oh . . where is Mr. Leete?

> *Not seeing him* MR. SMALLPEICE *skips as excitedly back into the dining-room.* DIMMUCK *returns and hangs up his cloak then goes towards* ABUD, *whom he surveys.*

DIMMUCK. Sir!

*With which insult he starts for the dining-room reaching the door
just in time to hold it open for* SIR GEORGE LEETE *who comes
out. He surveys* ABUD *for a moment, then explodes.*

SIR GEORGE LEETE. Damn you . . stand in the presence of your
grandfather-in-law.

ABUD *stands up.* CARNABY *returns coughing, and* SIR GEORGE
looks him up and down.

SIR GEORGE LEETE. I shall attend your funeral.

CARNABY. My daughter Sarah still needs me.

SIR GEORGE LEETE. I wonder at you, my son.

CARNABY. Have you any money to spare?

SIR GEORGE LEETE. No.

CARNABY. For Sarah, my housekeeper; I foresee a busy session.

ABUD *is now gingerly walking up the stairs.*

SIR GEORGE LEETE. Carnaby . . look at that.

CARNABY. Sound in wind and limb. Tread boldly, son-in-law.

ABUD *turns, stands awkwardly for a moment and then goes into
the dining-room.*

SIR GEORGE LEETE [*relapsing into a pinch of snuff*]. I'm calm.

CARNABY. Regard this marriage with a wise eye . . as an
amusing little episode.

SIR GEORGE LEETE. Do you?

CARNABY. And forget its oddity. Now that the humiliation is
irrevocable, is it a personal grievance to you?

SIR GEORGE LEETE. Give me a dinner a day for the rest of my
life and I'll be content.

CARNABY. Lately, one by one, opinions and desires have been
failing me . . a flicker and then extinction. I shall shortly attain
to being a most able critic upon life.

SIR GEORGE LEETE. Shall I tell you again? You came into this
world without a conscience. That explains you and it's all that
does. That such a damnable coupling as this should be permitted
by God Almighty . . or that the law shouldn't interfere! I've
said my say.

MR. SMALLPEICE *again comes out of the dining-room.*

MR. SMALLPEICE. Mr. Leete.

CARNABY [*ironically polite*]. Mr. Smallpeice.

MR. SMALLPEICE. Mr. Crowe is proposing your health.

MR. CROWE *comes out. A crop-headed beefy-looking farmer of
sixty.*

MR. CROWE. Was.

CARNABY. There's a good enemy!

6

MR. CROWE. Get out of my road . . lawyer Smallpeice.

CARNABY. Leave enough of him living to attend to my business.

MR. SMALLPEICE [*wriggling a bow at* CARNABY]. Oh . . dear sir!

SIR GEORGE LEETE [*disgustedly to* MR. SMALLPEICE]. You!

MR. SMALLPEICE. Employed in a small matter . . as yet.

CARNABY [*to* CROWE]. I hope you spoke your mind of me.

MR. CROWE. Not behind your back, sir.

> MRS. GEORGE LEETE *leads* LADY LEETE *from the dining-room.* LADY LEETE *is a very old, blind and decrepit woman.* DOLLY *is a buxom young mother; whose attire borders on the gaudy.*

CARNABY [*with some tenderness*]. Well . . Mother . . dear?

MR. CROWE [*bumptiously to* SIR GEORGE LEETE]. Did my speech offend you, my lord?

SIR GEORGE LEETE [*sulkily*]. I'm a baronet.

LADY LEETE. Who's this here?

CARNABY. Carnaby.

DOLLY. Step down . . grandmother.

LADY LEETE. Who did ye say you were?

DOLLY. Mrs. George Leete.

LADY LEETE. Take me to the fire-side.

> *So* CARNABY *and* DOLLY *lead her slowly to a chair by the fire where they carefully bestow her.*

MR. SMALLPEICE [*to* FARMER CROWE]. He's leaving Markswayde, you know . . and me agent.

LADY LEETE [*suddenly bethinking her*]. Grace was not said. Fetch my chaplain . . at once.

MR. SMALLPEICE. I will run.

> *He runs into the dining-room.*

DOLLY [*calling after with her country accent*]. Not parson Remnant . . t'other one.

LADY LEETE [*demanding*]. Snuff.

CARNABY [*to his father*]. Sir . . my hand is a little unsteady.

> SIR GEORGE *and* CARNABY *between them give* LADY LEETE *her snuff.*

MR. CROWE. Dolly . . ought those children to be left so long?

DOLLY. All right, father . . I have a maid.

> LADY LEETE *sneezes.*

SIR GEORGE LEETE. She'll do that once too often altogether.

LADY LEETE. I'm cold.

DOLLY. I'm cold . . I lack my shawl.

CROWE. Call out to your man for it.

DOLLY [*going to the dining-room door*]. Will a gentleman please ask Mr. George Leete for my Cache-y-mire shawl?

MR. CROWE [*to* CARNABY]. And I drank to the health of our grandson.

CARNABY. Now suppose George were to assume your name, Mr. Crowe?

MR. TOZER *comes out of the dining-room. Of the worst type of eighteenth century parson, for which one may see Hogarth's 'Harlot's Progress.' He is very drunk.*

SIR GEORGE LEETE [*in his wife's ear*]. Tozer!

LADY LEETE. When . . why!

SIR GEORGE LEETE. To say grace.

LADY LEETE *folds her withered hands.*

MR. TOZER [*through his hiccoughs*]. Damn you all.

LADY LEETE [*reverently, thinking it is said*]. Amen.

MR. TOZER. Only my joke.

CARNABY [*rising to the height of the occasion*]. Mr. Tozer, I am indeed glad to see you, upon this occasion so delightfully drunk.

MR. TOZER. Always a gen'elman . . by nature.

SIR GEORGE LEETE. Lie down . . you dog.

GEORGE *comes out carrying the cashmere shawl.*

GEORGE [*to his father*]. Dolly wants her father to rent Markswayde, sir.

MR. CROWE. Not me, my son. You're to be a farmer-baronet.

SIR GEORGE. Curse your impudence!

CARNABY. My one regret in dying would be to miss seeing him so.

GEORGE *goes back into the dining-room.*

MR. CROWE. I am tickled to think that the man marrying your daughter wasn't good enough for mine.

CARNABY. And yet at fisticuffs, I'd back John Abud against our son George.

DR. REMNANT *has come out of the dining-room.* TOZER *has stumbled towards him and is wagging an argumentative finger.*

MR. TOZER. . . Marriage means enjoyment!

DR. REMNANT [*controlling his indignation*]. I repeat that I have found in my own copy of the prayer book no insistence upon a romantic passion.

MR. TOZER. My 'terpretation of God's word is 'bove criticism.

MR. TOZER *reaches the door and falls into the dining-room.*

CARNABY [*weakly to* DR. REMNANT]. Give me your arm for a moment.

DR. REMNANT. I think Lady Cottesham has Mrs. John Abud prepared to start, sir.

CARNABY. I trust Ann will take no chill walking through the mud.

DR. REMNANT. Won't you sit down, sir?

CARNABY. No.

> *For some moments* CROWE *has been staring indignantly at* SIR GEORGE. *Now he breaks out.*

MR. CROWE. The front door of this mansion is opened to a common gardener and only then to me and mine!

SIR GEORGE LEETE [*virulently*]. Damn you and yours and damn them . . and damn you again for the worse disgrace.

MR. CROWE. Damn *you*, sir . . have you paid him to marry the girl?

> *He turns away, purple faced and* SIR GEORGE *chokes impotently.* ABUD *and* MR. PRESTIGE *come out talking. He is younger and less assertive than* FARMER CROWE.

MR. PRESTIGE [*pathetically*]. All our family always has got drunk at weddings.

ABUD [*in remonstrance*]. Please, uncle.

CARNABY. Mr. Crowe . . I have been much to blame for not seeking you sooner.

MR. CROWE [*mollified*]. Shake hands.

CARNABY [*offering his with some difficulty*]. My arm is stiff . . . from an accident. This is a maid's marriage, I assure you.

MR. PRESTIGE [*open mouthed to* DR. REMNANT]. One could hang bacon here!

DOLLY [*very high and mighty*]. The family don't.

CARNABY [*to his father*]. And won't you apologise for your remarks to Mr. Crowe, sir?

LADY LEETE [*demanding*]. Snuff!

CARNABY. And your box to my mother, sir.

> SIR GEORGE *attends to his wife.*

DOLLY [*anxiously to* DR. REMNANT]. Can a gentleman change his name?

MR. CROWE. Parson . . once noble always noble, I take it.

DR. REMNANT. Certainly . . but I hope you have money to leave them, Mr. Crowe.

DOLLY [*to* ABUD]. John.

ABUD. Dorothy.

DOLLY. You've not seen my babies yet.

> LADY LEETE *sneezes.*

SIR GEORGE LEETE. Carnaby . . d'ye intend to murder that Crowe fellow . . or must I?

MR. SMALLPEICE *skips from the dining-room.*

MR. SMALLPEICE. Mr. John Abud . .

MR. CROWE [*to* DR. REMNANT *as he nods towards* CARNABY]. Don't tell me he's got over that fever yet.

MR. SMALLPEICE. . . The ladies say . . are you ready or are you not?

MR. PRESTIGE. I'll get thy cloak, John.

MR. PRESTIGE *goes for the cloak.* CARNABY *has taken a pistol from the mantel-piece and now points it at* ABUD.

CARNABY. He's fit for heaven!

GEORGE LEETE *comes from the dining-room and noticing his father's action says sharply . .*

GEORGE. I suppose you know that pistol's loaded.

Which calls everyone's attention. DOLLY *shrieks.*

CARNABY. What if there had been an accident!

And he puts back the pistol. ABUD *takes his cloak from* PRESTIGE.

ABUD. Thank you, uncle.

MR. PRESTIGE. I'm a proud man, Mr. Crowe . .

CARNABY. Pride!

GEORGE [*has a sudden inspiration and strides up to* ABUD]. Here ends the joke, my good fellow. Be off without your wife.

ABUD *stares, as do the others. Only* CARNABY *suddenly catches* REMNANT's *arm.*

MR. PRESTIGE [*solemnly*]. But it's illegal to separate them.

GEORGE [*giving up*]. Mr. Prestige . . you are the backbone of England.

CARNABY [*to* REMNANT]. Where are your miracles?

MRS. PRESTIGE *comes out. A motherly farmer's wife, a mountain of a woman.*

MRS. PRESTIGE. John . . kiss your aunt.

ABUD *goes to her, and she obliterates him in an embrace.*

GEORGE [*to his father*]. Sense of humour . . Sense of humour!

LADY LEETE. Snuff.

But no one heeds her this time.

CARNABY. It doesn't matter.

GEORGE. Smile. Let's be helpless gracefully.

CARNABY. There are moments when I'm not sure—

GEORGE. It's her own life.

TOZER *staggers from the dining-room drunker than ever. He falls against the baluster and waves his arms.*

MR. TOZER. Silence there for the corpse!

MR. CROWE. You beast!

MR. TOZER. Respect my cloth . . Mr. Prestige.

MR. CROWE. That's not my name.

MR. TOZER. I'll have you to know that I'm Sir George Leete's baronet's most boon companion and her la'ship never goes nowhere without me. [*He subsides into a chair.*]

LADY LEETE [*tearfully*]. Snuff.

> *From the dining-room comes* ANN; *her head bent. She is crossing the hall when* SARAH *follows, calling her.*

SARAH. Ann!

> ANN *turns back to kiss her. The rest of the company stand gazing.*
> SIR GEORGE *gives snuff to* LADY LEETE.

ANN. Good-bye, Sally.

SARAH [*in a whisper*]. Forget us.

GEORGE [*relieving his feelings*]. Good-bye, everybody . . good-bye, everything.

> ABUD *goes to the front door and opening it stands waiting for her. She goes coldly, but timidly to her father, to whom she puts her face up to be kissed.*

ANN. Good-bye, Papa.

CARNABY [*quietly, as he kisses her cheek*]. I can do without you.

SIR GEORGE LEETE [*raging at the draught*]. Shut that door.

ANN. I'm gone.

> *She goes with her husband.* MRS. OPIE *comes hurriedly out of the dining-room, too late.*

MRS. OPIE. Oh!

DR. REMNANT. Run . . Mrs. Opie.

CARNABY. There has started the new century!

> MRS. OPIE *opens the front door to look after them.*

SIR GEORGE LEETE [*with double energy*]. Shut that door.

> LADY LEETE *sneezes and then chokes. There is much commotion in her neighbourhood.*

SIR GEORGE. Now she's hurt again.

DOLLY. Water!

MR. CROWE. Brandy!

SARAH [*going*]. I'll fetch both.

GEORGE. We must all die . . some day.

MR. TOZER [*who has struggled up to see what is the matter*]. And go to—

DR. REMNANT. Hell. You do believe in that, Mr. Toper.

MRS. OPIE [*fanning the poor old lady*]. She's better.

CARNABY [*to his guests*]. Gentlemen . . punch.

> PRESTIGE *and* SMALLPEICE; MRS. PRESTIGE, GEORGE *and*
> DOLLY *move towards the dining-room.*

MR. PRESTIGE [*to* SMALLPEICE]. You owe all this to me.

MR. CROWE. Dolly . . I'm going.

MRS. PRESTIGE [*to her husband as she nods towards* CARNABY].
Nathaniel . . look at 'im.

GEORGE [*to his father-in-law*]. Must we come too?

MRS. PRESTIGE [*as before*]. I can't help it . . a sneerin', carpin'
cavillin' devil!

MRS. OPIE. Markswayde is to let . . as I hear . . Mr. Leete?

CARNABY. Markswayde is to let.

> *He goes on his way to the dining-room meeting* SARAH *who comes
> out carrying a glass of water and a decanter of brandy.* SIR
> GEORGE LEETE *is comfortably warming himself at the fire.*

* * * * * * * * * * *

> *The living room of* JOHN ABUD'S *new cottage has bare plaster walls and
> its ceilings and floor are of red brick; all fresh looking but not
> new. In the middle of the middle wall there is a latticed window,
> dimity curtained; upon the plain shelf in front are several flower-
> pots.*
>
> *To the right of this, a door, cross beamed and with a large lock to it
> besides the latch.*
>
> *Against the right hand wall is a dresser, furnished with dishes and
> plates: below it is a common looking grandfather clock; below
> this a small door which when opened shows winding stairs
> leading to the room above. In the left hand wall there is a door
> which is almost hidden by the fireplace which juts out below it.
> In the fireplace a wood fire is laid but not lit. At right angles to
> this stands a heavy oak settle opposite a plain deal table, just
> beyond which is a little bench. On either side of the window is a
> Windsor armchair. Between the window and the door hangs a
> framed sampler.*
>
> *In the darkness the sound of the unlocking of a door and of* ABUD *entering
> is heard. He walks to the table, strikes a light upon a tinder-box
> and lights a candle which he finds there.* ANN *is standing in the
> doorway.* ABUD *is in stocking feet.*

ABUD. Don't come further. Here are your slippers.

> *He places one of the Windsor chairs for her on which she sits while
> he takes off her wet shoes and puts on her slippers which he found on*

the table. Then he takes her wet shoes to the fireplace. She sits still.
Then he goes to the door and brings in his own boots from the little
porch and puts them in the fireplace too. Then he locks the door
and hangs up the key beside it. Then he stands looking at her;
but she does not speak, so he takes the candle, lifts it above his
head and walks to the dresser.

ABUD [*encouragingly*]. Our dresser . . Thomas Jupp made that.
Plates and dishes. Here's Uncle Prestige's clock.

ANN. Past seven.

ABUD. That's upstairs. Table and bench, deal. Oak settle . .
solid.

ANN. Charming.

ABUD. Windsor chairs . . Mother's sampler.

ANN. Home.

ABUD. Is it as you wish? I have been glad at your not seeing it
until to-night.

ANN. I'm sinking into the strangeness of the place.

ABUD. Very weary? It's been a long nine miles.

She does not answer. He goes and considers the flower-pots in the
window.

ANN. I still have on my cloak.

ABUD. Hang it behind the door there . . no matter if the wet
drips.

ANN. . . I can wipe up the puddle.

She hangs up her cloak. He selects a flower-pot and brings it to her.

ABUD. Hyacinth bulbs for the spring.

ANN [*after a glance*]. I don't want to hold them.

He puts back the pot, a little disappointed.

ABUD. Out there's the scullery.

ANN. It's very cold.

ABUD. If we light the fire now that means more trouble in the
morning.

She sits on the settle.

ANN. Yes, I am very weary.

ABUD. Go to bed.

ANN. Not yet. [*After a moment.*] How much light one candle
gives! Sit where I may see you.

He sits on the bench. She studies him curiously.

ANN. Well . . this is an experiment.

ABUD [*with reverence*]. God help us both.

ANN. Amen. Some people are so careful of their lives. If we
fail miserably we'll hold our tongues . . won't we?

ABUD. I don't know . . I can't speak of this.

ANN. These impossible things which are done mustn't be talked of . . that spoils them. We don't want to boast of this, do we?

ABUD. I fancy nobody quite believes that we are married.

ANN. Here's my ring . . real gold.

ABUD [*with a sudden fierce throw up of his head*]. Never you remind me of the difference between us.

ANN. Don't speak to me so.

ABUD. Now I'm your better.

ANN. My master . . The door's locked.

ABUD [*nodding*]. I know that I must be . . or be a fool.

ANN [*after a moment*]. Be kind to me.

ABUD [*with remorse*]. Always I will.

ANN. You are master here.

ABUD. And I've angered you?

ANN. And if I fail . . I'll never tell you . . to make a fool of you. And you're trembling. [*She sees his hand, which is on the table, shake.*]

ABUD. Look at that now.

ANN [*lifting her own*]. My white hands must redden. No more dainty appetite . . no more pretty books.

ABUD. Have you learned to scrub?

ANN. Not this floor.

ABUD. Mother always did bricks with a mop. To-morrow I go to work. You'll be left for all day.

ANN. I must make friends with the other women around.

ABUD. My friends are very curious about you.

ANN. I'll wait to begin till I'm seasoned.

ABUD. Four o'clock's the hour for getting up.

ANN. Early rising always was a vice of mine.

ABUD. Breakfast quickly . . . and I take my dinner with me.

ANN. In a handkerchief.

ABUD. Hot supper, please.

ANN. It shall be ready for you.

There is silence between them for a little. Then he says timidly.

ABUD. May I come near to you?

ANN [*in a low voice*]. Come.

He sits beside her, gazing.

ABUD. Wife . . I never have kissed you.

ANN. Shut your eyes.

ABUD. Are you afraid of me?

ANN. We're not to play such games at love.

ABUD. I can't help wanting to feel very tender towards you.

ANN. Think of me . . not as a wife . . but as a mother of your children . . if it's to be so. Treat me so.

ABUD. You are a part of me.

ANN. We must try and understand it . . as a simple thing.

ABUD. But shall I kiss you?

ANN [lowering her head]. Kiss me.

But when he puts his arms round her she shrinks.

ANN. No.

ABUD. But I will. It's my right.

Almost by force he kisses her. Afterwards she clenches her hands and seems to suffer.

ABUD. Have I hurt you?

She gives him her hand with a strange little smile.

ANN. I forgive you.

ABUD [encouraged]. Ann . . we're beginning life together.

ANN. Remember . . work's enough . . no stopping to talk.

ABUD. I'll work for you.

ANN. I'll do my part . . something will come of it.

For a moment they sit together hand in hand. Then she leaves him and paces across the room.

There is a slight pause.

ANN. Papa . . I said . . we've all been in too great a hurry getting civilised. False dawn. I mean to go back.

ABUD. He laughed.

ANN. So he saw I was of no use to him and he's penniless and he let me go. When my father dies what will he take with him? . . . for you do take your works with you into Heaven or Hell, I believe. Much wit. Sally is afraid to die. Don't you aspire like George's wife. I was afraid to live . . and now . . I am content.

She walks slowly to the window and from there to the door against which she places her ear. Then she looks round at her husband.

ANN. I can hear them chattering.

Then she goes to the little door and opens it. ABUD *takes up the candle.*

ABUD. I'll hold the light . . the stairs are steep.

He lights her up the stairs.

THE VOYSEY INHERITANCE

A play in five acts

"The Voysey Inheritance" was first played at the Court Theatre, Sloane Square, on the afternoon of November 7th, 1905.

MR. VOYSEY..*A. E. George*

MRS. VOYSEY..*Miss Florence Haydon*

TRENCHARD VOYSEY, K.C.................................*Eugene Mayeur*

HONOR VOYSEY....................................*Miss Geraldine Olliffe*

MAJOR BOOTH VOYSEY....................................*Charles Fulton*

MRS. BOOTH VOYSEY.................................*Miss Grace Edwin*

CHRISTOPHER..*Harry C. Duff*

EDWARD VOYSEY ....*Thalberg Corbett*

HUGH VOYSEY...*Dennis Eadie*

MRS. HUGH VOYSEY............................*Miss Henrietta Watson*

ETHEL VOYSEY..................................*Miss Alexandra Carlisle*

DENIS TREGONING...*Frederick Lloyd*

ALICE MAITLAND ....*Miss Mabel Hackney*

MR. BOOTH..*O. B. Clarence*

THE REV. EVAN COLPUS...............................*Edmund Gwenn*

PEACEY ....*Trevor Lowe*

PHOEBE...*Miss Gwynneth Galton*

MARY ....*Mrs. Fordyce*

THE VOYSEY INHERITANCE

THE FIRST ACT

The Office of Voysey and Son is in the best part of Lincoln's Inn. Its panelled rooms give out a sense of grandmotherly comfort and security, very grateful at first to the hesitating investor, the dubious litigant. MR. VOYSEY's *own room, into which he walks about twenty past ten of a morning, radiates enterprise besides. There is polish on everything; on the windows, on the mahogany of the tidily packed writing-table that stands between them, on the brass-work of the fireplace in the other wall, on the glass of the firescreen which preserves only the pleasantness of a sparkling fire, even on* MR. VOYSEY's *hat as he takes it off to place it on the little red-curtained shelf behind the door.* MR. VOYSEY *is sixty or more and masterful; would obviously be master anywhere from his own home outwards, or wreck the situation in his attempt. Indeed there is sometimes a buccaneering air in the twist of his glance, not altogether suitable to a family solicitor. On this bright October morning,* PEACEY, *the head clerk, follows just too late to help him off with his coat, but in time to take it and hang it up with a quite unnecessary subservience. Relieved of his coat,* MR. VOYSEY *carries to his table the bunch of beautiful roses he is accustomed to bring to the office three times a week and places them for a moment only near the bowl of water there ready to receive them while he takes up his letters. These lie ready too, opened mostly, one or two private ones left closed and discreetly separate. By this time the usual salutations have passed,* PEACEY's *"Good morning, sir";* MR. VOYSEY's *"Morning, Peacey." Then as he gets to his letters* MR. VOYSEY *starts his day's work.*

MR. VOYSEY. Any news for me?

PEACEY. I hear bad accounts of Alguazils Preferred, sir.

MR. VOYSEY. Oh . . . who from?

PEACEY. Merrit and James's head clerk in the train this morning.

MR. VOYSEY. They looked all right on . . . Give me the Times.

[PEACEY *goes to the fireplace for the* Times; *it is warming there.* MR. VOYSEY *waves a letter, then places it on the table.*] Here, that's for you . . . Gerrard's Cross business. Anything else?

PEACEY [*as he turns the* Times *to its Finance page*]. I've made the usual notes.

MR. VOYSEY. Thank'ee.

PEACEY. Young Benham isn't back yet.

MR. VOYSEY. Mr. Edward must do as he thinks fit about that. Alguazils, Alg—oh, yes.

> *He is running his eye down the columns.* PEACEY *leans over the letters.*

PEACEY. This is from Mr. Leader about the codicil . . . You'll answer that?

MR. VOYSEY. Mr. Leader. Yes. Alguazils. Mr. Edward's here, I suppose.

PEACEY. No, sir.

MR. VOYSEY [*his eye twisting with some sharpness*]. What!

PEACEY [*almost alarmed*]. I beg pardon, sir.

MR. VOYSEY. Mr. Edward.

PEACEY. Oh, yes, sir, been in his room some time. I thought you said Headley; he's not due back till Thursday.

> MR. VOYSEY *discards the* Times *and sits to his desk and his letters.*

MR. VOYSEY. Tell Mr. Edward I've come.

PEACEY. Yes, sir. Anything else?

MR. VOYSEY. Not for the moment. Cold morning, isn't it?

PEACEY. Quite surprising, sir.

MR. VOYSEY. We had a touch of frost down at Chislehurst.

PEACEY. So early!

MR. VOYSEY. I want it for the celery. All right, I'll call through about the rest of the letters.

> PEACEY *goes, having secured a letter or two, and* MR. VOYSEY *having sorted the rest (a proportion into the waste-paper basket) takes up the forgotten roses and starts setting them into a bowl with an artistic hand. Then his son* EDWARD *comes in.* MR. VOYSEY *gives him one glance and goes on arranging the roses, but says cheerily . . .*

MR. VOYSEY. Good morning, my dear boy.

> EDWARD *has little of his father in him and that little is undermost. It is a refined face, but self-consciousness takes the place in it of imagination, and in suppressing traits of brutality in his character it looks as if the young man had suppressed his sense of humour too. But whether or no, that would not be much in evidence now,*

for EDWARD *is obviously going through some experience which is
scaring him (there is no better word). He looks not to have slept
for a night or two, and his standing there, clutching and unclutching
the bundle of papers he carries, his eyes on his father, half appealingly but half accusingly too, his whole being altogether so unstrung
and desperate, makes* MR. VOYSEY's *uninterrupted arranging of
the flowers seem very calculated indeed. At last the little tension of
silence is broken.*

EDWARD. Father . . .

MR. VOYSEY. Well?

EDWARD. I'm glad to see you.

*This is a statement of fact. He doesn't know that the commonplace
phrase sounds ridiculous at such a moment.*

MR. VOYSEY. I see you've the papers there.

EDWARD. Yes.

MR. VOYSEY. You've been through them?

EDWARD. As you wished me . . .

MR. VOYSEY. Well? [EDWARD *doesn't answer. Reference to the papers
seems to overwhelm him with shame.* MR. VOYSEY *goes on with cheerful
impatience.*] Now, now, my dear boy, don't take it like this. You're
puzzled and worried, of course. But why didn't you come down to
me on Saturday night? I expected you . . . I told you to come.
Your mother was wondering why you weren't with us for dinner
yesterday.

EDWARD. I went through everything twice. I wanted to make
quite sure.

MR. VOYSEY. I told you to come to me.

EDWARD [*he is very near crying*]. Oh, Father!

MR. VOYSEY. Now look here, Edward, I'm going to ring and
dispose of these letters. Please pull yourself together. [*He pushes
the little button on his table.*]

EDWARD. I didn't leave my rooms all day yesterday.

MR. VOYSEY. A pleasant Sunday! You must learn, whatever
the business may be, to leave it behind you at the office. Life's
not worth living else.

PEACEY *comes in to find* MR. VOYSEY *before the fire ostentatiously
warming and rubbing his hands.*

Oh, there isn't much else, Peacey. Tell Simmons that if he
satisfies you about the details of this lease it'll be all right. Make
a note for me of Mr. Granger's address at Mentone.

PEACEY. Mr. Burnett . . . Burnett and Marks . . . has just
come in, Mr. Edward.

EDWARD [*without turning*]. It's only fresh instructions. Will you take them?

PEACEY. All right.

PEACEY *goes, lifting his eyebrows at the queerness of* EDWARD'S *manner. This* MR. VOYSEY *sees, returning to his table with a little scowl.*

MR. VOYSEY. Now sit down. I've given you a bad forty-eight hours, have I? Well, I've been anxious about you. Never mind, we'll thresh the thing out now. Go through the two accounts. Mrs. Murberry's first . . . how do you find it stands?

EDWARD [*his feelings choking him*]. I hoped you were playing some joke on me.

MR. VOYSEY. Come now.

EDWARD *separates the papers precisely and starts to detail them; his voice quite toneless. Now and then his father's sharp comments ring out in contrast.*

EDWARD. We've got the lease of her present house, several agreements . . . and here's her will. Here's an expired power of attorney . . . over her securities and her property generally . . . it was made out for six months.

MR. VOYSEY. She was in South Africa.

EDWARD. Here's the Sheffield mortgage and the Henry Smith mortgage with Banker's receipts . . . her Banker's to us for the interest up to date . . . four and a half and five per cent. Then . . . Fretworthy Bonds. There's a note scribbled in your writing that they are at the Bank; but you don't say what bank.

MR. VOYSEY. My own.

EDWARD [*just dwelling on the words*]. Your own. I queried that. There's eight thousand five hundred in three and a half India stock. And there are her Banker's receipts for cheques on account of those dividends. I presume for those dividends.

MR. VOYSEY. Why not?

EDWARD [*gravely*]. Because then, Father, there are her Banker's half-yearly receipts for other sums amounting to an average of four hundred and twenty pounds a year. But I find no record of any capital to produce this.

MR. VOYSEY. Go on. What do you find?

EDWARD. Till about three years back there seems to have been eleven thousand in Queenslands which would produce . . . did produce exactly the same sum. But after January of that year I find no record of them.

MR. VOYSEY. In fact the Queenslands are missing, vanished?

EDWARD [*hardly uttering the word*]. Yes.

MR. VOYSEY. From which you conclude?

EDWARD. I supposed at first that you had not handed me all the papers. . . .

MR. VOYSEY. Since Mrs. Murberry evidently still gets that four twenty a year, somehow; lucky woman.

EDWARD [*in agony*]. Oh!

MR. VOYSEY. Well, we'll return to the good lady later. Now let's take the other.

EDWARD. The Hatherley Trust.

MR. VOYSEY. Quite so.

EDWARD [*with one accusing glance*]. Trust.

MR. VOYSEY. Go on.

EDWARD. Father . . .

　　His grief comes uppermost again and MR. VOYSEY *meets it kindly.*

MR. VOYSEY. I know, my dear boy. I shall have lots to say to you. But let's get quietly through with these details first.

EDWARD [*bitterly now*]. Oh, this is simple enough. We're young Hatherley's trustees till he comes of age. The property was thirty-eight thousand invested in Consols. Certain sums were to be allowed for his education; we seem to be paying them.

MR. VOYSEY. Regularly?

EDWARD. Quite. But where's the capital?

MR. VOYSEY. No record?

EDWARD. Yes . . . a note by you on a half sheet: Refer Bletchley Land Scheme.

MR. VOYSEY. Oh . . . we've been out of that six years or more! He's credited with the interest on his capital?

EDWARD. With the Consol interest.

MR. VOYSEY. Quite so.

EDWARD. The Bletchley scheme paid seven and a half.

MR. VOYSEY. At one time. Have you taken the trouble to calculate what will be due from us to the lad?

EDWARD. Yes . . . capital and interest . . . about forty-six thousand pounds.

MR. VOYSEY. A respectable sum. In five years' time?

EDWARD. When he comes of age.

MR. VOYSEY. That gives us, say, four years and six months in which to think about it.

　　EDWARD *waits, hopelessly, for his father to speak again; then says . . .*

EDWARD. Thank you for showing me these, sir. Shall I put them back in your safe now?

7

MR. VOYSEY. Yes, you'd better. There's the key. [EDWARD *reaches for the bunch, his face hidden.*] Put them down. Your hand shakes . . . why, you might have been drinking. I'll put them away later. It's no use having hysterics, Edward. Look your trouble in the face.

> EDWARD'S *only answer is to go to the fire, as far from his father as the room allows. And there he leans on the mantelpiece, his shoulders heaving.*

I'm sorry, my dear boy. I wouldn't tell you if I could help it.

EDWARD. I can't believe it. And that you should be telling me . . . such a thing.

MR. VOYSEY. Let yourself go . . . have your cry out, as the women say. It isn't pleasant, I know. It isn't pleasant to inflict it on you.

EDWARD [*able to turn to his father again; won round by the kind voice*]. How long has it been going on? Why didn't you tell me before? Oh, I know you thought you'd pull through. But I'm your partner . . . I'm responsible too. Oh, I don't want to shirk that . . . don't think I mean to shirk that, Father. Perhaps I ought to have discovered . . . but those affairs were always in your hands. I trusted . . . I beg your pardon. Oh, it's us . . . not you. Everyone has trusted us.

MR. VOYSEY [*calmly and kindly still*]. You don't seem to notice that I'm not breaking my heart like this.

EDWARD. What's the extent of . . . ? Are there other accounts . . . ? When did it begin? Father, what made you begin it?

MR. VOYSEY. I didn't begin it.

EDWARD. You didn't? Who then?

MR. VOYSEY. My father before me. [EDWARD *stares*] That calms you a little.

EDWARD. But how terrible! Oh, my dear father . . . I'm glad. But . . .

MR. VOYSEY [*shaking his head*]. My inheritance, Edward.

EDWARD. My dear Father!

MR. VOYSEY. I had hoped it wasn't to be yours.

EDWARD. But you mean to tell me that this sort of thing has been going on here for years? For more than thirty years!

MR. VOYSEY. Yes.

EDWARD. That's a little hard to understand . . . just at first, sir.

MR. VOYSEY [*sententiously*]. We do what we must in this world, Edward. I have done what I had to do.

EDWARD [*his emotion well cooled by now*]. Perhaps I'd better just listen while you explain.

MR. VOYSEY [*concentrating*]. You know that I'm heavily into Northern Electrics.

EDWARD. Yes.

MR. VOYSEY. But you don't know how heavily. When I got the tip the Municipalities were organising the purchase, I saw of course the stock must be up to a hundred and forty-five—a hundred and fifty in no time. Now Leeds has quarrelled with the rural group . . . there'll be no general settlement for ten years. I bought at ninety-five. What are they to-day?

EDWARD. Seventy-two.

MR. VOYSEY. Seventy-one and a half. And in ten years I may be . . . ! I'm not a young man, Edward. That's mainly why you've had to be told.

EDWARD. With whose money are you so heavily into Northern Electrics?

MR. VOYSEY. The firm's money.

EDWARD. Clients' money?

MR. VOYSEY. Yes.

EDWARD [*coldly*]. Well . . . I'm waiting for your explanation, sir.

MR. VOYSEY [*with a shrug*]. Children always think the worst of their parents, I suppose. I did of mine. It's a pity.

EDWARD. Go on, sir, go on. Let me know the worst.

MR. VORSEY. There's no immediate danger. I should think anyone could see that from the figures there. There's no real risk at all.

EDWARD. Is that the worst?

MR. VOYSEY [*his anger rising*]. Have you studied these two accounts or have you not?

EDWARD. Yes, sir.

MR. VOYSEY. Well, where's the deficiency in Mrs. Murberry's income . . . has she ever gone without a shilling? What has young Hatherley lost?

EDWARD. He stands to lose . . .

MR. VOYSEY. He stands to lose nothing if I'm spared for a little, and you will only bring a little common sense to bear and try to understand the difficulties of my position.

EDWARD. Father, I'm not thinking ill of you . . . that is, I'm trying not to. But won't you explain how you're justified . . . ?

MR. VOYSEY. In putting our affairs in order?

EDWARD. Are you doing that?

MR. VOYSEY. What else?

EDWARD [*starting patiently to examine the matter*]. How bad were things when you came into control?

MR. VOYSEY. Oh, I forget.

EDWARD. You can't forget.

MR. VOYSEY. Well . . . pretty bad.

EDWARD. How was it my grandfather . . . ?

MR. VOYSEY. Muddlement . . . timidity! Had a perfect mania for petty speculation. He'd no capital . . . no real credit . . . and he went in terror of his life. My dear Edward, if I hadn't found out in time, he'd have confessed to the first man who came and asked for a balance sheet.

EDWARD. How much was he to the bad then?

MR. VOYSEY. Oh . . . a tidy sum.

EDWARD. But it can't have taken all these years to pay off. . . .

MR. VOYSEY. O, hasn't it!

EDWARD [*making his point*]. Then how does it happen, sir, that such a recent trust as young Hatherley's has been broken into?

MR. VOYSEY. Well, what could be safer? There is no one to interfere, and we haven't to settle up for five years.

EDWARD [*utterly beaten*]. Father, are you mad?

MR. VOYSEY. Mad? I wish everybody were as sane. As a trustee the law permits me to earn for a fund three and a half per cent . . . and that I do . . . punctually and safely. Now as to Mrs. Murberry . . . those Fretworthy Bonds at my bank . . . I've borrowed five thousand on them. But I can release them to-morrow if need be.

EDWARD. Where's the five thousand?

MR. VOYSEY. I needed it . . . temporarily . . . to complete a purchase . . . there was that and four thousand more out of the Skipworth fund.

EDWARD. But, my dear father—

MR. VOYSEY. Well?

EDWARD [*summing it all up very simply*]. It's not right.

MR. VOYSEY *considers his son for a moment with a pitying shake of the head.*

MR. VOYSEY. That is a word, Edward, which one should learn to use very carefully. You mean that from time to time I have had to go beyond the letter of the law. But consider the position I found myself in. Was I to see my father ruined and disgraced without lifting a finger to help him? I paid back to the man who was most involved in my father's mistakes every penny of his capital . . . and he never even knew the danger he'd been in . . . never had one uneasy moment. It was I that lay awake. I have now somewhere a letter from that man written as he lay dying . . . I'll tell you who it was, old Thomson the physiologist . . . saying that only his perfect confidence in our conduct of his affairs had enabled him to do his life's work in peace. Well, Edward, I went beyond the letter of the law to do that service . . . to my father . . . to old Thomson . . to Science . . to Humanity. Was I right or wrong?

EDWARD. In the result, sir, right.

MR. VOYSEY. Judge me by the result. I took the risk of failure . . . I should have suffered. I could have kept clear of the danger if I'd liked.

EDWARD. But that's all past. The thing that concerns me is what you are doing now.

MR. VOYSEY [gently reproachful]. My boy, can't you trust me a little? It's all very well for you to come in at the end of the day and criticise. But I who have done the day's work know how that work had to be done. And here's our firm, prosperous, respected and without a stain on its honour. That's the main point, isn't it?

EDWARD [quite irresponsive to this pathetic appeal]. Very well, sir. Let's dismiss from our minds any prejudice about behaving as honest firms of solicitors do behave. . . .

MR. VOYSEY. We need do nothing of the sort. If a man gives me definite instructions about his property I follow them. And more often than not he suffers.

EDWARD. But if Mrs. Murberry knew . . .

MR. VOYSEY. Well, if you can make her understand her affairs . . . financial or other . . . it's more than I ever could. Go and knock it into her head, then, if you can, that four hundred and twenty pounds of her income hasn't, for the last eight years, come from the place she thinks it's come from, and see how happy you'll make her.

EDWARD. But is that four hundred and twenty a year as safe as it was before you . . . ?

MR. VOYSEY. Why not?

EDWARD. What's the security?

MR. VOYSEY [putting his coping stone on the argument]. My financial ability.

EDWARD [really not knowing whether to laugh or cry]. Why, one'd think you were satisfied with this state of things.

MR. VOYSEY. Edward, you really are most unsympathetic and unreasonable. I give all I have to the firm's work . . . my brain . . . my energies . . . my whole life. I can't, so to speak, cash in my abilities at par . . . I wish I could. If I could establish every one of these people with a separate and consistent bank balance to-morrow . . . naturally I should do it.

EDWARD [*thankfully able to meet anger with anger*]. Do you mean to tell me that you couldn't somehow have put things straight before now?

MR. VOYSEY. So easy to talk, isn't it?

EDWARD. If thirty years of this sort of thing hasn't brought you hopelessly to grief . . . why, there must have been opportunities . . .

MR. VOYSEY. Must there! Well, I hope that when I'm under the ground, you may find them.

EDWARD. I?

MR. VOYSEY. And put everything right with a stroke of your pen, if it's so easy!

EDWARD. I!

MR. VOYSEY. You're my partner and my son. You inherit the problem.

EDWARD [*realising at last that he has been led to the edge of this abyss*]. Oh no, Father.

MR. VOYSEY. Why else have I had to tell you all this?

EDWARD [*very simply*]. Father, I can't. I can't possibly. I don't think you've any right to ask me.

MR. VOYSEY. Why not, pray?

EDWARD. It's perpetuating the dishonesty.

MR. VOYSEY *hardens at the unpleasant word.*

MR. VOYSEY. You don't believe that I've told you the truth.

EDWARD. I want to believe it.

MR. VOYSEY. It's no proof . . . my earning these twenty or thirty people their incomes for the last . . . how many years?

EDWARD. Whether what you've done has been wrong or right . . . I can't meddle in it.

For the moment MR. VOYSEY *looks a little dangerous.*

MR. VOYSEY. Very well. Forget all I've said. Go back to your room. Get back to your drudgery. A life's work—my life's work—ruined! What does that matter?

EDWARD. Whatever did you expect of me?

MR. VOYSEY [*making a feint at his papers*]. Oh nothing. [*Then he slams them down with great effect.*] Here's a great edifice built up by years of labour and devotion and self-sacrifice . . . a great arch

you may call it . . . a bridge to carry our firm to safety with
honour. My work! And it still lacks the key-stone. Just that! And
it may be I am to die with my work incomplete. Then is there
nothing that a son might do? Do you think I shouldn't be proud
of you, Edward . . . that I shouldn't bless you from . . . wherever
I may be, when you had completed my life's work . . . with
perhaps just one kindly thought of your father?

In spite of this oratory, the situation is gradually impressing
EDWARD.

EDWARD. What will happen if I leave the firm now?

MR. VOYSEY. I shall see that you are not held responsible.

EDWARD. I wasn't thinking of myself, sir.

MR. VOYSEY. Well, I shan't mind the exposure. It won't make
me blush in my coffin. And you're not so quixotic, I hope, as to
be thinking of the feelings of your brothers and sisters. Considering how simple it would have been for me to go to my grave and
let you discover the whole thing afterwards, the fact that I
didn't, that I take thought for the future of you all . . . well, I
did hope it might convince you that I . . . ! But there . . . consult
your own safety.

EDWARD *has begun to pace the room; indecision growing upon*
him.

EDWARD. It's a queer dilemma to be facing.

MR. VOYSEY. My dear boy . . . don't think I can't appreciate
the shock it has been to you. After all, I had to go through it,
you know. And worse!

EDWARD. Why worse?

MR. VOYSEY. Well . . . I was a big younger. And my poor dear
Dad was on the edge of the precipice . . . all but over it. I'm not
landing you in any such mess, Edward. On the contrary! On
the contrary!

EDWARD. Yes, I came this morning thinking that next week
would see us in the dock together.

MR. VOYSEY. And I suppose if I'd broken down and begged
your pardon for my folly, you'd have done anything for me, gone
to prison smiling, eh?

EDWARD. I suppose so.

MR. VOYSEY. Oh, it's easy enough to forgive. I'm sorry I can't
assume sack-cloth and ashes to oblige you. [*Now he begins to rally*
his son; easy in his strength.] My dear Edward, you've lived a quiet
humdrum life up to now, with your poetry and your sociology
and your agnosticism and your ethics of this and your ethics of

that! . . . and you've never before been brought face to face with any really vital question. Now don't make a fool of yourself just through inexperience. I'm not angry at what you've said to me. I'm willing to forget it. And it's for your own sake and not for mine, Edward, that I do beg you to . . . to . . . be a man and take a man's view of the position you find yourself in. It's not a pleasant position, I know . . . but we must take this world as we find it, my dear boy.

EDWARD. You should have told me before you took me into partnership.

Oddly enough it is this last flicker of rebellion which breaks down MR. VOYSEY's *caution. Now he lets fly with a vengeance.*

MR. VOYSEY. Should I be telling you at all if I could help it? Don't I know you're about as fit for the job as a babe unborn? I've been hoping and praying for these three years past that you'd show signs of shaping into something. But I'm in a corner . . . and am I to see things come to smash simply because of your scruples? If you're a son of mine you'll do as I tell you. Hadn't I the same choice to make? D'you suppose I didn't have scruples? If you run away from this, Edward, you're a coward. My father was a coward and he suffered for it to the end of his days. I was more of a sick-nurse to him here than a partner. Good lord! . . . of course it's pleasant and comfortable to keep within the law . . . then the law will look after you. Otherwise you have to look pretty sharp after yourself. You have to cultivate your own sense of right and wrong . . . deal your own justice. But that makes a bigger man of you, let me tell you. How easily . . . how easily could I have walked out of my father's office and left him to his fate! But I didn't. I thought it my better duty to stay and . . . yes, I say it with all reverence . . . to take up my cross. Well, I've carried that cross pretty successfully. And what's more, it's made a happy . . . a self-respecting man of me. I don't want what I've been saying to influence you, Edward. You are a free agent. You must consult your conscience and decide upon your own course of action. Now don't let's discuss the matter any more for the moment.

EDWARD *looks at his father with clear eyes.*

EDWARD. Don't forget to put these papers away.

MR. VOYSEY. Are you coming down to Chislehurst soon? We've got Hugh and his wife, and Booth and Emily, and Christopher for two or three days, till he goes back to school.

EDWARD. How is Chris?

MR. VOYSEY. All right again now . . . grows more like his father. Booth's very proud of him. So am I.

EDWARD. I think I can't face them all just at present.

MR. VOYSEY. Nonsense.

EDWARD [*a little wave of emotion going through him*]. I feel as if this thing were written on my face. How I shall get through business I don't know!

MR. VOYSEY. You're weaker than I thought, Edward.

EDWARD [*a little ironically*]. I've always wondered why I was such a disappointment to you, Father. Though you've been very kind about it.

MR. VOYSEY. No, no. I say things I don't mean sometimes.

EDWARD. You should have brought one of the others into the firm . . . Trenchard or Booth.

MR. VOYSEY [*hardening*]. Trenchard! [*He dismisses that.*] Heavens, you're a better man than Booth. Edward, you mustn't imagine that the whole world is standing on its head merely because you've had an unpleasant piece of news. Come down to Chislehurst to-night . . . well, say to-morrow night. It'll be good for you . . . stop your brooding. That's your worst vice, Edward. You'll find the household as if nothing had happened. Then you'll remember that nothing really has happened. And presently you'll see that nothing need happen, if you keep your head. I remember times . . . when things have seemed at their worst . . . what a relief it's been to me . . . my romp with you all in the nursery just before your bed-time. And, my dear boy, if I knew that you were going to inform the next client you met of what I've just told you . . .

EDWARD [*with a shudder*]. Father!

MR. VOYSEY . . . and that I should find myself in prison to-morrow, I wouldn't wish a single thing I've ever done undone. I have never wilfully harmed man or woman. My life's been a happy one. Your dear mother has been spared to me. You're most of you good children and a credit to what I've done for you.

EDWARD [*the deadly humour of this too much for him*]. Father!

MR. VOYSEY. Run along now, run along. I must finish my letters and get into the City.

He might be scolding a schoolboy for some trifling fault. EDWARD *turns to have a look at the keen unembarrassed face.* MR. VOYSEY *smiles at him and proceeds to select from the bowl a rose for his buttonhole.*

EDWARD. I'll think it over, sir.

MR. VOYSEY. That's right! And don't brood.

> *So* EDWARD *leaves him; and having fixed the rose in his buttonhole to his satisfaction he rings his table telephone and calls through to the listening clerk.*

Send Atkinson to me, please.

> *Then he gets up, keys in hand, to lock away Mrs. Murberry's and the Hatherley Trust papers.*

THE SECOND ACT

The Voysey *dining-room at Chislehurst, when children and grandchildren are visiting, is dining-table and very little else. And at the moment in the evening when five or six men are sprawling back in their chairs, and the air is clouded with smoke, it is a very typical specimen of the middle-class English domestic temple. It has the usual red-papered walls, the usual varnished woodwork which is known as grained oak; there is the usual hot, mahogany furniture; and, commanding point of the whole room, there is the usual black-marble sarcophagus of a fireplace. Above this hangs one of the two or three oil-paintings, which are all that break the red pattern of the walls, the portrait, painted in 1880, of an undistinguished-looking gentleman aged sixty; he is shown sitting in a more graceful attitude than it could ever have been comfortable for him to assume.* MR. VOYSEY's *father it is, and the brass plate at the bottom of the frame tells us that the portrait was a presentation one. On the mantelpiece stands, of course, a clock; at either end a china vase filled with paper spills. And in front of the fire—since that is the post of vantage—stands at this moment* MAJOR BOOTH VOYSEY. *He is the second son, of the age that it is necessary for a Major to be, and of the appearance of many ordinary Majors in ordinary regiments. He went into the army because he thought it would come up to a schoolboy's idea of it; and, being there, he does his little all to keep it to this. He stands astride, hands in pockets, coat-tails through his arms, half-smoked cigar in mouth, moustache bristling. On either side of him sits at the table an old gentleman; the one is* MR. EVAN COLPUS, *the vicar of their parish, the other* MR. GEORGE BOOTH, *a friend of long standing, and the Major's godfather.* MR. COLPUS *is a harmless enough anachronism, except for the comparative waste of £400 a year in which his stipend involves the community. Leaving most of his parochial work to an energetic curate, he devotes his serious attention to the composition of two sermons a week.* MR. GEORGE BOOTH, *on the contrary, is as gay an old gentleman as can be found in Chislehurst. An only son, his father left him at the age of twenty-five a fortune of a hundred thousand pounds. At the same time he had the good sense*

*to dispose of his father's business, into which he had been most
unwillingly introduced five years earlier, for a like sum before he
was able to depreciate its value. It was* MR. VOYSEY's *invaluable
assistance in this transaction which first bound the two together in
great friendship. Since that time* MR. BOOTH *has been bent on
nothing but enjoying himself. He has even remained a bachelor
with that object. Money has given him all he wants, therefore he
loves and reverences money; while his imagination may be estimated
by the fact that he has now reached the age of sixty-five, still
possessing more of it than he knows what to do with. At the head
of the table, meditatively cracking walnuts, sits* MR. VOYSEY. *He
has his back to the conservatory door. On* MR. VOYSEY's *left is*
DENIS TREGONING, *a nice enough young man. And at the other
end of the table sits* EDWARD, *not smoking, not talking, hardly
listening, very depressed. Behind him is the ordinary door of the
room, which leads out into the dismal, draughty hall. The*
MAJOR'S *voice is like the sound of a cannon through the tobacco
smoke.*

MAJOR BOOTH VOYSEY. Certainly . . . I am hot and strong for
conscription . . . and the question will be to the fore again very
shortly.

MR. GEORGE BOOTH. My dear boy . . . the country won't hear
of it . . .

MAJOR BOOTH VOYSEY. I differ from you. If we . . . the army
. . . if the men who have studied the subject . . . the brains of the
army . . . say as one man to the country: Conscription is once
more necessary for your safety . . . what answer has the country?
What? There you are! None.

TREGONING. You try . . . and you'll see.

MAJOR BOOTH VOYSEY. If the international situation grows more
threatening I shall seriously consider going on half-pay for a bit
and entering the House. And . . . I'm not a conceited man . . .
but I believe that if I speak out upon a subject I understand, and
only upon that subject, the House . . . and the country . . . will
listen.

MR. GEORGE BOOTH. The gentlemen of England have always
risen to an emergency. Why . . . old as I am . . . I would
shoulder a musket myself if need be. But . . .

MAJOR BOOTH VOYSEY. Just one moment. Our national safety
is not the only question. There's the stamina of the race . . .
deplorably deteriorated! You should just see the fellars that try

to enlist nowadays. Horrid little runts . . . with their stinkin'
little fags . . . hangin' out of the corners of their slobberin' little
mouths. What England wants is chest. Chest and discipline. And
conscription . . .

MR. VOYSEY [*with the crack of a nut*]. Your godson talks a deal,
don't he? You know, when our Major gets into a club, he gets on
the committee . . . gets on any committee to enquire into anything . . . and then goes on at 'em just like this. Don't you,
Booth?

BOOTH *knuckles under easily enough to his father's sarcasm.*

MAJOR BOOTH VOYSEY. Well, sir, people tell me I'm a useful
man on committees.

MR. VOYSEY. I don't doubt it . . . your voice must drown all
discussion.

MAJOR BOOTH VOYSEY. You can't say I don't listen to you, sir.

MR. VOYSEY. I don't . . . and I'm not blaming you. But I must
say I often think what a devil of a time the family will have with
you when I'm gone. Fortunately for your poor mother, she's deaf.

MAJOR BOOTH VOYSEY. Well, sir . . . it might be my duty . . .
as eldest son . . . Trenchard not counting . . .

MR. VOYSEY [*with the crack of another nut*]. Trenchard not
counting. Oh, certainly . . . bully them. Never mind whether
you're right or wrong . . . bully them. I don't manage things
that way myself, but I think it's your best chance.

MAJOR BOOTH VOYSEY [*with some discomfort*]. Ha! If I were a
conceited man, sir, I could trust you to take it out of me.

MR. VOYSEY [*as he taps* MR. BOOTH *with the nut-crackers*]. Help
yourself, George, and drink to your godson's health. Long may
he keep his chest notes! Never heard him on parade, have you?

TREGONING. There's one thing you learn in the army . . . and
that's how to display yourself. Booth makes a perfect firescreen.
But I believe after mess that position is positively rushed.

MAJOR BOOTH VOYSEY [*cheered to find an opponent he can tackle*]. If
you want a bit of fire, say so, you sucking Lord Chancellor.
Because I mean to allow you to be my brother-in-law, you think
you can be impertinent.

So TREGONING *moves to the fire and that changes the conversation.*

MR. VOYSEY. Vicar, the port's with you. Help yourself and send
it on.

MR. COLPUS. Thank you . . . I have had my quantum.

MR. VOYSEY. Nonsense!

MR. COLPUS. Well . . . a teeny weeny drain!

MR. VOYSEY. By the way . . . did you see Lady Mary yesterday?
Is she going to help us clear off the debt on the chapel?

MR. COLPUS. Well, no . . . I'm afraid she isn't.

MR. VOYSEY. Why not?

MR. COLPUS. Well . . . the fact is she's quite angry.

MR. VOYSEY. What about?

MR. COLPUS. I regret to tell you . . . it's about Hugh's fresco.

MAJOR BOOTH VOYSEY. Ah . . . I knew there'd be trouble!

MR. COLPUS. Someone has let it out to her that the Apostles are
all portraits of people . . . and she strongly disapproves.

MAJOR BOOTH VOYSEY. So do I.

MR. COLPUS. Indeed, I fear she's writing to you to say that as
Hugh is your son she thinks you should have kept him under
better control. I said I'd done all I could. And I did argue with
him. First of all, you know, he wanted to make them local people
. . . the butcher and the plumber and old Sandford. He said the
fifteenth-century Florentines always did it. I said: My dear Hugh,
we are not fifteenth-century Florentines . . .

MAJOR BOOTH VOYSEY. Hugh's no good at a likeness. I don't
believe anyone would have known.

MR. COLPUS. But all he said was: Ha! Ha! Then I didn't see
the thing for a week, and . . . oh, far worse! . . . he'd made them
all quite well-known public characters! And as it was in tempera,
he couldn't alter it without taking the wall down.

MR. VOYSEY. What's the debt now?

MR. COLPUS. Three hundred pounds nearly.

MR. VOYSEY. I shall have to stump up, I suppose.

MAJOR BOOTH VOYSEY. Anonymously. What?

MR. VOYSEY. George Booth . . . will you go halves?

MR. GEORGE BOOTH. Certainly not. I can't see what we wanted
the chapel at all for. Eight hundred pounds and more . . . !

MR. COLPUS. People do drop in and pray. Oh . . . I've seen them.

MR. GEORGE BOOTH. Well, Vicar . . . it's your business, of
course . . . but I call it a mistake to encourage all this extra
religion. Work on week-days . . . church on Sundays. That was
the rule when I was young.

MR. VOYSEY. You can't stop people praying.

MR. GEORGE BOOTH. But why make a show of it? What's the
result? Hugh's a case in point. When he was a boy . . . mad about
religion! Used to fast on Fridays! I remember your punishing
him for it. Now look at him. What his beliefs are now . . . well,
I'd rather not know. And with Edward here . . .

EDWARD. With me?

MR. GEORGE BOOTH. Up at Cambridge . . . wanted to turn Papist, didn't you? And now . . . I suppose you call yourself a free-thinker.

EDWARD. I don't call myself anything.

MR. GEORGE BOOTH. Keep to the middle of the road . . . that's what I'd tell any young man.

TREGONING. Safety first.

MR. GEORGE BOOTH. Certainly. For what should be a man's aim in life? I have always known mine, and . . . though far be it from me to boast . . . I look back to nothing I need regret . . . nothing the whole world might not know. I don't speak of quite personal affairs. Like most other men, I have been young. But all that sort of thing is nobody's business but one's own. I inherited a modest fortune. I have not needed to take the bread out of other men's mouths by working. My money has been wisely administered . . . well, ask your father about that . . . and has . . . not diminished. I have paid my taxes without grumbling. I have never wronged any man. I have never lied about anything that mattered. I have left theories to take care of themselves and tried to life the life of an English gentleman. And I consider there is no higher . . . at any rate no more practical ideal.

MAJOR BOOTH VOYSEY [*not to be outdone by this display of virtue*]. Well, I'm not a conceited man, but—

TREGONING. I hope you're sure of that, Booth.

MAJOR BOOTH VOYSEY. Shut up. I was going to say when my young cub of a brother-in-law-to-be interrupted me, that Training, for which we all have to be thankful to you, sir, has much to do with it. [*Suddenly he pulls his trousers against his legs.*] I say, I'm scorching. Try one of those new cigars, Denis?

TREGONING. No, thank you.

MAJOR BOOTH VOYSEY. I will.

> *He glances round;* TREGONING *sees a box on the table and reaches it. The Vicar gets up.*

MR. COLPUS. Must be taking my departure.

MR. VOYSEY. Already!

MAJOR BOOTH VOYSEY [*frowning upon the cigar-box*]. No, not those. The Ramon Allones. Why on earth doesn't Honor see they're here?

MR. VOYSEY. Spare time for a chat with my wife before you go. She has ideas about a children's tea-fight.

MR. COLPUS. Certainly I will.

MAJOR BOOTH VOYSEY [*scowling helplessly around*]. My goodness! . . . one can never find anything in this house.

MR. VOYSEY. My regards to Mrs. Colpus. Hope her lumbago will be better.

MR. COLPUS. These trials are sent us.

He is sliding through the half-opened door when ETHEL *meets him, flinging it wide. She is the younger daughter, the baby of the family, but twenty-three now.*

MR. VOYSEY. I say! It's cold again to-night! An ass of an architect who built this place . . . such a draught between these two doors.

He gets up to draw the curtain. When he turns MR. COLPUS *has disappeared, while* ETHEL *has been followed into the room by* ALICE MAITLAND, *who shuts the door after her.* MISS ALICE MAITLAND *is a young lady of any age to thirty. Nor need her appearance alter for the next fifteen years; since her nature is healthy and well-balanced. It mayn't be a pretty face, but it has alertness and humour; and the resolute eyes and eyebrows are a more innocent edition of* MR. VOYSEY'S, *who is her uncle.* ETHEL *goes straight to her father (though her glance is on* DENIS *and his on her) and chirps, birdlike, in her spoiled-child way.*

ETHEL. We think you've stayed in here quite long enough.

MR. VOYSEY. That's to say, Ethel thinks Denis has been kept out of her pocket much too long.

ETHEL. Ethel wants billiards. . . . Father . . . what a dessert you've eaten. Greedy pig!

ALICE *is standing behind* EDWARD, *considering his hair-parting apparently.*

ALICE. Crack me a filbert, please, Edward . . . I had none.

EDWARD [*jumping up, rather formally well-mannered*]. I beg your pardon, Alice. Won't you sit down?

ALICE. No.

MR. VOYSEY [*taking* ETHEL *on his knee*]. Come here, puss. Have you made up your mind yet what you want for a wedding present?

ETHEL [*rectifying a stray hair on his forehead*]. After mature consideration, I decide on a cheque.

MR. VOYSEY. Do you!

ETHEL. Yes. I think that a cheque will give most scope to your generosity. If you desire to add any trimmings in the shape of a piano or a Persian carpet you may . . . and Denis and I will be grateful. But I think I'd let yourself go over a cheque.

MR. VOYSEY. You're a minx.

MAJOR BOOTH VOYSEY [*giving up the cigar search*]. Here, who's going to play?

MR. GEORGE BOOTH [*pathetically, as he gets up*]. Well, if my wrist will hold out . . .

MAJOR BOOTH VOYSEY [*to* TREGONING]. No, don't you bother to look for them. [*He strides from the room, his voice echoing through the hall.*] Honor, where are those Ramon Allones?

ALICE [*calling after*]. She's in the drawing-room with Auntie and Mr. Colpus.

MR. VOYSEY. Now I suggest that you and Denis go and take off the billiard table cover. You'll find folding it up a very excellent amusement.

He illustrates his meaning with his table napkin and by putting together the tips of his forefingers, roguishly.

MR. GEORGE BOOTH. Ah ha! I remember that being done in some play . . .

ETHEL. Dear father . . . you must try not to be roguish. You won't get a blush or a giggle out of either of us. Denis . . . come here and kiss me . . . before everybody.

TREGONING. I shall do nothing of the sort.

ETHEL. If you don't I swear I won't marry you. Come along. I detest self-conscious people. Come on. [DENIS *gives her a shame-faced peck on one cheek.*] That's a nice sort of kiss, too! If it wasn't for having to send back the presents I wouldn't marry you.

She goes off.

DENIS. Women have no shame.

The Major comes stalking back, followed in a fearful flurry by his elder sister HONOR. DENIS *follows* ETHEL. *Poor* HONOR (*her female friends are apt to refer to her as Poor* HONOR) *is a phenomenon common to most large families. From her earliest years she has been bottle-washer to her brothers. They were expensively educated, but she was grudged schooling. Her fate is a curious survival of the intolerance of parents towards daughters until the vanity of their hunger for sons has been gratified. In a less humane society she would have been exposed at birth. Yet* HONOR *is not unhappy in her survival, even if at this moment her life is a burden.*

MAJOR BOOTH VOYSEY. Honor, they are not in the dining-room.

HONOR. But they must be!—where else can they be?

She has a habit of accentuating one word in each sentence and often the wrong one.

MAJOR BOOTH VOYSEY. That's what you ought to know.

8

MR. VOYSEY [*as he moves towards the door*]. Well . . . will you have a game?

MR. GEORGE BOOTH. I'll play you fifty up, not more. I'm getting old.

MR. VOYSEY [*stopping at a dessert dish*]. Yes, these are good apples of Bearman's. Six of my trees spoilt this year.

HONOR. Here you are, Booth.

> *She triumphantly discovers the discarded box, at which the Major becomes pathetic with indignation.*

MAJOR BOOTH VOYSEY. Oh, Honor, don't be such a fool. I want the Ramon Allones.

HONOR. I don't know the difference.

MAJOR BOOTH VOYSEY. No, you don't, but you might learn.

MR. VOYSEY [*in a voice like the crack of a very fine whip*]. Booth!

MAJOR BOOTH VOYSEY [*subduedly*]. What is it, sir?

MR. VOYSEY. Look for your cigars yourself. Honor, go back to your reading or your sewing or whatever you were fiddling at, and fiddle in peace.

> MR. VOYSEY *departs, leaving the room rather hushed.* MR. BOOTH *has not waited for this parental display. Then* ALICE *insinuates a remark very softly.*

ALICE. Have you looked in the library?

MAJOR BOOTH VOYSEY [*relapsing to an injured mutter*]. Where's Emily?

HONOR. Upstairs with little Henry, he woke up and cried.

MAJOR BOOTH VOYSEY. Letting her wear herself to rags over the child . . .

HONOR. Well, she won't let me go.

MAJOR BOOTH VOYSEY. Why don't you stop looking for those cigars?

HONOR. If you don't mind I want a lace doily now I am here.

MAJOR BOOTH VOYSEY. I daresay they're in the library. What a house!

> *He departs.*

HONOR. Booth is so trying.

ALICE. Honor, why do you put up with it?

HONOR. Someone has to.

ALICE [*discreetly nibbling a nut, which* EDWARD *has cracked for her*]. I'm afraid I think Master Major Booth ought to have been taken in hand early . . . with a cane.

HONOR [*as she vaguely burrows into corners*]. Papa did. But it's never prevented him booming at us . . . oh, ever since he was a baby. Now he's flustered me so I simply can't remember which set of them it was.

ALICE. The Pettifers wished to be remembered to you, Edward.

HONOR. I'd better take one of each. [*But she goes on looking*]. I sometimes think, Alice, that we're a very difficult family . . . except perhaps Edward.

EDWARD. Why except me?

HONOR. And you were always difficult . . . to yourself. [*Then she starts to go, threading her way through the disarranged chairs.*] Mr. Colpus will shout so at Mother, and she doesn't like people to think she's so very deaf. . . . I thought Mary Pettifer looking old . . .

She talks herself out of the room.

ALICE [*after her*]. She's getting old. I was glad not to spend August abroad for once. We drove into Cheltenham to a dance. I golfed a lot.

EDWARD. How long were you with them?

ALICE. A fortnight. It doesn't seem three months since I was here.

EDWARD. I'm down so seldom.

ALICE. I might be one of the family . . . almost.

EDWARD. You know they're always pleased.

ALICE. Well, being a homeless person! But what a cartload to descend . . . yesterday and to-day. The Major and Emily. . . Emily's not at all well. Hugh and Mrs. Hugh. And me. Are you staying?

EDWARD. No. I must get a word with my father.

ALICE. Edward . . . you look more like half-baked pie-crust than usual. I wish you didn't sit over your desk quite so much.

EDWARD [*a little enviously*]. You're very well.

ALICE. I'm always well and nearly always happy.

MAJOR BOOTH *returns. He has the right sort of cigar in his mouth and is considerably mollified.*

ALICE. You found them?

MAJOR BOOTH VOYSEY. Of course they were there. Thank you very much, Alice. Now I want a knife.

ALICE. I must give you a cigar-cutter for Christmas, Booth.

MAJOR BOOTH VOYSEY. Beastly things, I hate 'em. [*He eyes the dessert disparagingly.*] Nothing but silver ones. [EDWARD *hands him a carefully opened pocket-knife.*] Thank you, Edward. And I must take one of the candles. Something's gone wrong with the library ventilator and you never can see a thing in that room.

ALICE. Is Mrs. Hugh there?

MAJOR BOOTH VOYSEY. Writing letters. Things are neglected here, Edward, unless one is constantly on the look out. The Pater only cares for his garden. I must speak seriously to Honor.

He has returned the knife, still open, and having now lit his cigar at the candle he carries this off.

EDWARD [*giving her a nut, about the fifteenth*]. Here. 'Scuse fingers.

ALICE. Thank you. [*Looking at him, with her head on one side and her face more humorous than ever.*] Edward, why have you given up proposing to me?

He starts, flushes; then won't be outdone in humour.

EDWARD. One can't go on proposing for ever.

ALICE. Have you seen anyone you like better?

EDWARD. No.

ALICE. Well . . . I miss it.

EDWARD. What satisfaction did you find in refusing me?

ALICE [*as she weighs the matter*]. I find satisfaction in feeling that I'm wanted.

EDWARD. Without any intention of giving . . . of throwing yourself away.

ALICE [*teasing his sudden earnestness*]. Ah, now we come from mere vanity to serious questions.

EDWARD. Mine was a very serious question.

ALICE. But, Edward, all questions are serious to you. You're a perfect little pocket-guide to life . . . every question answered; what to eat, drink and avoid, what to believe and what to say. Some things are worth bothering over . . . and some aren't.

EDWARD. One lays down principles.

ALICE. I prefer my plan. I always do what I know I want to do. Crack me another nut.

EDWARD. Haven't you had enough?

ALICE. I know I want one more.

He cracks another with a sigh which sounds ridiculous in that connection.

I know it just as I knew I didn't want to marry you . . . each time. I didn't say no on principle . . . or because I thought it wouldn't be wise. That's why I want you to keep on asking me. Because at any moment I might say Yes. And then I suppose I should find that it was simply a habit you'd got into . . . and that you didn't want me after all. Still, take another chance. Take it now!

EDWARD. No . . . I think not . . . now.

ALICE. Edward! There's nothing wrong, is there?

EDWARD. Nothing at all.

> *They are interrupted by the sudden appearance of* MRS. HUGH
> VOYSEY, *a brisk, bright little woman, in an evening gown which
> she has bullied a cheap dressmaker into making look exceedingly
> smart.* BEATRICE *is hard and clever. But if she keeps her feelings
> buried pretty deep it is because they are precious to her; and if she
> is impatient with fools it is because her own brains have had to
> win her everything in the world, so perhaps she does overvalue them
> a little. She speaks always with great decision and little effort.*

BEATRICE. I believe I could write business letters upon an
island in the middle of Fleet Street. But while Booth is poking at
a ventilator with a billiard cue . . . no, I can't. The Vicar's in
the drawing-room . . . and my bedroom's like an ice-house.

> *She goes to the fireplace, waving her half-finished letter.* BOOTH
> *appears at the door, billiard cue in hand, and says solemnly . . .*

MAJOR BOOTH VOYSEY. Edward, I wish you'd come and have a
look at this ventilator, like a good fellow.

> *Then he turns and goes again, obviously with the weight of an
> important matter on his shoulders. With the ghost of a smile*
> EDWARD *gets up and follows him.*

ALICE. No one has a right to be as good and kind as Edward is.
It encourages the rotters.

> *With which comment she joins* BEATRICE *at the fireplace.*

BEATRICE. A satisfactory day's shopping?

ALICE. 'M. The baby bride and I bought clothes all the
morning. Then we had lunch with Denis and bought furniture.

BEATRICE. Nice furniture?

ALICE. Very good and very new. They neither of them know
what they want. [*Then suddenly throwing up her chin and exclaiming.*]
Beatrice . . . why do women get married? Oh, of course . . . if
you're caught young! With Ethel and Denis now . . . they're two
little birds building their nest and it's all ideal. They'll soon forget
they've ever been apart.

> *Now* HONOR *flutters into the room, patient but wild-eyed.*

HONOR. Mother wants last week's Notes and Queries. Have
you seen it?

BEATRICE [*exasperated at the interruption*]. No.

HONOR. It ought not to be here. [*So she proceeds to look for it.*]
Hugh had it.

BEATRICE. Lit his pipe with it.

HONOR. Oh, d'you think so?

> *So she gives up the search and flutters out again.*

ALICE. This is a most unrestful house.

BEATRICE. I once thought of putting the Voyseys into a book of mine. Then I concluded they'd be as dull there as they are anywhere else.

ALICE. They're not duller than most of the rest of us.

BEATRICE. But how very dull that is!

ALICE. They're a little noisier and perhaps not quite so well-mannered. But I love them . . . in a sort of way.

BEATRICE. I don't. I should have thought love was just what they couldn't inspire.

ALICE. Hugh's not like the others.

BEATRICE. He has most of their bad points. But I don't love Hugh.

ALICE [*her eyebrows up, though she smiles*]. Beatrice, you shouldn't say so.

BEATRICE. Sounds affected, doesn't it?

ALICE [*her face growing a little thoughtful*]. Beatrice . . . were you in love with Hugh when you married him? Don't answer if you don't want to.

BEATRICE. I married him for his money.

ALICE. He hadn't much.

BEATRICE. I had none . . . and I wanted to chuck journalism and write books. Yes, I loved him enough to marry him. But with some of us . . . that's not much.

ALICE. But you thought you'd be happy?

BEATRICE [*considering carefully*]. No, I didn't. I hoped he'd be happy. Dear Alice, how ever should you understand these things? You've eight hundred a year.

ALICE. What has that to do with it?

BEATRICE [*putting her case very precisely*]. Fine feelings, my dear, are as much a luxury as clean gloves. From seventeen to twenty-eight I had to earn my own living . . . and I'm no genius. So there wasn't a single thing I ever did quite genuinely for its own sake. No . . . always with an eye to bread-and-butter . . . pandering to the people who were to give me that. I warned Hugh . . . he took the risk.

ALICE. What risk?

BEATRICE. That one day I'd find I could get on better without him.

ALICE. And if he can't without you?

BEATRICE. One should never let one's happiness depend on other people. It's degrading . . .

The conservatory door opens and through it come MR. VOYSEY *and* MR. BOOTH *in the midst of a discussion.*

MR. VOYSEY. My dear man, stick to the shares and risk it.

MR. GEORGE BOOTH. No, of course if you seriously advise me. . . .

MR. VOYSEY. I never advise greedy children; I let 'em overeat 'emselves and take the consequences.

ALICE [*shaking a finger*]. Uncle Trench, you've been in the garden without a hat after playing billiards in that hot room.

MR. GEORGE BOOTH. We had to give up . . . my wrist was bad. They've started pool.

BEATRICE. Is Booth going to play?

MR. VOYSEY. We left him instructing Ethel how to hold a cue.

BEATRICE. I can finish my letter.

Off she goes. ALICE *is idly following with a little paper her hand has fallen on behind the clock.*

MR. VOYSEY. Don't run away, my dear.

ALICE. I'm taking this to Auntie. . . . Notes and Queries . . . she wants it.

MR. VOYSEY. This room's cold. Why don't they keep the fire up? [*He proceeds to put coals on it.*]

MR. GEORGE BOOTH. It was too hot in the billiard room. You know, Voysey . . . about those Alguazils?

MR. VOYSEY [*through the rattling of the coals*]. What?

MR. GEORGE BOOTH [*trying to pierce the din*]. Those Alguazils.

MR. VOYSEY *with surprising inconsequence points a finger at the silk handkerchief across* MR. BOOTH'S *shirt front.*

MR. VOYSEY. What have you got your handkerchief there for?

MR. GEORGE BOOTH. Measure of precau— [*at that moment he sneezes*]. Damn it . . . if you've given me a chill dragging me through your infernal garden . . .

MR. VOYSEY [*slapping him on the back*]. You're an old crock.

MR. GEORGE BOOTH. Well, I'll be glad of a winter in Egypt. [*He returns to his subject.*] And if you think seriously that I ought to sell out of the Alguazils before I go . . . ? Well . . . you'll have them. You can sell out if things look bad.

At this moment PHOEBE, *the middle-aged parlourmaid, comes in, tray in hand. Like an expert fisherman* MR. VORSEY *lets loose the thread of the conversation.*

MR. VOYSEY. D'you want to clear?

PHOEBE. It doesn't matter, sir.

MR. VOYSEY. No, go on . . . go on.

So MARY, *the young housemaid, comes in as well, and the two*
start to clear the table. All of which fidgets poor MR. BOOTH
considerably. He sits shrivelled up in the armchair by the fire; and
now MR. VOYSEY *attends to him.*

MR. VOYSEY. George . . . I've told you again and again that
you ought not to run after high interest as you do.

MR. GEORGE BOOTH. Yes . . . but one ought to see that one's
money's put to good use.

MR. VOYSEY. You're an old gambler.

MR. GEORGE BOOTH [*propitiatingly*]. Ah, but then I've you to
advise me. I do what you tell me in the end . . . you can't deny
that.

MR. VOYSEY. The man who don't know must trust in the man
who do.

MR. GEORGE BOOTH [*modestly insisting*]. There's ten thousand in
Alguazils. What else could we put it into?

MR. VOYSEY. I can get you something at four and a half.

MR. GEORGE BOOTH. Oh, Lord!

MR. VOYSEY [*with a sudden serious friendliness*]. I sometimes wish,
George, that you'd look after your own affairs a little more than
you do. You leave far too much in my hands. If I were a crook
I could play Old Harry with them . . . and I doubt if you'd ever
find out.

MR. GEORGE BOOTH. But, of course, I shouldn't trust anybody.
It's a question of knowing one's man . . . as I know you. Ah, my
friend, what'll happen to your firm when you depart this life! . . .
not before my time, I hope.

MR. VOYSEY [*with a little frown*]. What d'ye mean?

MR. GEORGE BOOTH. Edward's no use.

MR. VOYSEY. I beg your pardon . . . very sound in business.

MR. GEORGE BOOTH. May be . . . but I tell you he's no use. No
personality.

MR. VOYSEY. I fear you don't much like Edward.

MR. GEORGE BOOTH [*with pleasant frankness*]. No, I don't.

MR. VOYSEY. That's a pity. That's a great pity.

MR. GEORGE BOOTH [*with a flattering smile*]. He's not his father
and never will be. What's the time?

MR. VOYSEY. Twenty past ten.

MR. GEORGE BOOTH. I must be trotting.

As he goes to the door he meets EDWARD, *who comes in apparently*
looking for his father; at any rate he catches his eye immediately,
while MR. BOOTH *obliviously continues.*

MR. GEORGE BOOTH. I'll look into the drawing-room for a second. Stroll home with me?

MR. VOYSEY. I can't.

MR. GEORGE BOOTH [mildly surprised at the short reply]. Well, good-night. Good-night, Edward.

He trots away.

MR. VOYSEY. Leave the table, Phoebe.

PHOEBE. Yes, sir.

MR. VOYSEY. You can come back in ten minutes.

PHOEBE *and* MARY *depart and the door is closed. Alone with his son* MR. VOYSEY *does not move. His face grows a little keener, that's all.*

MR. VOYSEY. Well, Edward?

EDWARD *starts to move restlessly about, like a cowed animal in a cage; silently for a moment or two. Then when he speaks his voice is toneless, and he does not look at his father.*

EDWARD. Would you mind, sir, dropping with me for the future all these protestations about putting the firm's affairs straight . . . about all your anxieties and sacrifices. I see now, of course . . . a cleverer man than I could have seen it yesterday . . . that for some time, ever since, I suppose, you recovered from the first shock and got used to the double dealing, this hasn't been your object at all. You've used your clients' capital to produce your own income . . . to bring us up and endow us with. That ten thousand pounds to Booth for his boys; what you're giving Ethel on her marriage . . . ! It's odd it never struck me yesterday that my own pocket-money as a boy must have been drawn from some client's account. I suppose about half the sum you've spent on us first and last would have put things right?

MR. VOYSEY. No, it would not.

EDWARD [appealing for the truth]. Come now . . . at some time or other!

MR. VOYSEY. Well, if there have been good times there have been bad. At present the three hundred a year I'm to allow your sister is going to be rather a pull.

EDWARD. Three hundred a year . . . with things as they are! Since it isn't lunacy, sir, I can only conclude that you're enjoying yourself.

MR. VOYSEY. Three trusts . . . two of them big ones . . . have been wound up within this last four years and the accounts have been above suspicion. What's the object of this rodomontade, Edward?

EDWARD. If I'm to remain in the firm it had better be with a very clear understanding of things as they are.

MR. VOYSEY [*firmly, not too anxiously*]. Then you do remain?

EDWARD [*in a v v low voice*]. I must remain.

MR. VOYSEY [*qui e gravely*]. That's wise of you. . . . I'm very glad.

EDWARD. But I make one condition. And I want some information.

MR. VOYSEY. Well?

EDWARD. Of course no one has ever discovered . . . and no one suspects this state of things?

MR. VOYSEY. Peacey knows.

EDWARD. Peacey!

MR. VOYSEY. His father found out.

EDWARD. Oh. Does he draw hush-money?

MR. VOYSEY [*curling a little at the word*]. I have made him a little present from time to time. But I might well have done that in any case. [*He becomes benevolent.*] Peacey's a devoted fellow. I couldn't do without him.

EDWARD [*with entire comprehension*]. No . . . it would hardly be wise to try. Well . . . the condition I make is a very simple one. It is that we should really try . . . as unobtrusively as you like . . . to put things straight.

MR. VOYSEY [*with a little polite shrug*]. I've no doubt you'll prove an abler man of business than I have been.

EDWARD. To begin with we can halve what I draw from the firm.

MR. VOYSEY. As you please.

EDWARD. And it seems to me that you can't give Ethel this thousand pounds dowry.

MR. VOYSEY [*shortly, with one of the quick twists of his eye*]. I have given my word to Denis . . .

EDWARD. Since the money isn't yours to give.

MR. VOYSEY [*in an indignant crescendo*]. I should not dream of depriving Ethel of what, as my daughter, she has every right to expect. I am surprised at your suggesting such a thing.

EDWARD [*pale and firm*]. I am set on this, Father.

MR. VOYSEY. Don't be such a fool, Edward. What would it look like . . . suddenly refusing without rhyme or reason? What would old Tregoning think?

EDWARD. Oh, can't you see it's my duty to prevent this?

MR. VOYSEY. Well . . . you can prevent it . . . by telling the nearest policeman. It is my duty to pay no more attention to such folly than a nurse pays to her child's tantrums. Understand, Edward, I don't want to force you to go on. Come with me gladly, or don't come at all.

EDWARD [*dully*]. It is my duty to be of what use I can to you, sir. Father, I want to save you if I can.

He flashes into this exclamation of almost broken-hearted affection. MR. VOYSEY *looks at his son for a moment and his lip quivers. Then he steels himself.*

MR. VOYSEY. Thank you! I have been saving myself quite satisfactorily for the last thirty years, and you must please believe that by this time I know my own business best.

EDWARD [*hopelessly*]. Can't we find the money some other way? How do you manage for your own income?

MR. VOYSEY. I have a bank balance and a cheque book, haven't I? I spend what I think well to spend. What's the use of earmarking this or that as my own? You say none of it is my own. I might say it's all my own. I think I've earned it.

EDWARD [*anger coming on him*]. That's what I can't forgive. If you'd lived poor . . . if you'd really done all you could for your clients and not thought of your own pocket . . . then, even though things were no better than they are now . . . why, in a queer sort of way, I could have been proud of you. But, Father, do own the truth . . . I've a right to that from you at least. Didn't you simply seize this chance as a means of money-making?

MR. VOYSEY [*with a sledge-hammer irony*]. Certainly. I sat that morning in my father's office, studying the helmet of the policeman in the street below, and thinking what a glorious path I had happened on to wealth and honour and renown. [*Then he begins to bully* EDWARD *in the kindliest way.*] My dear boy, you don't grasp the A.B.C. of my position. What has carried me to victory? The confidence of my clients. What has earned me that confidence? A decent life, my integrity, my brains? No, my reputation for wealth . . . that, and nothing else. Business now-a-days is run on the lines of the confidence trick. What makes old George Booth so glad to trust me with every penny he possesses? Not affection . . . he's never cared for anything in his life but his collection of French prints.

EDWARD [*stupified, helpless*]. Is he involved?

MR. VOYSEY. Of course he's involved, and he's always after high interest, too . . . it's little one makes out of him. But there's a further question here, Edward. Should I have had confidence in

myself, if I'd remained a poor man? No, I should not. In this
world you must either be the master of money or its servant. And
if one is not opulent in one's daily life one loses that wonderful
. . . financier's touch. One must be confident oneself . . . and I
saw from the first that I must at any cost inspire confidence. My
whole public and private life has tended to that. All my sur-
roundings . . . you and your brothers and sisters that I have
brought into, and up, and put out in the world so worthily . . .
you in your turn inspire confidence.

EDWARD. I sat down yesterday to try and make a list of the
people who are good enough to trust their money to us. From
George Booth with his money piling up while he sleeps . . . so he
fancies . . . to Nursie with her savings, which she brought you so
proudly to invest. But you've let those be, at least.

MR. VOYSEY. Five hundred pounds. I don't know what I did
with it.

EDWARD. But that's damnable.

MR. VOYSEY. Indeed? I give her seventy-five pounds a year for
it. Would you like to take charge of that account, Edward? I'll
give you five hundred to invest to-morrow.

EDWARD, *hopelessly beaten, falls into an almost comic state of
despair.*

EDWARD. My dear father, putting every moral question aside
. . . it's all very well your playing Robin Hood in this magnificent
manner; but have you given a moment's thought to the sort of
inheritance you'll be leaving me?

MR. VOYSEY [*pleased for the first time*]. Ah! that's a question you
have every right to ask.

EDWARD. If you died to-morrow could we pay eight shillings
in the pound . . . or seventeen . . . or five? Do you know?

MR. VOYSEY. And the answer is, that by your help I have every
intention, when I die, of leaving a personal estate that will run
into six figures. D'you think I've given my life and my talents
for a less result than that? I'm fond of you all . . . and I want you
to be proud of me . . . and I mean that the name of Voysey shall
be carried high in the world by my children and grandchildren.
Don't you be afraid, Edward. Ah, you lack experience, my boy
. . . you're not full-grown yet . . . your impulses are a bit chaotic.
You emotionalise over your work, and you reason about your
emotions. You must sort yourself. You must realise that money-
making is one thing, and religion another, and family life a
third . . . and that if we apply our energies whole-heartedly to

each of these in turn, and realise that different laws govern each, that there is a different end to be served, a different ideal to be striven for in each . . .

His coherence is saved by the sudden appearance of his wife, who comes round the door smiling benignly. Not in the least put out, in fact a little relieved, he greets her with an affectionate shout, for she is very deaf.

MR. VOYSEY. Hullo, Mother!

MRS. VOYSEY. Oh, there you are, Trench. I've been deserted.

MR. VOYSEY. George Booth gone?

MRS. VOYSEY. Are you talking business? Perhaps you don't want me.

MR. VOYSEY. No, no . . . no business.

MRS. VOYSEY [*who has not looked for his answer*]. I suppose the others are in the billiard room.

MR. VOYSEY [*vociferously*]. We're not talking business, old lady.

EDWARD. I'll be off, sir.

MR. VOYSEY [*genial as usual*]. Why don't you stay? I'll come up with you in the morning.

EDWARD. No, thank you, sir.

MR. VOYSEY. Then I'll be up about noon.

EDWARD. Good-night, Mother.

MRS. VOYSEY *places a plump, kindly hand on his arm and looks up affectionately.*

MRS. VOYSEY. You look tired.

EDWARD. No, I'm not.

MRS. VOYSEY. What did you say?

EDWARD [*too weary to repeat himself*]. Nothing, Mother dear.

He kisses her cheek, while she kisses the air.

MR. VOYSEY. Good-night, my boy.

Then he goes. MRS. VOYSEY *is carrying her Notes and Queries. This is a dear old lady, looking older too than probably she is. Placid describes her. She has had a life of little joys and cares, has never measured herself against the world, never even questioned the shape and size of the little corner of it in which she lives. She has loved an indulgent husband and borne eight children, six of them surviving, healthy. That is her history.*

MRS. VOYSEY. George Booth went some time ago. He said he thought you'd taken a chill walking round the garden.

MR. VOYSEY. I'm all right.

MRS. VOYSEY. D'you think you have?

MR. VOYSEY [*in her ear*]. No.

MRS. VOYSEY. You should be careful, Trench. What did you put on?

MR. VOYSEY. Nothing.

MRS. VOYSEY. How very foolish! Let me feel your hand. You are quite feverish.

MR. VOYSEY [*affectionately*]. You're a fuss-box, old lady.

MRS. VOYSEY [*coquetting with him*]. Don't be rude, Trench.

> HONOR *descends upon them. She is well into that nightly turmoil of putting everything and everybody to rights which always precedes her bed-time. She carries a shawl which she clasps round her mother's shoulders, her mind and gaze already on the next thing to be done.*

HONOR. Mother, you left your shawl in the drawing-room. Oh . . . can't they finish clearing?

MR. VOYSEY [*arranging the folds of the shawl with real tenderness*]. Now who's careless!

> PHOEBE *comes into the room.*

HONOR. Phoebe, finish here and then you must bring in the tray for Mr. Hugh.

MRS. VOYSEY [*having looked at the shawl and* HONOR, *and connected the matter in her mind*]. Thank you, Honor. You'd better look after your father; he's been walking round the garden without his cape.

HONOR. Papa!

MR. VOYSEY. Phoebe, you get that little kettle and boil it, and brew me some whiskey and water. I shall be all right.

HONOR [*fluttering more than ever*]. I'll get it. Where's the whiskey? And Hugh coming back at ten o'clock with no dinner. No wonder his work goes wrong. Here it is! Papa, you do d e s e r v e to be ill.

> *Clasping the whiskey decanter she is off again.* MRS. VOYSEY *sits at the dinner-table and adjusts her spectacles. She returns to Notes and Queries, one elbow firmly planted and her plump hand against her plump cheek. This is her favourite attitude; and she is apt, when reading, to soliloquize in her deaf woman's voice. At least, whether she considers it soliloquy or conversation is not easy to discover.* MR. VOYSEY *stands with his back to the fire, grumbling and pulling faces.*

MRS. VOYSEY. This is a very perplexing correspondence about the Cromwell family. One can't deny the man had good blood in him . . . his grandfather Sir Henry, his uncle Sir Oliver . . .

MR. VOYSEY. There's a pain in my back.

MRS. VOYSEY. . . . and it's difficult to discover where the taint crept in.

MR. VOYSEY. I believe I strained myself putting in those straw-berry plants.

MARY, *the house-parlourmaid, carries in a tray of warmed-up dinner for* HUGH *and plants it on the table.*

MRS. VOYSEY. Yes, but then how was it he came to disgrace himself so? I believe the family disappeared. Regicide is a root and branch curse. You must read the letter signed C. W. A. . . . it's quite interesting. There's a misprint in mine about the first umbrella-maker . . . now where was it . . . [*and so the dear lady will ramble on indefinitely*].

THE THIRD ACT

The dining-room looks very different in the white light of a July noon. Moreover, on this particular day, it isn't even its normal self. There is a peculiar luncheon spread on the table and on it are decanters of port and sherry; sandwiches, biscuits and an uncut cake; two little piles of plates and one little pile of napkins. There are no table decorations, and indeed the whole room has been made as bare and as tidy as possible. Such preparations denote one of the recognised English festivities, and the appearance of PHOEBE, the maid, who has just completed them, the set solemnity of her face and the added touches of black to her dress and cap, suggest that this is probably a funeral. When MARY comes in, the fact that she has evidently been crying and that she decorously does not raise her voice above an unpleasant whisper makes it quite certain.

MARY. Phoebe, they're coming back . . . and I forgot one of the blinds in the drawing-room.

PHOEBE. Well, pull it up quick and make yourself scarce. I'll open the door.

MARY got rid of, PHOEBE composes her face still more rigorously into the aspect of formal grief and with a touch to her apron as well goes to admit the funeral party. The first to enter are MRS. VOYSEY and MR. BOOTH, she on his arm; and the fact that she is in widow's weeds makes the occasion clear. The little old man leads his old friend very tenderly.

MR. GEORGE BOOTH. Will you come in here?

MRS. VOYSEY. Thank you.

With great solicitude he puts her in a chair; then takes her hand.

MR. GEORGE BOOTH. Now I'll intrude no longer.

MRS. VOYSEY. You'll take some lunch?

MR. GEORGE BOOTH. No.

MRS. VOYSEY. Not a glass of wine?

MR. GEORGE BOOTH. If there's anything I can do just send round.

MRS. VOYSEY. Thank you.

He reaches the door only to be met by the Major and his wife. He shakes hands with them both.

MR. GEORGE BOOTH. My dear Emily! My dear Booth!

EMILY is a homely, patient, pale little woman of about thirty-five. She looks smaller than usual in her heavy black dress and is meeker than usual on an occasion of this kind. The Major, on the other hand, though his grief is most sincere, has an irresistible air of being responsible for, and indeed rather proud of, the whole affair.

MAJOR BOOTH VOYSEY. I think it all went off as he would have wished.

MR. GEORGE BOOTH [*feeling that he is called on for praise*]. Great credit . . . great credit.

He makes another attempt to escape and is stopped this time by TRENCHARD VOYSEY, *to whom he is extending a hand and beginning his formula. But* TRENCHARD *speaks first.*

TRENCHARD. Have you the right time?

MR. GEORGE BOOTH [*taken aback and fumbling for his watch*]. I think so . . . I make it fourteen minutes to one. [*He seizes the occasion.*] Trenchard, as a very old and dear friend of your father's, you won't mind me saying how glad I was that you were present to-day. Death closes all. Indeed . . . it must be a great regret to you that you did not see him before . . . before . . .

TRENCHARD [*his cold eye freezing this little gush*]. I don't think he asked for me.

MR. GEORGE BOOTH [*stoppered*]. No? No! Well . . . well . . .

At this third attempt to depart he actually collides with someone in the doorway. It is HUGH VOYSEY.

MR. GEORGE BOOTH. My dear Hugh . . . I won't intrude.

Determined to escape, he grasps his hand, gasps out his formula and is off. TRENCHARD *and* HUGH, *eldest and youngest son, are as unlike each other as it is possible for Voyseys to be, but that isn't very unlike.* TRENCHARD *has the cocksure manner of the successful barrister;* HUGH *the sweetly querulous air of diffidence and scepticism belonging to the unsuccessful man of letters or artist. The self-respect of* TRENCHARD'S *appearance is immense, and he cultivates that air of concentration upon any trivial matter, or even upon nothing at all, which will some day make him an impressive figure upon the Bench.* HUGH *is always vague, searching Heaven or the corners of the room for inspiration; and even on this occasion his tie is abominably crooked. The inspissated gloom of this assembly, to which each member of the family as he arrives adds his share, is unbelievable.* HUGH *is depressed partly at the inadequacy of his grief:* TRENCHARD *conscientiously preserves an air of the indifference which he feels;* BOOTH *stands statuesque at*

9

the mantelpiece; while EMILY *is by* MRS. VOYSEY, *whose face in its quiet grief is nevertheless a mirror of many happy memories of her husband.*

MAJOR BOOTH VOYSEY. I wouldn't hang over her, Emily.

EMILY. No, of course not.

Apologetically she sits by the table.

TRENCHARD. I hope your wife is well, Hugh?

HUGH. Thank you, Trench: I think so. Beatrice is in America . . . giving some lectures there.

TRENCHARD. Really!

Then comes in a small, well-groomed, bullet-headed schoolboy. This is the Major's eldest son. Looking scared and solemn, he goes straight to his mother.

EMILY. Now be very quiet, Christopher.

Then DENIS TREGONING *appears.*

TRENCHARD. Oh, Tregoning, did you bring Honor back?

DENIS. Yes.

MAJOR BOOTH VOYSEY [*at the table*]. A glass of wine, Mother?

MRS. VOYSEY. What?

BOOTH *hardly knows how to turn his whisper decorously into enough of a shout for his mother to hear. But he manages it.*

MAYOR BOOTH VOYSEY. Have a glass of wine?

MRS. VOYSEY. Sherry, please.

While he pours it out with an air of its being medicine on this occasion and not wine at all, EDWARD *comes quickly into the room, his face very set, his mind obviously on other matters than the funeral. No one speaks to him for the moment and he has time to observe them all.* TRENCHARD *is continuing his talk to* DENIS.

TRENCHARD. Give my love to Ethel. Is she ill that . . .

TREGONING. Not exactly, but she couldn't very well be with us. I thought perhaps you might have heard. We're expecting . . .

He hesitates with the bashfulness of a young husband.

TRENCHARD. Indeed. I congratulate you. I hope all will be well. Please give my best love to Ethel.

MAJOR BOOTH VOYSEY [*in an awful voice*]. Lunch, Emily?

EMILY [*scared*]. I suppose so, Booth, thank you.

MAJOR BOOTH VOYSEY. I think the boy had better run away and play . . . [*He checks himself on the word.*] Well, take a book and keep quiet; d'ye hear me, Christopher?

CHRISTOPHER, *who looks incapable of a sound, gazes at his father with round eyes.* EMILY *whispers "Library" to him and*

adds a kiss in acknowledgement of his good behaviour. After a
moment he slips out, thankfully.

EDWARD. How's Ethel, Denis?

TREGONING. A little smashed, of course, but no harm done . . .
I hope. The doctor's a bit worried about her, though.

ALICE MAITLAND *comes in, brisk and businesslike; a little*
impatient of this universal cloud of mourning.

ALICE. Edward, Honor has gone to her room; I must take her
some food and make her eat it. She's very upset.

EDWARD. Make her drink a glass of wine, and say it is necessary
she should come down here. And d'you mind not coming back
yourself, Alice?

ALICE [*her eyebrows up*]. Certainly, if you wish.

MAJOR BOOTH VOYSEY [*overhearing*]. What's this? What's this?

ALICE *gets her glass of wine and goes. The Major is suddenly*
full of importance.

MAJOR BOOTH VOYSEY. What is this, Edward?

EDWARD. I have something to say to you all.

MAJOR BOOTH VOYSEY. What?

EDWARD. Well, Booth, you'll hear when I say it.

MAJOR BOOTH VOYSEY. Is it business? . . . because I think this
is scarcely the time for business.

EDWARD. Why?

MAJOR BOOTH VOYSEY. Do you find it easy to descend from your
natural grief to the consideration of money? . . . I do not. [*He*
finds TRENCHARD *at his elbow.*] I hope you are getting some
lunch, Trenchard.

EDWARD. This is business and rather more than business,
Booth. I choose now, because it is something I wish to say to the
family, not write to each individually . . . and it will be difficult
to get us all together again.

MAJOR BOOTH VOYSEY [*determined at any rate to give his sanction*].
Well, Trenchard, as Edward is in the position of trustee . . .
executor . . . I don't know your terms . . . I suppose . . .

TRENCHARD. I don't see what your objection is.

MAJOR BOOTH VOYSEY [*with some superiority*]. Don't you? I
should not call myself a sentimental man, but . . .

EDWARD. You had better stay, Denis; you represent Ethel.

TREGONING [*who has not heard the beginning of this*]. Why?

HONOR *has obediently come down from her room. She is pale and*
thin, shaken with grief and worn out besides; for needless to say
the brunt of her father's illness, the brunt of everything, has been

on her. Six weeks' nursing, part of it hopeless, will exhaust anyone. Her handkerchief is to her eyes, and every minute or two they flood over with tears. EDWARD *goes and affectionately puts his arm round her.*

EDWARD. My dear Honor, I am sorry to be so . . . so merciless. There! . . . there! [*He hands her into the room; then turns and once more surveys the family, who this time mostly return the compliment. Then he says shortly.*] I think you might all sit down. [*And then, since* BOOTH *happens to be conveniently near . . .*] Shut the door, Booth.

MAJOR BOOTH VOYSEY. Shut the door!

But he does so, with as much dignity as possible. EDWARD *goes close to his mother and speaks very distinctly, very kindly.*

EDWARD. Mother, we're all going to have a little necessary talk over matters . . . now, because it's most convenient. I hope it won't . . . I hope you won't mind. Will you come to the table?

MRS. VOYSEY *looks up as if understanding more than he says.*

MRS. VOYSEY. Edward . . .

EDWARD. Yes, Mother dear?

MAJOR BOOTH VOYSEY [*commandingly*]. You'll sit here, Mother, of course.

He places her in her accustomed chair at the foot of the table. One by one the others sit down, EDWARD *apparently last. But then he discovers that* HUGH *has lost himself in a corner of the room and is gazing into vacancy.*

EDWARD [*with a touch of kindly exasperation*]. Hugh, would you mind attending?

HUGH. What is it?

EDWARD. There's a chair.

HUGH *takes it. Then for a moment—while* EDWARD *is trying to frame in coherent sentences what he must say to them—for a minute there is silence, broken only by* HONOR'S *sniffs, which culminate at last in a noisy little cascade of tears.*

MAJOR BOOTH VOYSEY. Honor, control yourself.

And to emphasize his own perfect control he helps himself majestically to a glass of sherry. Then says . . .

MAJOR BOOTH VOYSEY. Well, Edward?

EDWARD. I'll come straight to the point which concerns you. Our father's will gives certain sums to you all . . . the gross amount would be something over a hundred thousand pounds. There will be no money.

He can get no further than the bare statement, which is received only with varying looks of bewilderment; until MRS. VOYSEY, *discovering nothing from their faces, breaks this second silence.*

MRS. VOYSEY. I didn't hear.

HUGH [*in his mother's ear*]. Edward says there's no money.

TRENCHARD [*precisely*]. I think you said . . . "will be."

MAJOR BOOTH VOYSEY [*in a tone of mitigated thunder*]. Why will there be no money?

EDWARD [*letting himself go*]. Because every penny by right belongs to the clients father spent his life in defrauding. I mean that in its worst sense . . . swindling . . . thieving. And now I must collect every penny, any money that you can give me; put the firm into bankruptcy; pay back all we can. I'll stand my trial . . . it'll come to that with me . . . and the sooner the better. [*He pauses, partly for breath, and glares at them all.*] Are none of you going to speak? Quite right, what is there to be said? [*Then with a gentle afterthought.*] I'm sorry to hurt you, Mother.

> *The* VOYSEY *family seems buried deep beneath this avalanche of horror. All but* MRS. VOYSEY, *who has been watching* EDWARD *closely, and now says very calmly . . .*

MRS. VOYSEY. I can't hear quite all you say, but I guess what it is. You don't hurt me, Edward . . . I have known of this for a long time.

EDWARD [*with a muted cry*]. Oh Mother, did he know you knew?

MRS. VOYSEY. What do you say?

TRENCHARD [*collected and dry*]. I may as well tell you, Edward; I suspected everything wasn't right about the time of my last quarrel with my father. As there was nothing I could do I did not pursue my suspicions. Was father aware that you knew, Mother?

MRS. VOYSEY. We never discussed it. There was once a great danger, I believe . . . when you were all younger . . . of his being found out. But we never discussed it.

EDWARD [*swallowing a fresh bitterness*]. I'm glad it isn't such a shock to all of you.

HUGH [*alive to the dramatic aspect of the matter*]. My God . . . before the earth has settled on his grave!

EDWARD. I thought it wrong to put off telling you.

> HONOR, *the word swindling having spelt itself out in her mind, at last gives way to a burst of piteous grief.*

HONOR. Oh poor papa! . . . poor papa!

EDWARD [*comforting her kindly*]. Honor, we shall want your help and advice.

The Major has recovered from the shock, to swell with importance. It being necessary to make an impression, he instinctively turns first to his wife.

MAJOR BOOTH VOYSEY. I think, Emily, there was no need for you to be present at this exposure, and that now you had better retire.

EMILY. Very well, Booth.

She gets up to go, conscious of her misdemeanour. But as she reaches the door, an awful thought strikes the Major.

MAJOR BOOTH VOYSEY. Good Heavens . . . I hope the servants haven't been listening! See where they are, Emily . . . and keep them away . . . distract them. Open the door suddenly. [*She does so, more or less, and there is no one behind it.*] That's all right.

Having watched his wife's departure, he turns with gravity to his brother.

MAJOR BOOTH VOYSEY. I have said nothing as yet, Edward. I am thinking.

TRENCHARD [*a little impatient at this exhibition*]. That's the worst of these family practices . . . a lot of money knocking around and no audit ever required. The wonder to me is to find an honest solicitor of that sort anywhere.

MAJOR BOOTH VOYSEY. Really, Trenchard!

TRENCHARD. Well, think of the temptation.

EDWARD. And most people are such innocents . . .

TRENCHARD. Of course the whole world is getting more and more into the hands of its experts . . .

EDWARD. Here were these funds . . . a kind of lucky bag into which he dipped.

TRENCHARD. But he must have kept accounts of some sort.

EDWARD. Scraps of paper. The separate funds . . . most of them I can't even trace. The capital doesn't exist.

MAJOR BOOTH VOYSEY. Where's it gone?

EDWARD [*very directly*]. You've been living on it.

MAJOR BOOTH VOYSEY. Good God!

TRENCHARD. What can you pay in the pound?

EDWARD. As we stand? . . . six or seven shillings, I daresay. But we must do better than that.

To which there is no response.

MAJOR BOOTH VOYSEY. All this is very dreadful. Does it mean beggary for the whole family?

EDWARD. Yes, it should.

TRENCHARD [*sharply*]. Nonsense.

EDWARD [*joining issue at once*]. What right have we to a thing we possess?

TRENCHARD. He didn't make you an allowance, Booth? Your capital's your own, isn't it?

MAJOR BOOTH VOYSEY [*awkwardly placed between the two of them*]. Really . . . I . . . I suppose so.

TRENCHARD. How long have you had it?

MAJOR BOOTH VOYSEY. Oh . . . when I married . . .

TRENCHARD. Then that's all right.

EDWARD [*vehemently*]. It was stolen money . . . it must have been.

TRENCHARD. Possibly . . . but possibly not. And Booth took it in good faith.

MAJOR BOOTH VOYSEY. I should hope so!

EDWARD [*dwelling on the words*]. It's stolen money.

MAJOR BOOTH VOYSEY [*bubbling with distress*]. I say, what ought I to do?

TRENCHARD. Do . . . my dear Booth? Nothing.

EDWARD [*with great indignation*]. Trenchard, we owe reparation.

TRENCHARD. No doubt. But to whom? From which client's account was Booth's money taken? You say yourself you don't know.

EDWARD [*grieved*]. Trenchard!

TRENCHARD. My dear Edward . . . the law will take anything it has a right to and all it can get; you needn't be afraid. But what about your position . . . can we get you clear?

EDWARD. Oh . . . I'll face the music.

BOOTH'S *head has been turning incessantly from one to the other and by this he is just a bristle of alarm.*

MAJOR BOOTH VOYSEY. But I say, you know, this is awful! Will the thing have to be made public?

TRENCHARD. No help for it.

The Major's jaw drops; he is speechless. MRS. VOYSEY'S *dead voice steals in.*

MRS. VOYSEY. What is all this?

TRENCHARD. I am explaining, Mother, that the family is not called upon to begger itself in order to pay back to every client to whom Father owed a pound perhaps eight shillings instead of seven.

MRS. VOYSEY. He will find that my estate has been kept separate.

TRENCHARD. I'm very glad to hear it, Mother.

EDWARD *hides his face in his hands.*

MRS. VOYSEY. When Mr. Barnes died, your father agreed to appointing another trustee.

TREGONING [*diffidently*]. I suppose, Edward, I'm involved?

EDWARD [*lifting his head quickly*]. Denis, I hope not. I didn't know that anything of yours. . . .

TREGONING. Yes . . . all I got under my aunt's will.

EDWARD. See how things are . . . I've not found a trace of that yet. We'll hope for the best.

TREGONING [*setting his teeth*]. It can't be helped.

> MAJOR BOOTH VOYSEY *leans over the table and speaks in the loudest of whispers.*

MAJOR BOOTH VOYSEY. Let me advise you to say nothing of this to Ethel at such a critical time.

TREGONING. Thank you, Booth . . . naturally I shan't.

> HUGH, *by a series of contortions, has lately been giving evidence of a desire or intention to say something.*

EDWARD. Well, what is it, Hugh?

HUGH. I have been wondering . . . if he can hear this conversation.

> *Up to now it has all been meaningless to* HONOR, *in her nervous dilapidation; but this remark brings a fresh burst of tears.*

HONOR. Oh, poor papa . . . poor papa!

MRS. VOYSEY. I think I'll go to my room. I can't hear what any of you are saying. Edward can tell me afterwards.

EDWARD. Would you like to go too, Honor?

HONOR [*through her sobs*]. Yes, please, I would.

TREGONING. I'll get out, Edward. Whatever you think fit to do . . . ! I'm on one side of the fence and Ethel's on the other, so to speak. I wish I'd more work on hand . . . for her sake . . . and the child's. That's all.

> *By this time* MRS. VOYSEY *and* HONOR *have been got out of the room.* TREGONING *follows them, and the four brothers are left together,* HUGH *is vacant,* EDWARD *does not speak,* BOOTH *looks at* TRENCHARD, *who settles himself to acquire information.*

TRENCHARD. How long have things been wrong?

EDWARD. He told me the trouble began in his father's time and that he'd been battling with it ever since.

TRENCHARD [*smiling*]. Oh, come now . . . that's hardly possible.

EDWARD. I believed him. Of course I've barely begun on the papers yet. But I doubt if I'll be able to trace anything more than twenty years back . . . unless it's to do with old George Booth's business.

MAJOR BOOTH VOYSEY. But the Pater never touched his money . . . why, he was a personal friend.

TRENCHARD. How long now since he told you?

EDWARD. Last autumn.

TRENCHARD. What has been happening since?

EDWARD. He got ill in November . . . which didn't make him any easier to deal with. I began by trying to make him put some of the smaller people right. He said that was penny wise and pound foolish. So I've been doing what I could myself this last month or so. Oh . . . nothing to count.

TRENCHARD. He didn't think you'd actually take a hand?

EDWARD. First it was that he was in a corner and I was to help him out. Then we were to clean up the whole mess and have a quarter of a million to the good. That was in February . . . when the new Kaffir boom was on.

TRENCHARD. He was in that, was he?

EDWARD. Up to the neck. And I believe he'd have made a pile if he hadn't been ill. As it was, he got out fifteen thousand to the good.

MAJOR BOOTH VOYSEY. Really!

EDWARD. I'm not sure he didn't only tell me because he wanted someone to boast to about his financial exploits.

TRENCHARD. Got more reckless as he got older, I suppose.

EDWARD. Oh . . . mere facts meant nothing to him. He drew up this will in May. He knew then he'd nothing to leave . . . on the balance. But there it all is . . . legacies to servants . . . and charities. And I'm the sole executor . . . with an extra thousand for my trouble!

TRENCHARD. Childish! Was I down for anything?

EDWARD. No.

TRENCHARD [without resentment]. How he did hate me!

EDWARD. You're spared the results of his affection anyway.

TRENCHARD. What on earth made you stay with him once you knew?

EDWARD *does not answer for a moment.*

EDWARD. I thought I might prevent things getting worse.

TRENCHARD. I'm afraid your position . . . at the best . . . is not a pleasant one.

EDWARD [bowing his head]. I know.

TRENCHARD, *the only one of the three who comprehends, looks at his brother for a moment with something that might almost be admiration. Then he stirs himself.*

TRENCHARD. I must be off. Work waiting . . . end of term.

MAJOR BOOTH VOYSEY. Shall I walk to the station with you?

TRENCHARD. I'll spend a few minutes with Mother. [*He says, at the door, very respectfully.*] You'll count on me for any professional help I can give, please, Edward.

EDWARD [*simply*]. Thank you, Trenchard.

> *So* TRENCHARD *goes. And the Major, who has been endeavouring to fathom his final attitude, then comments—*

MAJOR BOOTH VOYSEY. No heart, y'know! Great brain! If it hadn't been for that distressing quarrel, he might have saved our poor father. Don't you think so, Edward?

EDWARD. Perhaps.

HUGH [*giving vent to his thoughts at last with something of a relish*]. The more I think this out, the more devilishly humorous it gets. Old Booth breaking down by the grave . . . Colpus reading the service. . . .

EDWARD. Yes, the Vicar's badly hit.

HUGH. Oh, the Pater had managed his business for years.

MAJOR BOOTH VOYSEY. Good God . . . how shall we ever look old Booth in the face again?

EDWARD. I don't worry about him; he can die quite comfortably enough on our six shillings in the pound. It's one or two of the smaller fry who will suffer.

MAJOR BOOTH VOYSEY. Now, just explain to me . . . I didn't interrupt while Trenchard was speaking . . . of what exactly did this defrauding consist?

EDWARD. Speculating with a client's capital. You pocket the gains . . . and you keep paying the client his ordinary income.

MAJOR BOOTH VOYSEY. So that he doesn't find it out?

EDWARD. Quite so.

MAJOR BOOTH VOYSEY. In point of fact, he doesn't suffer?

EDWARD. He doesn't suffer till he finds it out.

MAJOR BOOTH VOYSEY. And all that's wrong now is that some of their capital is missing.

EDWARD [*half amused, half amazed at this process of reasoning*]. Yes, that's all that's wrong.

MAJOR BOOTH VOYSEY. What is the—ah—deficit? [*The word rolls from his tongue.*]

EDWARD. Anything between two and three hundred thousand pounds.

MAJOR BOOTH VOYSEY [*impressed, and not unfavourably*]. Dear me . . . this is a big affair!

HUGH [*following his own line of thought*]. Quite apart from the rights and wrongs of this, only a very able man could have kept a straight face to the world all these years, as the Pater did.

MAJOR BOOTH VOYSEY. But he often made money by these speculations?

EDWARD. Very often. His own expenditure was heavy . . . as you know.

MAJOR BOOTH VOYSEY [*with gratitude for favours received*]. He was a very generous man.

HUGH. Did nobody ever suspect?

EDWARD. You see, Hugh, when there was any pressing danger . . . if a trust had to be wound up . . . he'd make a great effort and put the accounts straight.

MAJOR BOOTH VOYSEY. Then he did put some accounts straight?

EDWARD. Yes, when he couldn't help himself.

BOOTH *looks very enquiring, and then squares himself up to the subject.*

MAJOR BOOTH VOYSEY. Now look here, Edward. You told us that he told you that it was the object of his life to put these accounts straight. Then you laughed at that. Now you tell me that he did put some accounts straight.

EDWARD [*wearily*]. My dear Booth, you don't understand.

MAJOR BOOTH VOYSEY. Well, let me understand . . . I am anxious to understand.

EDWARD. We can't pay ten shillings in the pound.

MAJOR BOOTH VOYSEY. That's very dreadful. But do you know that there wasn't a time when we couldn't have paid five?

EDWARD [*acquiescent*]. Perhaps.

MAJOR BOOTH VOYSEY. Very well, then! If it was true about his father and all that . . . and why shouldn't we believe him if we can? . . . and he did effect an improvement, that's to his credit, isn't it? Let us at least be just, Edward.

EDWARD [*patiently polite*]. I am sorry if I seem unjust. But he has left me in a rather unfortunate position.

MAJOR BOOTH VOYSEY. Yes, his death was a tragedy. It seems to me that if he had been spared he might have succeeded at length in this tremendous task and restored to us our family honour.

EDWARD. Yes, Booth, he sometimes spoke very feelingly of that.

MAJOR BOOTH VOYSEY [*irony lost upon him*]. I can well believe it. And I can tell you that now . . . I may be right or I may be wrong . . . I am feeling far less concerned about the clients' money than I am at the terrible blow to the Family which this exposure will strike. Money, after all, can to a certain extent be done without . . . but honour. . . .

> *This is too much for* EDWARD.

EDWARD. Our honour! Does any one of you mean to give me a single penny towards undoing all the wrong that has been done?

MAJOR BOOTH VOYSEY. I take Trenchard's word for it that that . . . is quite unnecessary.

EDWARD. Then don't talk to me about honour.

MAJOR BOOTH VOYSEY [*somewhat nettled at this outburst*]. I am thinking of the public exposure. Edward, can't that be prevented?

EDWARD [*with quick suspicion*]. How?

MAJOR BOOTH VOYSEY. Well, how was it being prevented before he died . . . before we knew anything about it?

EDWARD [*appealing to the spirits that watch over him*]. Oh, listen to this! First Trenchard . . . and now you! You've the poison in your blood, every one of you. Who am I to talk! I daresay so have I.

MAJOR BOOTH VOYSEY [*reprovingly*]. I am beginning to think that you have worked yourself into rather an hysterical state over this unhappy business.

EDWARD [*rating him*]. Perhaps you'd have been glad . . . glad if I'd gone on lying and cheating . . . and married and begotten a son to go on lying and cheating after me . . . and to pay you your interest in the lie and the cheat.

MAJOR BOOTH VOYSEY [*with statesman-like calm*]. Look here, Edward, this rhetoric is exceedingly out of place. The simple question before us is . . . what is the best course to pursue?

EDWARD. There is no question before us. There's only one course to pursue.

MAJOR BOOTH VOYSEY [*crushingly*]. You will let me speak, please. In so far as our poor father was dishonest to his clients, I pray that he may be forgiven. In so far as he spent his life honestly endeavouring to right a wrong which he had found already committed . . . I forgive him . . . I admire him, Edward . . . and I feel it my duty to—er—reprobate most strongly the—er—gusto with which you have been holding him up in memory to us . . . ten minutes after we'd been standing round his grave . . . as a monster of wickedness. I think I knew him as well as you . . . better. And . . . thank God! . . . there was not between him and me this . . . this unhappy business to warp my judgment of him. [*He warms to his subject.*] Did you ever know a more

charitable man . . . a larger-hearted? He was a faithful husband
. . . and what a father to all of us! . . . putting us out into the
world and fully intending to leave us comfortably settled there.
Further . . . as I see this matter, Edward . . . when as a young
man he was told this terrible secret and entrusted with such a
frightful task . . . did he turn his back on it like a coward? No.
He went through it heroically to the end of his life. And, as he
died, I imagine there was no more torturing thought than that
he had left his work unfinished. [*He is pleased with this peroration.*]
And now . . . if all these clients can be kept receiving their
natural incomes . . . and if father's plan could be carried out, of
gradually replacing the capital. . . .

    EDWARD *at this raises his head and stares with horror.*

    EDWARD. You're asking me to carry on this. . . ? Oh, you don't
know what you're talking about.

    The Major, having talked himself back to a proper eminence,
    remains good tempered.

    MAJOR BOOTH VOYSEY. Well, I'm not a conceited man . . . but
I do think that I can understand a simple financial problem
when it has been explained to me.

    EDWARD. You don't know the nerve . . . the unscrupulous
daring it requires to. . . .

    MAJOR BOOTH VOYSEY. Of course, if you're going to argue round
your own incompetence. . . .

    EDWARD [*very straight*]. D'you want your legacy?

    MAJOR BOOTH VOYSEY [*with dignity*]. In one moment I shall get
very angry. Here am I doing my best to help you and your clients
. . . and there you sit imputing to me the most sordid motives.
Do you suppose I should touch, or allow to be touched, the money
which father has left us till every client's claim was satisfied?

    EDWARD. My dear Booth, I know you mean well . . .

    MAJOR BOOTH VOYSEY. I'll come down to your office and work
with you.

    At this cheerful prospect even poor EDWARD *can't help smiling.*

    EDWARD. I'm sure you would.

    MAJOR BOOTH VOYSEY [*feeling that it is a chance lost*]. If the Pater
had ever consulted me. . . .

    At this point TRENCHARD *looks round the door to say* . . .

    TRENCHARD. Are you coming, Booth?

    MAJOR BOOTH VOYSEY. Yes, certainly. I'll talk this over with
Trenchard. [*As he gets up and automatically stiffens, he is reminded of
the occasion and his voice drops.*] I say . . . we've been speaking very

loud. You must do nothing rash. I've no doubt he and I can devise something which will obviate . . . and then I'm sure I shall convince you. . . . [*Glancing into the hall he apparently catches his eldest brother's impatient eye, for he departs abruptly, saying. . .*] All right, Trenchard, you've eight minutes.

  BOOTH's *departure leaves* HUGH, *at any rate, really at his ease.*

HUGH. This is an experience for you, Edward!

EDWARD [*bitterly*]. And I feared what the shock might be to you all! Booth has made a good recovery.

HUGH. You wouldn't have him miss such a chance of booming at us.

EDWARD. It's strange that people will believe you can do right by means which they know to be wrong.

HUGH [*taking great interest in this*]. Come, what do we know about right and wrong? Let's say legal and illegal. You're so down on the governor because he has trespassed against the etiquette of your own profession. But now he's dead . . . and if there weren't any scandal to think of . . . it's no use the rest of us pretending to feel him a criminal. Because we don't. Which just shows that money . . . and property . . .

  At this point he becomes conscious that ALICE MAITLAND *is standing behind him, her eyes fixed on his brother. So he interrupts himself to ask . . .*

HUGH. D'you want to speak to Edward?

ALICE. Please, Hugh.

HUGH. I'll go.

  He goes; a little martyr-like, to conclude the evolution of his theory in soliloquy. His usual fate. ALICE *still looks at* EDWARD, *and he at her rather appealingly.*

ALICE. Auntie has told me.

EDWARD. He was fond of you. Don't think worse of him than you can help.

ALICE. I'm thinking of you.

EDWARD. I may just escape.

ALICE. So Trenchard says.

EDWARD. My hands are clean, Alice.

ALICE. I know that.

EDWARD. Mother's not very upset.

ALICE. She'd expected a smash in his lifetime.

EDWARD. I'm glad that didn't happen.

ALICE. Yes. I've put Honor to bed. It was a mercy to tell her just at this moment. She can grieve for his death and his disgrace at the same time . . . and the one grief will soften the other perhaps.

EDWARD. Oh, they're all shocked enough at the disgrace . . . but will they open their purses to lessen the disgrace?

ALICE. Will it seem less disgraceful to have stolen ten thousand pounds than twenty?

EDWARD. I should think so.

ALICE. I should think so; but I wonder if that's the Law. If it isn't, Trenchard wouldn't consider the point. I'm sure Public Opinion doesn't say so . . . and that's what Booth is considering.

EDWARD [with contempt]. Yes.

ALICE [ever so gently ironical]. Well, he's in the Army . . . he's almost in Society . . . and he has got to get on in both; one mustn't blame him.

EDWARD [very serious]. But when one thinks how the money was obtained!

ALICE. When one thinks how most money is obtained!

EDWARD. They've not earned it.

ALICE [her eyes humorous]. If they had they might have given it you and earned more. Did I ever tell you what my guardian said to me when I came of age?

EDWARD. I'm thankful you're out of the mess.

ALICE. I shouldn't have been, but I was made to look after my affairs myself . . . much against my will. My guardian was a person of great character and no principles, the best and most lovable man I've ever met . . . I'm sorry you never knew him, Edward . . . and he said once to me: you've no moral right to your money . . . you've not earned it or deserved it in any way. So don't be either surprised or annoyed when any enterprising person tries to get it from you. He has at least as much moral right to it as you . . . if he can use it better perhaps he has more. Shocking sentiments, aren't they? But perhaps that's why I've less pity for some of these clients than you have, Edward.

EDWARD shakes his head, treating these paradoxes as they deserve.

EDWARD. Alice . . . one or two of them will be beggared.

ALICE [sincerely]. Yes, that is bad. What's to be done?

EDWARD. There's old nurse . . . with her poor little savings gone!

ALICE. Something can be done for her . . . surely.

EDWARD. The Law's no respecter of persons . . . that's its boast. Old Booth with more than he wants will keep enough and to spare. My old nurse, with just enough, may starve. But it'll be a relief to clear out this nest of lies, even though one suffers one's self. I've been ashamed to walk into that office. I'll hold my head high in prison though.

  He shakes himself stiffly erect, his chin high. ALICE *quizzes him.*

ALICE. Edward, I'm afraid you're feeling heroic.

EDWARD. I!

ALICE. You looked quite like Booth for the moment. [*This effectually removes the starch.*] Please don't glory in your martyrdom. It will be very stupid to send you to prison, and you must do your very best to keep out. [*Her tone is most practical.*] We were talking about these people who'll be beggared.

EDWARD [*simply*]. I didn't mean to be heroic.

ALICE. I know. But there's the danger in acting on principle . . . one begins to think more of one's attitude than of the use of what one is doing.

EDWARD. But I've no choice in the matter. There's only the one thing I can do.

ALICE. Run the ship ashore? Well . . . if you say so!

EDWARD. Unless you expect me to take Booth's advice . . . turn honest cheat . . . juggle and speculate in the hope that . . .! Oh, my dear Alice . . . no! If it were only a question of a few thousands . . . ! But I'm no good at that sort of thing anyway. It'd simply make matters worse. I've been sitting down . . . self-pityingly . . . under the shame of it all these months. I did . . . take a hand . . . and stop one affair going from bad to worse. I'd no right to. Sheer favouritism! I shall suffer for it now.

ALICE. That's nobody's business but your own.

EDWARD. I could go on doing that . . . putting the worst cases straight . . . say for a year . . . or till I'm found out . . . as I almost certainly should be. For don't think I'd be any good at the game, Alice [*Then his tone changes; he is glancing inward.*] But you know . . . there's something in me that'd rather like to try. [*He looks her full in the face.*] What do you say?

ALICE [*catching her breath*]. Dear Edward . . . I can't advise.

EDWARD [*with grimly whimsical humour*]. You've undermined my principles. I must have some help in exchange.

ALICE. I'm lawless at heart, I fear. Most women are. What would happen at the end of the year?

EDWARD. Then I should have to do what I ought to do now . . . send round a polite letter: Dear Sir or Madam . . . I am a thief . . . please call the police. For I can't succeed. Understand that. I can't make up a quarter of a million by careful management.

ALICE. Will it be much worse for you . . . if at last they do call the police?

EDWARD. That . . . as you said . . . would be nobody's business but my own.

ALICE. I'd do anything to help you . . . anything. That sounds like dear Booth . . . and it's just as silly.

EDWARD. Suppose I tackle the job?

ALICE. Not because I want you to?

EDWARD. Do you? No . . . you shan't have to think that.

ALICE. But my dear . . . I shall be so proud of you.

EDWARD. When I've failed?

ALICE. I shan't think it failure.

EDWARD. Booth and Hugh and the rest must hold their tongues. I needn't have told them.

ALICE. They'll do that much for you.

EDWARD. But I rather liked telling them too.

She is looking at him with suddenly shining eyes.

ALICE. Edward . . . I'm so happy. Suddenly . . . you're a different man.

EDWARD. Am I?

ALICE. You've begun to be. It was in you to be . . . and I knew it.

His face darkens.

EDWARD. I wonder . . . I wonder if I'm not . . . already!

ALICE. Why . . .?

EDWARD. And if my father didn't begin . . . just like this? He told me he did. Doing the right thing in the wrong way . . . then doing the wrong thing . . . and coming to be what he was . . . and bringing me to this. Alice, suppose it's not failure I'm risking . . . but success. Yes, you're right . . . I feel a different man.

She brings him help.

ALICE. I'll take that risk, my dear. I'll risk your turning crook. And it's a pretty big risk now for me.

He accepts it.

EDWARD. Then there's no more to be said, is there?

ALICE. Not for the moment. [*He does not ask what she means by this*]. I must go back to Honor. Horrid . . . if one knew it . . . to look comic when one is suffering. [*As she opens the door.*] And here's Booth back again.

EDWARD. Shall I tell him he has convinced me?

ALICE [*mischievously*]. It would delight him. But I shouldn't.

10

THE FOURTH ACT

MR. VOYSEY'S *room at the office is* EDWARD'S *room now. It has somehow lost that brilliancy which the old man's occupation seemed to give it. Perhaps it is only because this December morning is dull and depressing; but the fire isn't bright and the panels and windows don't shine as they did. There are no roses on the table either.* EDWARD, *walking in as his father did, hanging his hat and coat where his father's used to hang, is certainly the palest shadow of that other masterful presence. A depressed, drooping shadow, too. This may be what* PEACEY *feels; for he looks very surly as he obeys the old routine of following his chief to this room on his arrival. Nor has* EDWARD *so much as a glance for his confidential clerk. They exchange the most formal of greetings.* EDWARD *sits at his desk, on which lies the morning's pile of letters, unopened now.*

PEACEY. Good morning, sir.

EDWARD. Good morning, Peacey. Any notes for me?

PEACEY. Well, I've hardly been through the letters yet, sir.

EDWARD [*his eyebrows meeting*]. Oh . . . and I'm late myself.

PEACEY. I'm very sorry, sir.

EDWARD. If Mr. Bullen calls, you had better show him those papers. Write to Metcalfe; say I've seen Mr. Vickery this morning and that we hope for a decision from Mr. Booth within a day or so. Better show me the letter.

PEACEY. Very good, sir.

EDWARD. That's all, thank you.

PEACEY *gets to the door, where he stops, looking not only surly but nervous now.*

PEACEY. May I speak to you a moment, sir?

EDWARD. Certainly.

PEACEY, *after a moment, makes an effort, purses his mouth and begins.*

PEACEY. Bills are beginning to come in upon me as is usual at this season, sir. My son's allowance at Cambridge is now rather a heavy item of my expenditure. I hope that the custom of the

firm isn't to be neglected now that you are the head of it, Mr.
Edward. Two hundred your father always made it at Christmas
. . . in notes if you please.

> *Towards the end of this* EDWARD *begins to pay attention. When
> he answers his voice is harsh.*

EDWARD. Oh to be sure . . . your hush money.

PEACEY [*bridling*]. That's not a very pleasant word.

EDWARD. This is an unpleasant subject.

PEACEY. Well, it's not one I wish to discuss. Mr. Voysey would
always give me the notes in an envelope when he shook hands
with me at Christmas.

EDWARD. Notes I understand. But why not a rise in salary?

PEACEY. Mr. Voysey's custom, sir, from before my time. My
father . . .

EDWARD. Yes. It's an hereditary pull you have over the firm,
isn't it?

PEACEY. When my father retired . . . he's been dead twenty-
six years, Mr. Edward . . . he simply said: I have told the
governor you know what I know. And Mr. Voysey said . . . I
treat you as I did your father, Peacey. Never another word with
him on the subject.

EDWARD. A very decent arrangement . . . and the thriftiest no
doubt. Of the raising of salaries there might have been no end.

PEACEY. Mr. Edward, that's uncalled for. We have served you
and yours most faithfully. I know my father would sooner have
cut off his hand than do anything to embarrass the firm.

EDWARD. But business is business, Peacey. Surely he could
have had a partnership for the asking.

PEACEY. That's another matter, sir.

EDWARD. Why?

PEACEY. A matter of principle, if you'll excuse me. I must not
be taken to approve of the firm's conduct. Nor did my dear father
approve. And at anything like a partnership he would certainly
have drawn the line.

EDWARD. My apologies.

PEACEY. That's all right, sir. Always a bit of friction in coming
to an understanding about anything, isn't there, sir?

> *He is going when* EDWARD's *question stops him.*

EDWARD. Why didn't you speak about this last Christmas?

PEACEY. You were so upset about your father's death.

EDWARD. My father died the summer before that.

PEACEY. Well . . . truthfully, Mr. Edward?

EDWARD. As truthfully as you think suitable.

The irony of this is wasted on PEACEY, *who becomes pleasantly candid.*

PEACEY. Well, I'd always thought there must be a smash when your father died . . . but it didn't come. I couldn't make you out. So I thought I'd better keep quiet for a bit and say nothing.

EDWARD. I see. Your son's at Cambridge?

PEACEY. Yes.

EDWARD. I wonder you didn't bring him into the firm.

PEACEY [*taking this very kind*]. Thank you. But James will go to the bar. He'll have to wait his chance, of course. But he's a clever lad. And it's a good use for one's savings.

EDWARD. I feel sure he'll do well. I'm glad to have had this little talk with you, Peacey. I'm sorry you can't have the money.

He returns to his letters, a little steely-eyed. PEACEY *quite at his ease, makes for the door yet again, saying* . . .

PEACEY. Oh, any time will do, sir.

EDWARD. You can't have it at all.

PEACEY [*brought up short*]. Can't I?

EDWARD. No. This was one of the first things I made up my mind about. The firm's business is not carried on quite as it used to be. You may have noticed that you don't get the same little matters passing through your hands. In fact, we no longer make illicit profits out of our clients. So there are none for you to share.

PEACEY *bridles.*

PEACEY. Mr. Edward . . . I'm sorry we began this discussion. You'll give me my two hundred, please . . . and we'll drop the subject.

EDWARD. Yes . . . I've no more to say.

PEACEY. I want the money. And it's hardly gentlemanly in you, Mr. Edward, to try and get out of giving it me. Your father'd never have made such an excuse.

EDWARD. D'you think I'm lying to you?

PEACEY. That is no business of mine, sir.

EDWARD. As long as the dividend is punctually paid.

PEACEY. And there's no need to be sarcastic.

EDWARD. Would you rather I told you plainly what I think of you?

PEACEY. That I'm a thief because I've taken money from a thief?

EDWARD. Worse! You're content to have others steal for you.

PEACEY. And who isn't?

EDWARD *is really pleased with the retort. He relaxes and changes his tone, which had indeed become a little bullying.*

EDWARD. Ah, my dear Peacey . . . I fear we mustn't begin to talk economics. The present point is that I myself no longer receive these particular stolen goods. Therefore I can throw a stone at you. I have thrown it.

PEACEY, *who would far sooner be bullied than talked to like this, turns very sulky indeed.*

PEACEY. Then I resign my position here.

EDWARD. Very well.

PEACEY. And I happen to think the secret's worth its price.

EDWARD. Perhaps someone will pay it you.

PEACEY [*feebly threatening*]. Don't presume upon it's not being worth my while to make use of what I know.

EDWARD [*not unkindly*]. But, my good fellow, it happens to be the truth I'm telling you. I am doing a thankless . . . and an unpleasant . . . and a quite unprofitable job here. How can you hope to blackmail a man who has everything to gain by exposure and nothing to lose?

PEACEY [*peeving*]. I don't want to ruin you, sir, and I have a great regard for the firm. But you must see that I can't have my income reduced in this way without a struggle.

EDWARD [*with great cheerfulness*]. Very well . . . struggle away.

PEACEY [*his voice rising high and thin*]. But is it fair dealing on your part to dock the money suddenly like this? I have been counting on it most of the year, and I have been led into heavy expenses. Why couldn't you have warned me?

EDWARD. Yes, that's true, Peacey ... it was stupid of me. I'm sorry.

PEACEY *is a little comforted by this quite candid acknowledgment.*

PEACEY. Things may get easier for you by and by.

EDWARD. Possibly.

PEACEY. Will you reconsider the matter then?

At this insinuation EDWARD *looks up, more than a little exasperated.*

EDWARD. Then you don't believe what I tell you?

PEACEY. Yes, I do.

EDWARD. But you think that the fascination of swindling one's clients will finally prove irresistible?

PEACEY. That's what your father found, I suppose you know.

This gives EDWARD *such pause that he drops his masterful tone.*

EDWARD. I didn't.

PEACEY. He got things as right as rain once.

EDWARD. Did he?

PEACEY. So my father told me. But he started again.

EDWARD. Are you sure of this?

PEACEY [*expanding pleasantly*]. Well, sir, I knew your father pretty well. And when I first came into the firm I simply hated him. He was that sour . . . so snappy with everyone . . . as if he had a grievance against the whole world.

EDWARD [*pensively*]. He had then . . . in those days!

PEACEY. His dealings with his clients were no business of mine. I speak as I find. He came to be very kind to me . . . thoughtful and considerate. He was pleasant and generous to everyone . . .

EDWARD. So you have hopes of me yet?

PEACEY [*who has a simple mind*]. No, Mr. Edward, no. You're different from your father . . . one must make up one's mind to that. And you may believe me or not, but I should be very glad to know that the firm was going straight again. I'm getting on in years myself, now. I'm not much longer for the business, and there've been times when I have sincerely regretted my connection with it. If you'll let me say so, I think it's very noble of you to have undertaken the work you have. [*Then, as everything seems smooth again.*] And if you'll give me enough to cover this year's extra expense, I think I may promise you that I shan't expect money again.

EDWARD [*good-tempered, as he would speak to an importunate child*]. No, Peacey, no.

PEACEY [*fretful again*]. Well, sir, you make things very difficult for me.

EDWARD. Here is a letter from Mr. Cartwright which you might attend to. If he wants an appointment with me, don't make one till the New Year. His case can't come on before February.

PEACEY [*taking the letter*]. I show myself anxious to meet you in every way. . . . [*He is handed another.*]

EDWARD. "Perceval Building Estate". . . that's yours too.

PEACEY [*putting them both down, resolutely*]. But I refuse to be ignored. I must consider my whole position. I hope I may not be tempted to make use of the power I possess. But if I am driven to proceed to extremities . . .

EDWARD [*breaking in upon this bunch of tags*]. My dear Peacey, don't talk nonsense . . . you couldn't proceed to an extremity to save your life. You've comfortably taken this money all these years. You'll find you're no longer capable of doing even such a

slightly uncomfortable thing as tripping up your neighbour.
   This does completely upset the gentle blackmailer. He loses one
   grievance in another.

PEACEY. Really, Mr. Edward, I am a considerably older man
than you. These personalities . . . !

EDWARD. I'm sorry. Don't forget the letters.

PEACEY. I will not, sir.
   He takes them with great dignity and is leaving the room.

PEACEY. There's Mr. Hugh waiting.

EDWARD. To see me? Ask him in.

PEACEY. Come in, Mr. Hugh, please.
   HUGH *comes in,* PEACEY *holding the door for him with a frigid*
   politeness of which he is quite oblivious. At this final slight
   PEACEY *goes out in dudgeon.*

EDWARD. How are you?

HUGH. I don't know.
   And he throws himself into the chair by the fire. EDWARD, *quite*
   used to this sort of thing, goes quietly on with his work, adding
   encouragingly after a moment . . .

EDWARD. How's Beatrice?

HUGH. Ink to the elbows. She's half-way through her new book.
   He studies his boots with the gloomiest expression. And indeed,
   they are very dirty and his turned-up trousers are muddy at the
   edge. As he is quite capable of sitting silently by the fire for a
   whole morning EDWARD *asks him at last* . . .

EDWARD. Do you want anything?

HUGH. Yes . . . I want five bob. I left home without a penny.
I've walked.

EDWARD. From Highgate?

HUGH. Yes . . . by Hornsey and Highbury and Hackney and
Hoxton. And I must have some lunch.

EDWARD. I can manage five bob . . .
   He puts them on his table.

HUGH. And Upper Holloway and Lower Holloway . . . and
Pentonville . . . and Clerkenwell . . .

EDWARD. I don't know any of them.

HUGH. Nobody does . . . except the million people who live
there. But that's London. And I also, my dear Edward, want it
destroyed.

EDWARD. We are warned that . . . under certain circumstances
. . . it may be.

HUGH. But why wait for mere foreigners to do the job? Why

not tackle it ourselves . . . and, in the inspiring words of Mr. Rockefeller, do it now?

EDWARD. And what about the people who live there?

HUGH. Why should they live there . . . or anywhere? Why should they live at all?

EDWARD. Well, they've their work to do . . . most of them. Incidentally . . . much as I love your society . . . so have I mine. And this morning I'm rather busy.

HUGH. Aha! There's the fatal word. We don't work, Edward, not one in a thousand of us. Work is creation. Is that what an outworn civilisation requires of us? Obviously not. It asks us to keep busy . . . and forget that to all these means there is no creative end at all. We've to keep our accounts straight . . . as you have to now . . . to keep the streets clean . . . and ourselves clean . . .

EDWARD. That at least may be called an end in itself.

HUGH. I'm not so sure. If it's merely a habit . . . all habits are bad habits. Why wash?

EDWARD. I seem to remember that, as a small boy, washing was not your strong point.

HUGH. I'm glad I had that much moral courage. On principle a man should not wash unless he feels an inward urge to wash. Did Michelangelo wash? Seldom!

EDWARD. Better his work than his company, then.

HUGH. I'm sick of this endless sham. But one can put some sort of an end to it . . . if not to all of it . . . to one's own small share in it. And I mean to. So that's that.

EDWARD. Suicide?

HUGH. Oh dear me no! Life's great fun if you could only live it. I mean to live it. Thanks for the five bob. [He pockets it.] And my first step is to hand you back for your wretched clients the money that the Pater settled on me . . . what there is left of it. And don't let me forget that I owe you this too.

EDWARD. But my dear Hugh, you can't afford . . .

HUGH. Aha! Another fatal word. Afford! Give a man an income . . . big or small . . . and he passes half his time thinking what he can or can't afford. The money has been a curse to me. It has never belonged to me . . .

EDWARD. No.

HUGH. Oh, never mind the legal . . . I mean in the real sense. How could it belong to me? I didn't create it . . . or even earn it. I've belonged to it. So there's the first step to being free. My

spiritual history is a very interesting one, Edward. If it weren't
for Beatrice I'd make a book of it.

EDWARD. Would it show her up badly?

HUGH. No . . . but writing's her job. One mustn't poach.

EDWARD. She might make a book of it.

HUGH. Oh, it doesn't interest her. D'you remember the row
there was at home when I said I meant to paint?

EDWARD. Very well.

HUGH. However . . . the Pater came down at last with two
hundred a year. Studio rent, velvet coat, mutton chop cooked
on the gas stove, and sardines for supper . . . that's what the art
of painting meant to him. Then I got married to Beatrice . . .
which was so unexpectedly moral of me that he sprang another
two hundred. Well . . . I've kept busy. And I've learnt how to
paint. And I do paint . . . other men's pictures.

EDWARD. Forgery?

HUGH. Yes . . . it is.

EDWARD. Are you joking?

HUGH. Not at all. Forty-nine out of fifty of us . . . if you put
us to paint that table and chair . . . to begin with we don't see
that table and chair! What we see is what we remember of some
painting by Matisse or Picasso of some other table and chair.
This world, my dear Edward, is growing fuller and fuller of
paintings of paintings . . . and of paintings of paintings of
paintings. And a couple of hundred of them must be mine. If I
could afford it . . . aha, afford! . . . I'd buy them back and burn
them. But the critics, dear Edward, much prefer paintings of
paintings to paintings . . . for they know what to say about them.
They rejoice when they see that bastard great-grandchild of
Picasso's . . .

EDWARD's *table telephone rings.*

EDWARD. Yes? Yes . . . in two minutes. I must turn you out,
Hugh. What does Beatrice say, by the bye?

HUGH. About the money? Yes, there's that. I can't quite leave
her with nothing.

EDWARD. Are you leaving her?

HUGH. We got married with the idea that we'd separate some
time. And I can't be free unless I do.

EDWARD. I thought you were so fond of each other.

HUGH. I suppose in a sort of way we still are We've always
disagreed about everything. That used to be stimulating. But
now when we argue we quarrel. And that's tiring.

EDWARD. Do they know down at home that you're not getting on?

HUGH. Emily may.

EDWARD. For heaven's sake keep a good face on things for Christmas.

HUGH. I don't believe I'll go down for Christmas.

EDWARD. Nonsense! You can't hurt Mother's feelings by . . .

HUGH. Do not expect me to pay homage to the Voysey family feelings. If we must have a hollow fraud to kow-tow before, there are many less brassy ones. Good lord . . . you're not still taken in by them, surely . . . after the way we've all treated you? Even I've shirked asking you how you've been getting on here . . . for fear you'd start telling me. How are things, though?

EDWARD. I've not done so badly. Better than I thought I should, really! I've righted what I thought the four most scandalous cases . . . somewhat to the prejudice of the rest.

HUGH. Then can't you cut free?

EDWARD. And go to gaol?

HUGH. [really startled by this]. But they won't . .

EDWARD. But they will.

HUGH. And at any moment . . .?

EDWARD. Yes. I live on the brink. For the first month or so I thought every knock at the door meant a push over it. But nothing happens. There are days . . . you wouldn't believe it . . . when I quite forget that I'm a criminal. And . . . it's possible . . . nothing may happen. And . . . at this moment . . . I really don't know whether I want it to or not.

HUGH. I should take the plunge.

EDWARD. Why?

HUGH. The longer you wait the worse it'll be for you, won't it?

EDWARD. Yes.

HUGH. The thing's telling on you too.

EDWARD. I know. My barber tries to sell me hair restorer.

HUGH. On your faculties. The damn thing is swallowing you up. Don't let it. You've no right to let your life be brought to nothing.

EDWARD. Does my life matter?

HUGH. But of course.

EDWARD [the iron in his soul]. That's where we differ. Still, now I've scavenged up the worst of the mess . . . and can only sit here drudging . . . improving things by thirty shillings here . . . and by seven pounds two and sixpence there . . . I do begin to understand Father a little better.

HUGH [*cheerfully*]. Oh . . . I'm all for the Pater. He played a great game. And what this civilization needs . . . if we can't smash it up altogether . . . is a lot more men like him. . . .

The door is opened and MR. GEORGE BOOTH *comes in. He looks older than he did and besides is evidently not in a happy frame of mind.*

MR. GEORGE BOOTH. Hullo, Hugh. How are you, Edward?

HUGH. But what I'm going to do is to step out of my front door with five bob in my pocket. And I'll tramp . . . and I'll paint for my bread . . . the farmer . . . the farmer's wife . . . or his dog or his cow . . . an honest bit of work done with despatch for just what he thinks it's worth to him. And if I can earn my bread I'll know I'm some good . . . and if I can't I'll drown myself.

EDWARD. I should wait till the summer comes.

HUGH. I'll begin with your office boy. For two shillings I will do him a sketch of his spotty little countenance. Edward, may I propose it to him?

EDWARD. You may not. To begin with he can't afford two shillings. . . .

HUGH. Aha! Afford! And of course he's very busy too?

EDWARD. If he isn't, I'll sack him.

HUGH. Good God . . . what a world! Good-bye.

HUGH departs, not, we may be sure, to tramp the roads; but he has thoroughly enjoyed hearing himself talk.

EDWARD. Will you come here . . . or will you sit by the fire?

MR. GEORGE BOOTH. This'll do. I shan't keep you long.

EDWARD. Well . . . here's the Vickery correspondence. He will pay the extra rent, but . . .

MR. GEORGE BOOTH [*nervously*]. Yes . . . it isn't really that I've come about.

EDWARD. No?

MR. GEORGE BOOTH. Something less pleasant, I'm afraid.

EDWARD. Litigation? I trust not.

MR. GEORGE BOOTH. No. . . . I'm getting too old to quarrel. No! I've made up my mind to withdraw my securities from the custody of your firm. I don't know what notice is usual.

He has got it out and feels better. EDWARD *has awaited such a shock for so long that now it has come he finds he feels nothing.*

EDWARD. To a good solicitor . . . five minutes. Ten for a poor one. Have you any particular reason for doing this, Mr. Booth?

MR. GEORGE BOOTH [*thankful to be able to talk and, so he thinks, stave off reproaches*]. Oh . . . naturally . . . naturally! You can't but know, Edward, that I have never been able to feel that implicit confidence in you . . . in your abilities, your personality, that's to say . . . which I reposed in your father. Well . . . hardly to be expected, was it?

EDWARD [*grimly acquiescent*]. Hardly.

MR. GEORGE BOOTH. It's nothing against you. Men like your father are few and far between. I don't doubt that things go on here as they have always done. But since he died . . . I have not been happy about my affairs. It is a new experience for me . . . to feel worried . . . especially about money. The possession of money has always been something of a pleasure to me. And my doctor . . . I saw him again yesterday . . . he keeps me on a diet now . . . quite unnecessary . . . but he said that above all things I was not to worry. And, as I made up my mind upon the matter some time ago . . . in point of fact more than a year before your father died it was clear to me that I could not leave my interests in your hands as I had in his. . . .

EDWARD [*but this strikes* EDWARD *with the shock of a bullet*]. Did he know that?

MR. GEORGE BOOTH. He must have guessed. I practically told him so. And I hoped he'd tell you . . . and so spare me the unpleasant necessity of hurting your feelings . . . as I fear I must be doing now.

EDWARD. Not at all. But we'll take it, if you please, that he never guessed. [*For with that thought of his father he really could not live.*] I can't induce you to change your mind?

MR. GEORGE BOOTH. No. And I'd sooner you wouldn't try. I shall make a point of telling the family that you are in no way to blame. My idea is for the future to let my Bank . . .

EDWARD. For it's my duty to if I can. . . .

MR. GEORGE BOOTH. Heavens above us, my dear Edward . . . the loss of one client . . . however important . . .!

EDWARD. I know. Well . . . here's the way out. And it isn't my fault.

MR. GEORGE BOOTH. Forgive me for saying that your conduct seems to me a little lacking in dignity.

EDWARD [*patient; ironic*]. I'm sure it must. Will you walk off with your papers now? They'll make rather a cart-load.

MR. GEORGE BOOTH. You'll have to explain matters a bit.

EDWARD [*grimly*]. Yes. I'd better. How much . . . Mr. Booth . . . do you think you're worth?

MR. GEORGE BOOTH. God bless me . . . I know what I'm worth. I'm not a baby . . . or a woman. I have it all written down . . . more or less . . . in a little book.

EDWARD. I should like to see that little book. You'll get not quite half of that out of us.

MR. GEORGE BOOTH. Don't be perverse, Edward. I said I had made up my mind to withdraw the whole . . . .

EDWARD. You should have made it up sooner.

MR. GEORGE BOOTH. What's this all about?

EDWARD. The greater part of what is so neatly written down in that little book doesn't exist.

MR. GEORGE BOOTH. Nonsense. It must exist. I don't want to realise. You hand me over the securities. I don't need to reinvest simply because . . .

EDWARD [*dealing his blow not unkindly, but squarely*]. I can't hand you over what I haven't got.

The old man hears the words. But their meaning . . . ?

MR. GEORGE BOOTH. Is anything . . . wrong?

EDWARD. How many more times am I to tell you that we have robbed you of half your property?

MR. GEORGE BOOTH [*his senses almost failing him*]. Say that again.

EDWARD. It's quite true.

MR. GEORGE BOOTH. My money . . . gone?

EDWARD. Yes.

MR. GEORGE BOOTH [*clutching at a straw of anger*]. You've been the thief . . . you . . . you . . .?

EDWARD. I wouldn't tell you so if I could help it . . . my father.

This actually calls MR. BOOTH *back to something like dignity and self-possession. He thumps* EDWARD's *table furiously.*

MR. GEORGE BOOTH. I'll make you prove that.

EDWARD. Oh, you've fired a mine.

MR. GEORGE BOOTH [*scolding him well*]. Slandering your dead father, and lying to me . . . revenging yourself by frightening me . . . because I detest you!

EDWARD. Why . . . haven't I thanked you for pushing me over the edge? I do . . . I promise you I do.

MR. GEORGE BOOTH [*shouting; and his courage fails him as he shouts*]. Prove it . . . prove it to me. You don't frighten me so easily. One can't lose half of all one has and then be told of it in two minutes . . . sitting at a table. [*His voice tails off to a piteous whimper.*]

EDWARD [*quietly now and kindly*]. If my father had told you this in plain words, you'd have believed him.

MR. GEORGE BOOTH [*bowing his head*]. Yes.

EDWARD *looks at the poor old thing with great pity.*

EDWARD. What on earth did you want to do this for? You need never have known . . . you could have died happy. Settling with all those charities in your will would have smashed us up. But proving your will is many years off yet, we'll hope.

MR. GEORGE BOOTH [*pathetic and bewildered*]. I don't understand. No, I don't understand . . . because your father . . .! But I must understand, Edward.

EDWARD. I shouldn't try to, if I were you. Pull yourself together, Mr. Booth. After all, this isn't a vital matter to you. It's not even as if you had a family to consider . . . like some of the others.

MR. GEORGE BOOTH [*vaguely*]. What others?

EDWARD. Don't imagine your money has been specially selected for pilfering.

MR. GEORGE BOOTH [*with solemn incredulity*]. One has read of this sort of thing. But I thought people always got found out.

EDWARD [*brutally humorous*]. Well . . . you've found us out.

MR. GEORGE BOOTH [*rising to the full appreciation of his wrongs*]. Oh . . . I've been foully cheated!

EDWARD [*patiently*]. Yes . . . I've told you so.

MR. GEORGE BOOTH [*his voice breaks, he appeals pitifully*]. But by you, Edward . . . say it's by you.

EDWARD [*unable to resist his quiet revenge*]. I've not the ability or the personality for such work, Mr. Booth . . . nothing but the remains of a few principles, which forbid me even to lie to you.

> *The old gentleman draws a long breath and then speaks with great awe, blending into grief.*

MR. GEORGE BOOTH. I think your father is in Hell. I loved him, Edward . . . I loved him. How he could have had the heart! We were friends for fifty years. And all he cared for was to cheat me.

EDWARD [*venturing the comfort of an explanation*]. No . . . he didn't value money quite as you do.

MR. GEORGE BOOTH [*with sudden shrill logic*]. But he took it. What d'you mean by that?

> EDWARD *leans back in his chair and changes the tenor of their talk.*

EDWARD. Well, you are master of the situation now. What are you going to do?

MR. GEORGE BOOTH. To get the money back?

EDWARD. No, that's gone.

MR. GEORGE BOOTH. Then give me what's left and—

EDWARD. Are you going to prosecute?

MR. GEORGE BOOTH [*shifting uneasily in his chair*]. Oh, dear . . . is that necessary? Can't somebody else do that? I thought the law . . .! What'll happen if I don't?

EDWARD. What do you suppose I'm doing here now?

MR. GEORGE BOOTH [*as if he were being asked a riddle*]. I don't know.

EDWARD [*earnestly*]. When my father died, I began to try and put things straight. Then I made up my accounts . . . they can see who has lost and who hasn't and do as they please about it. And now I've set myself to a duller sort of work. I throw penny after penny hardly earned into the half-filled pit of our deficit. I've been doing that . . . for what it's worth . . . till this should happen. If you choose to let things alone . . . and hold your tongue . . . I can go on with the job till the next threat comes . . . and I'll beg that off too if I can. I've thought this my duty . . . and it's my duty to ask you to let me go on. [*He searches* MR. BOOTH's *face and finds there only disbelief and fear. He bursts out.*] Oh you might at least believe me. It can't hurt you to believe me.

MR. GEORGE BOOTH. You must admit, Edward, it isn't easy to believe anything in this office . . . just for the moment.

EDWARD [*bowing to the extreme reasonableness of this*]. I suppose not. I can prove it to you. I'll take you through the books . . . you won't understand them . . . but I could prove it.

MR. GEORGE BOOTH. I think I'd rather not. Ought I to hold any further friendly communication with you now at all?

        And at this he takes his hat.

EDWARD [*with a little explosion of contemptuous anger*]. Certainly not. Prosecute . . . prosecute!

MR. GEORGE BOOTH [*with dignity*]. Don't lose your temper. It's my place to be angry with you.

EDWARD. I shall be grateful if you'll prosecute.

MR. GEORGE BOOTH. It's all very puzzling. I suppose I must prosecute. I believe you're just trying to practise on my goodness of heart. Certainly I ought to prosecute. Oughtn't I? I suppose I must consult another solicitor.

EDWARD [*his chin in the air*]. Why not write to The Times about it?

MR. GEORGE BOOTH [*shocked and grieved at his attitude*]. Edward how can you be so cool and heartless?

EDWARD [*changing his tone*]. D'you think I shan't be glad to sleep at night?

MR. GEORGE BOOTH. You may be put in prison.

EDWARD. I am in prison . . . a less pleasant one than Wormwood Scrubbs. But we're all prisoners, Mr. Booth.

MR. GEORGE BOOTH [*wagging his head*]. Yes. This is what comes of your free-thinking and philosophy. Why aren't you on your knees?

EDWARD. To you?

> *This was not what* MR. BOOTH *meant, but he assumes a vicarious dignity of that sort.*

MR. GEORGE BOOTH. And why should you expect me to shrink from vindicating the law?

EDWARD [*shortly*]. I don't. I've explained you'll be doing me a kindness. When I'm wanted you'll find me here at my desk. [*Then as an afterthought.*] If you take long to decide . . . don't alter your behaviour to my family in the meantime. They know the main points of the business, and . . .

MR. GEORGE BOOTH [*knocked right off his balance*]. Do they? Good God! And I'm going there to dinner the day after tomorrow. It's Christmas Eve. The hypocrites!

EDWARD [*unmoved*]. I shall be there . . . that will have given you two days. Will you tell me then?

MR. GEORGE BOOTH [*protesting violently*]. But I can't go . . . I can't have dinner with them. I must be ill.

EDWARD [*with a half-smile*]. I remember I went to dine at Chislehurst to tell my father of my decision.

MR. GEORGE BOOTH [*testily*]. What decision?

EDWARD. To remain in the firm when I first learned what was happening.

MR. GEORGE BOOTH [*interested*]. Was I there?

EDWARD. I daresay.

> MR. BOOTH *stands, hat, stick, gloves in hand, shaken by this experience, helpless, at his wits' end. He falls into a sort of fretful reverie, speaking half to himself, but yet as if he hoped that* EDWARD, *who is wrapt in his own thoughts, would have the decency to answer, or at least listen to what he is saying.*

MR. GEORGE BOOTH. Yes, how often I dined with him! Oh, it was monstrous! [*His eyes fall on the clock.*] It's nearly lunch time now. D'you know I can still hardly believe it all. I wish I hadn't found it out. If he hadn't died, I should never have found it out. I hate to have to be vindictive . . . it's not my nature. I'm sure

I'm more grieved than angry. But it isn't as if it were a small sum. And I don't see that one is called upon to forgive crimes . . . or why does the law exist? This will go near to killing me. I'm too old to have such troubles. It isn't right. And if I have to prosecute . . .

EDWARD [*at last throwing in a word*]. Well . . . you need not.

MR. GEORGE BOOTH [*thankful for the provocation*]. Don't you attempt to influence me, sir. [*He turns to go.*]

EDWARD. And what's more . . . with the money you have left . . .

EDWARD *follows him politely.* MR. BOOTH *flings the door open.*

MR. GEORGE BOOTH. You'll make out a cheque for that at once, sir, and send it to me.

EDWARD. You might . . .

MR. GEORGE BOOTH [*clapping his hat on, stamping his stick*]. I shall do the right thing, sir . . . never fear.

So he marches off in fine style, he thinks, having had the last word and all. But EDWARD, *closing the door after him, mutters* . . .

EDWARD. Save your soul . . . I'm afraid I was going to say.

11

THE FIFTH ACT

Naturally it is the dining-room which bears the brunt of what an English household knows as Christmas decorations. They consist chiefly of the branches of holly, stuck cock-eyed behind the top edges of the pictures. The one picture conspicuously not decorated is that which hangs over the fireplace, a portrait of MR. VOYSEY, *with its new gilt frame and its brass plate marking it also as a presentation. Otherwise the only difference between the dining-room's appearance at half-past nine on Christmas Eve and on any other evening in the year is that little piles of queer-shaped envelopes seem to be lying about, and quite a lot of tissue paper and string is to be seen peeping from odd corners. The electric light has been reduced to one bulb, but when the maid opens the door showing in* MR. GEORGE BOOTH *she switches on the rest.*

MR. GEORGE BOOTH. No, No . . . in here will do. Just tell Mr. Edward.

PHOEBE. Very well, sir.

She leaves him to fidget towards the fireplace and back, not removing his comforter or his coat, scarcely turning down the collar, screwing his cap in his hands. In a very short time EDWARD *comes in, shutting the door and taking stock of the visitor before he speaks.*

EDWARD. Well?

MR. GEORGE BOOTH [*feebly*]. I hope my excuse for not coming to dinner was acceptable. I did have . . . I have a very bad headache.

EDWARD. I daresay they believed it.

MR. GEORGE BOOTH. I have come at once to tell you my decision.

EDWARD. What is it?

MR. GEORGE BOOTH. I couldn't think the matter out alone. I went this afternoon to talk it over with the Vicar. After your father, he's my oldest friend now. [*At this* EDWARD's *eyebrows contract and then rise.*] What a terrible shock to him!

EDWARD. Oh, three of his four thousand pounds are quite safe.

MR. GEORGE BOOTH. That you and your father . . . you, whom he baptized . . . should have robbed him! I never saw a man so utterly prostrate with grief. That it should have been your father! And his poor wife . . . though she never got on with your father.

EDWARD [*with cheerful irony*]. Oh, Mrs. Colpus knows too, does she?

MR. GEORGE BOOTH. Of course he told Mrs. Colpus. This is an unfortunate time for the storm to break on him. What with Christmas Day and Sunday following so close they're as busy as can be. He has resolved that during this season of peace and good-will he must put the matter from him if he can. But once Christmas is over . . .! [*He envisages the old Vicar giving* EDWARD *a hell of a time then.*]

EDWARD [*coolly*]. So you mean to prosecute. If you don't, you've inflicted on the Colpuses a lot of unnecessary pain and a certain amount of loss by telling them.

MR. GEORGE BOOTH [*naïvely*]. I never thought of that. No, Edward, I have decided not to prosecute.

EDWARD *hides his face for a moment.*

EDWARD. And I've been hoping to escape! Well, it can't be helped [*and he sets his teeth*].

MR. GEORGE BOOTH [*with touching solemnity*]. I think I could not bear to see the family I have loved brought to such disgrace. And I want to ask your pardon, Edward, for some of the hard thoughts I have had of you. I consider this effort of yours a very striking one. You devote all the firm's earnings, I gather, to restoring the misappropriated capital. Very proper.

EDWARD. Mr. Booth . . . as I told you, you could help me . . . if you would. Your affairs, you see, are about the heaviest burden I carry.

MR. GEORGE BOOTH. Why is that?

EDWARD. My father naturally made freest with the funds of the people who trusted him most.

MR. GEORGE BOOTH. Naturally . . . you call it. Most unnatural, I think.

EDWARD [*finely*]. That also is true. And if you really want to help me, you could cut your losses . . . take interest only on the investments which do still exist. . . .

MR. GEORGE BOOTH. No . . . forgive me . . . I have my own plan.

EDWARD. By prosecuting you'd be no better off . . .

MR. GEORGE BOOTH. Quite so. The very first thing the Vicar

said. He has an excellent head for business. Of course his interests are small beside mine. But we stand together . . .

> EDWARD *scents mischief and he looks straight at* MR. BOOTH . . . *very straight indeed.*

EDWARD. What is your plan?

MR. GEORGE BOOTH. Its moral basis . . . I quote the Vicar . . . is this. You admit, I take it, that there were degrees of moral turpitude in your father's conduct . . . that his treachery was blacker by far in some cases than in others.

EDWARD. I think I won't make that admission for the moment.

MR. GEORGE BOOTH. What . . . to cheat and betray a life-long friend . . . and . . . and a man of God like the Vicar . . . is that no worse than a little ordinary trickiness? Now where are my notes? Our conditions are . . . one: we refrain from definitely undertaking not to prosecute . . . two: such securities as you have intact are to be returned to us at once . . .

EDWARD. Oh, certainly.

MR. GEORGE BOOTH. Three: the interest upon those others that have been made away with is to be paid.

EDWARD. As it has been so far.

MR. GEORGE BOOTH. We admit that. Four: the repayment of our lost capital is to be a first charge upon the . . . surplus earnings of the firm. There you are. And the Vicar and I both consider it very fair dealing.

EDWARD. Do you!

> *He goes off into peals of laughter.*

MR. GEORGE BOOTH. Edward . . . don't laugh!

EDWARD. But it's very, very funny!

MR. GEORGE BOOTH. Stop laughing, Edward.

EDWARD. You refrain from undertaking not to prosecute . . . that's the neatest touch. That would keep me under your thumb, wouldn't it? [*Then with a sudden savage snarl.*] Oh, you Christian gentlemen!

MR. GEORGE BOOTH. Don't be abusive, sir.

EDWARD. I'm giving my soul and body to restoring you and the rest of you to your precious money-bags. And you'll wring me dry . . . won't you? Won't you?

MR. GEORGE BOOTH. Don't be rhetorical. The money was ours . . . we want it back. That's reasonable.

EDWARD [*at the height of irony*]. Oh . . . most!

MR. GEORGE BOOTH. Any slight amendments to the plan . . . I'm willing to discuss them.

EDWARD [*as to a dog*]. Go to the devil.

MR. GEORGE BOOTH. And don't be rude.

EDWARD. I'm sorry.

There is a knock at the door.

EDWARD. Come in.

HONOR intrudes an apologetic head.

HONOR. Am I interrupting business?

EDWARD [*mirthlessly joking*]. No. Business is over . . . quite over. Come in, Honor.

HONOR puts on the table a market basket bulging with little paper parcels, and, oblivious of MR. BOOTH's distracted face, tries to fix his attention.

HONOR. I thought, dear Mr. Booth, perhaps you wouldn't mind carrying round this basket of things yourself. It's so very damp underfoot that I don't want to send one of the maids out to-night if I can possibly avoid it . . . and if one doesn't get Christmas presents the very first thing on Christmas morning quite half the pleasure in them is lost, don't you think?

MR. GEORGE BOOTH. Yes . . . yes.

HONOR [*fishing out the parcels one by one*]. This is a bell for Mrs. Williams . . . something she said she wanted so that you can ring for her, which saves the maids; cap and apron for Mary; cap and apron for Ellen; shawl for Davis when she goes out to the larder . . . all useful presents. And that's something for you . . . but you're not to look at it till the morning.

Having shaken each of them at the old gentleman, she proceeds to re-pack them. He is now trembling with anxiety to escape before any more of the family find him there.

MR. GEORGE BOOTH. Thank you . . . thank you. I hope my lot has arrived. I left instructions . . .

HONOR. Quite safely . . . and I have hidden them. Presents are put on the breakfast-table to-morrow.

EDWARD [*with an inconsequence that still further alarms MR. BOOTH*]. When we were children our Christmas breakfast was mostly made off chocolates.

Before the basket is packed, MRS. VOYSEY sails slowly into the room, as smiling and as deaf as ever. MR. BOOTH does his best not to scowl at her.

MRS. VOYSEY. Are you feeling better, George Booth?

MR. GEORGE BOOTH. No. [*Then he elevates his voice with a show of politeness.*] No, thank you; . . . I can't say I am.

MRS. VOYSEY. You don't look better.

MR. GEORGE BOOTH. I still have my headache. [*With a distracted shout.*] Headache!

MRS. VOYSEY. Bilious, perhaps. I quite understand you didn't care to dine. But why not have taken your coat off? How foolish in this warm room!

MR. GEORGE BOOTH. Thank you. I'm . . . just going.

He seizes the market basket. At that moment MRS. HUGH *appears.*

BEATRICE. You shawl, Mother. [*And she clasps it round* MRS. VOYSEY'S *shoulders.*]

MRS. VOYSEY. Thank you, Beatrice. I thought I had it on. [*Then to* MR. BOOTH, *who is now entangled in his comforter.*] A merry Christmas to you.

BEATRICE. Good evening, Mr. Booth.

MR. GEORGE BOOTH. I beg your pardon. Good evening, Mrs. Hugh.

HONOR [*with sudden inspiration, to the company in general*]. Why shouldn't I write in here . . . now the table's cleared?

MR. GEORGE BOOTH [*sternly, now he is safe by the door*]. Will you see me out, Edward?

EDWARD. Yes.

He follows the old man and his basket, leaving the others to distribute themselves about the room. It is a custom of the female members of the VOYSEY *family, about Christmas time, to return to the dining-room, when the table has been cleared, and occupy themselves in various ways which involve space and untidiness.* BEATRICE *has a little work-basket containing a buttonless glove and such things, which she is rectifying.* HONOR'S *writing is done with the aid of an enormous blotting book, which bulges with apparently a year's correspondence. She sheds its contents upon the end of the dining-table and spreads them abroad.* MRS. VOYSEY *settles to the table near to the fire, opens the Nineteenth Century and is instantly absorbed in it.*

BEATRICE. If there's anywhere else left in this house where one can write or sew or sit, I'd be glad to know of it. Christmas Tree in the back drawing-room and all the furniture in the front! Presents piled up under dusters in the library! My heap is very soft and bulgy. Honor . . . if you've given me an eiderdown quilt I'll never forgive you.

HONOR. Oh, I haven't . . . I shouldn't think of it.

BEATRICE. And to-morrow this room will look like a six P.M. bargain counter.

HONOR. But . . . Beatrice . . . it's Christmas.

BEATRICE. Noel . . . Noel! Where's Emily?

HONOR. Well . . . I'm afraid she's talking to Booth.

BEATRICE. If you mean that Booth is listening to her, I don't believe it. She has taken my fine scissors.

HONOR. And I think she's telling him about you.

BEATRICE. What . . . in particular . . . about me?

HONOR. About you and Hugh.

BEATRICE. Now whose fault is this? We agreed that nothing more was to be said till after Christmas.

HONOR. But Edward knows . . . and Mother knows . . .

BEATRICE. I warned Mother a year ago.

HONOR. And Emily told me. And everyone seems to know except Booth. And it would be fearful if he found out. So I said: Tell him one night when he's in bed and very tired. But Emily didn't seem to think that would . . .

> At this moment EMILY comes in, looking rather trodden upon. HONOR concludes in the most audible of whispers . . .

HONOR. Don't say anything . . . it's my fault.

BEATRICE [fixing her with a severe forefinger]. Emily . . . have you taken my fine scissors?

EMILY [timidly]. No, Beatrice.

HONOR [who is diving into the recesses of the blotting book]. Oh, here they are! I must have taken them. I do apologise!

EMILY [more timidly still]. I'm afraid Booth's rather cross. He's gone to look for Hugh.

BEATRICE [with a shake of her head]. Honor . . . I've a good mind to make you do this sewing for me.

> In comes the Major, strepitant. He takes, so to speak, just enough time to train himself on BEATRICE and then fires.

MAJOR BOOTH VOYSEY. Beatrice, what on earth is this Emily has been telling me?

BEATRICE [with elaborate calm]. Emily, what have you been telling Booth?

MAJOR BOOTH VOYSEY. Please . . . please do not prevaricate. Where is Hugh?

MRS. VOYSEY [looking over her spectacles]. What did you say, Booth?

MAJOR BOOTH VOYSEY. I want Hugh, Mother.

MRS. VOYSEY. I thought you were playing billiards together.

> EDWARD strolls back from despatching MR. BOOTH, his face thoughtful.

MAJOR BOOTH VOYSEY [insistently]. Edward, where is Hugh?

EDWARD [*with complete indifference*]. I don't know.

MAJOR BOOTH VOYSEY [*in trumpet tones*]. Honor, will you oblige me by finding Hugh and saying I wish to speak to him here immediately.

> HONOR, *who has leapt at the sound of her name, flies from the room without a word.*

BEATRICE. I know quite well what you want to talk about, Booth. Discuss the matter by all means if it amuses you . . . but don't shout.

MAJOR BOOTH VOYSEY. I use the voice Nature has gifted me with, Beatrice.

BEATRICE [*as she searches for a glove button*]. Nature did let herself go over your lungs.

MAJOR BOOTH VOYSEY [*glaring round with indignation*]. This is a family matter . . . otherwise I should not feel it my duty to interfere . . . as I do. Any member of the family has a right to express an opinion. I want Mother's. Mother, what do you think?

MRS. VOYSEY [*amicably*]. What about?

MAJOR BOOTH VOYSEY. Hugh and Beatrice separating.

MRS. VOYSEY. They haven't separated.

MAJOR BOOTH VOYSEY. But they mean to.

MRS. VOYSEY. Fiddle-de-dee!

MAJOR BOOTH VOYSEY. I quite agree with you.

BEATRICE [*with a charming smile*]. Such reasoning would convert a stone.

MAJOR BOOTH VOYSEY. Why have I not been told?

BEATRICE. You have just been told.

MAJOR BOOTH VOYSEY [*thunderously*]. Before.

BEATRICE. The truth is, dear Booth, we're all so afraid of you.

MAJOR BOOTH VOYSEY [*a little mollified*]. Ha . . . I should be glad to think that.

BEATRICE [*sweetly*]. Don't you?

MAJOR BOOTH VOYSEY [*intensely serious*]. Beatrice, your callousness shocks me. That you can dream of deserting Hugh . . . a man who, of all others, requires constant care and attention.

BEATRICE. May I remark that the separation is as much Hugh's wish as mine?

MAJOR BOOTH VOYSEY. I don't believe that.

BEATRICE [*her eyebrows up*]. Really!

MAJOR BOOTH VOYSEY. I don't imply that you're lying. But you must know that it's Hugh's nature to wish to do anything that he things anybody wishes him to do. All my life I've had to stand up for him . . . and, by Jove, I'll continue to do so.

EDWARD [*from the depths of his arm-chair*]. Booth . . . if you could manage to let this alone . . .

The door is flung almost off its hinges by HUGH, *who then stands stamping and pale green with rage.*

HUGH. Look here, Booth . . . I will not have you interfering with my private affairs. Is one never to be free from your bullying?

MAJOR BOOTH VOYSEY. You ought to be grateful.

HUGH. Well, I'm not.

MAJOR BOOTH VOYSEY. This is a family affair.

HUGH. It is not!

MAJOR BOOTH VOYSEY [*at the top of his voice*]. If all you can do is to contradict me . . . you'd better listen to what I've got to say . . . quietly.

HUGH, *quite shouted down, flings himself petulantly into a chair. A hushed pause.*

EMILY [*in a still small voice*]. Would you like me to go, Booth?

MAJOR BOOTH VOYSEY [*severely*]. No, Emily. Unless anything has been going on which cannot be discussed before you. [*More severely still.*] And I trust that is not so.

BEATRICE. Nothing at all appropriate to that tone of voice has been . . . going on. We swear it.

MAJOR BOOTH VOYSEY. Why do you wish to separate?

HUGH. What's the use of telling you? You won't understand.

BEATRICE [*who sews on undisturbed*]. We don't get on well together.

MAJOR BOOTH VOYSEY [*amazedly*]. Is that all?

HUGH [*snapping at him*]. Yes, that's all. Can you find a better reason?

MAJOR BOOTH VOYSEY [*with brotherly contempt*]. I've given up expecting common sense from you. But Beatrice . . .! [*His tone implores her to be reasonable.*]

BEATRICE. Common sense is dry diet for the soul, you know.

MAJOR BOOTH VOYSEY [*protesting*]. My dear girl . . . that sounds like a quotation from your latest book.

BEATRICE. It isn't. I do think you might read that book . . . for the honour of the Family.

MAJOR BOOTH VOYSEY [*successfully side-tracked*]. I bought it at once, Beatrice, and . . .

BEATRICE. That's the principal thing, of course.

MAJOR BOOTH VOYSEY [... *and discovering it*]. But do let us keep to the subject.

BEATRICE [*with flattering sincerity*]. Certainly, Booth. And there is hardly any subject that I wouldn't ask your advice about. But upon this ... please let me know better. Hugh and I will be happier apart.

MAJOR BOOTH VOYSEY [*obstinately*]. Why?

BEATRICE [*with resolute patience, having vented a little sigh*]. Hugh finds that my opinions distress him. And I have at last lost patience with Hugh.

MRS. VOYSEY [*who has been trying to follow this through her spectacles*]. What does Beatrice say?

MAJOR BOOTH VOYSEY [*translating into a loud sing-song*]. That she wishes to leave her husband because she has lost patience.

MRS. VOYSEY [*with considerable acrimony*]. Then you must be a very ill-tempered woman. Hugh has a sweet nature.

HUGH [*shouting self-consciously*]. Nonsense, Mother.

BEATRICE [*shouting good humouredly*]. I quite agree with you, Mother. [*She continues to her husband in an even, just tone.*] You have a sweet nature, Hugh, and it is most difficult to get angry with you. I have been seven years working up to it. But now that I am angry I shall never get pleased again.

The Major returns to his subject refreshed by a moment's repose.

MAJOR BOOTH VOYSEY. How has he failed in his duty? Tell us. I'm not bigoted in his favour. I know your faults, Hugh. [*He wags his head at* HUGH, *who writhes with irritation.*]

HUGH. Why can't you leave them alone ... leave us alone?

BEATRICE. I'd state my case against Hugh if I thought he'd retaliate.

HUGH [*desperately rounding on his brother*]. If I tell you, you won't understand. You understand nothing! Beatrice thinks I ought to prostitute my art to make money.

MAJOR BOOTH VOYSEY [*glancing at his wife*]. Please don't use metaphors of that sort.

BEATRICE [*reasonably*]. Yes, I think Hugh ought to earn more money.

MAJOR BOOTH VOYSEY [*quite pleased to be getting along at last*]. Well, why doesn't he?

HUGH. I don't want money.

MAJOR BOOTH VOYSEY. How can you not want money? As well say you don't want bread.

BEATRICE [*as she breaks off her cotton*]. It's when one has known what it is to be a little short of both . . .

> *Now the Major spreads himself and begins to be very wise; while* HUGH, *to whom this is more intolerable than all, can only clutch his hair.*

MAJOR BOOTH VOYSEY. You know I never considered art a very good profession for you, Hugh. And you won't even stick to one department of it. It's a profession that gets people into very bad habits, I consider. Couldn't you take up something else? You could still do those wood-cuts in your spare time to amuse yourself.

HUGH [*commenting on this with two deliberate shouts of simulated mirth*]. Ha! Ha!

MAJOR BOOTH VOYSEY. Well, it wouldn't much matter if you didn't do them at all.

HUGH. True!

> MRS. VOYSEY *leaves her arm-chair for her favourite station at the dining-table.*

MRS. VOYSEY. Booth is the only one of you that I can hear at all distinctly. But if you two foolish young people think you want to separate . . . try it. You'll soon come back to each other and be glad to. People can't fight against nature for long. And marriage is a natural state . . . once you're married.

MAJOR BOOTH VOYSEY [*with intense approval*]. Quite right, Mother.

MRS. VOYSEY. I know.

> *She resumes the Nineteenth Century. And the Major, to the despair of everybody, makes yet another start; trying oratory this time.*

MAJOR BOOTH VOYSEY. My own opinion is, Beatrice and Hugh, that you don't realise the meaning of the word marriage. I don't call myself a religious man . . . but, dash it all, you were married in Church. And you then entered upon a lawful compact . . .! Surely, as a woman, Beatrice, the religious point of it ought to appeal to you. Good Lord . . . suppose everybody were to carry on like this! And have you considered that . . . whether you are right, or whether you are wrong . . . if you desert Hugh you cut yourself off from the Family.

BEATRICE [*with the sweetest of smiles*]. That will distress me terribly.

MAJOR BOOTH VOYSEY [*not doubting her for a moment*]. Of course.

> HUGH *flings up his head, and finds relief at last in many words.*

HUGH. I wish to God I'd ever been able to cut myself off from the Family! Look at Trenchard!

MAJOR BOOTH VOYSEY [*gobbling a little at this unexpected attack*]. I do not forgive Trenchard for his quarrel with the Pater.

HUGH. He quarrelled because that was his best way of escape.

MAJOR BOOTH VOYSEY. Escape from what?

HUGH. From tyranny . . . from hypocrisy . . . from boredom!
. . . from his Happy English Home.

BEATRICE [kindly]. Now, my dear . . . it's no use . . .

MAJOR BOOTH VOYSEY [attempting sarcasm]. Speak so that
Mother can hear you!

But HUGH *isn't to be stopped now.*

HUGH. Why are we all dull, cubbish, uneducated . . . hopelessly
middle-class!

MAJOR BOOTH VOYSEY [taking this as very personal]. Cubbish!

BEATRICE. Middle-class! Hugh . . . do think what you're saying.

HUGH. Upper middle-class, then. Yes . . . and snobbish too!
What happens to you when you're born into that estate? What
happened to us, anyhow? We were fed . . . we were clothed . . .
we were taught and trained . . . and we were made comfortable.
And that was the watchword given us: Comfort! You must work
for a comfortable livelihood. You must practise a comfortable
morality . . . and go to your parson for spiritual comfort . . . and
he'll promise you everlasting comfort in heaven. Far better be
born in a slum . . . with a drunkard for a father and a drab for
a mother . . .

MAJOR BOOTH VOYSEY. I never heard such lunacy.

HUGH. If you're nothing and nobody, you may find it in you
to become something and somebody . . . and at least you learn
what the world wants of you and what it doesn't. But do you
think the world to-day couldn't do without u s? Strip yourself of
your comfortable income . . . as Edward here told you to . . .
and step out into the street and see.

MAJOR BOOTH VOYSEY [ponderously]. I venture to think . . .

HUGH. Oh no, you don't. You don't do either . . . and you'd
better not try . . . for a little thinking might tell you that we and
our like have ceased to exist at all. Yes, I mean it. Trenchard
escaped in time. You went into the army . . . so how could you
discover what a back number you are? But I found out soon
enough . . . when I tried to express myself in art . . . that there
was nothing to express . . . except a few habits, and tags of other
people's thoughts and feelings. There is no Me . . . that's what's
the matter. I'm an illusion. Not that it does matter to anyone
but me. And look at Honor . . .

MAJOR BOOTH VOYSEY. Honor leads a useful life . . . and a
happy one. We all love her.

HUGH. Yes . . . and what have we always called her? Mother's right hand! I wonder they bothered to give her a name. By the time little Ethel came they were tired of training children. She was alive . . . in a silly, innocent sort of way. And then . . .

BEATRICE. Poor little Ethel!

MAJOR BOOTH VOYSEY. Poor Ethel!

They speak as one speaks of the dead.

HUGH. And though your luck has been pretty poor, Edward, you've come up against realities at least . . . against something that could make a man of you. [*Then back to his humorous savagery.*] But if Booth thinks this world will stand still because he and his like want to be comfortable . . . that's where he's wrong.

MAJOR BOOTH VOYSEY [*dignified and judicious*]. We will return, if you please, to the original subject of discussion. This question of a separation . . .

HUGH *jumps up, past all patience.*

HUGH. Beatrice and I mean to separate. And nothing you may say will prevent it. The only trouble is money. She says we must have enough to live apart comfortably.

BEATRICE [*in kindly irony*]. Yes . . . comfortably!

HUGH. And I daresay she's right . . . she generally is. So the question is: Can we raise it?

MAJOR BOOTH VOYSEY. Well?

HUGH. Well . . . for the moment we can't.

MAJOR BOOTH VOYSEY. Well then?

HUGH. So we can't separate.

MAJOR BOOTH VOYSEY. Then what in heaven's name have we been discussing it for?

HUGH. I haven't discussed it. I don't want to discuss it. Why can't you mind your own business? Now I'll go back to the billiard-room and my book.

He is gone before the Major can recover his breath.

MAJOR BOOTH VOYSEY. I am not an impatient man . . . but really . . . !

BEATRICE. Hugh's tragedy is that he is just clever enough to have found himself out . . . and no cleverer.

MAJOR BOOTH VOYSEY [*magnanimous but stern*]. I will be frank. You have never made the best of Hugh.

BEATRICE. No . . . at the worst it never came to that.

MAJOR BOOTH VOYSEY. I am glad . . . for both your sakes . . . that you can't separate.

BEATRICE. As soon as I am earning enough I shall walk off from him.

The Major's manly spirit stirs.

MAJOR BOOTH VOYSEY. You will do nothing of the sort, Beatrice.

BEATRICE [*unruffled*]. How will you stop me, Booth?

MAJOR BOOTH VOYSEY. I shall tell Hugh he must command you to stay.

BEATRICE [*with a little smile*]. I wonder would that make the difference. It was one of the illusions of my girlhood that I'd love a man who would master me.

MAJOR BOOTH VOYSEY. Hugh must assert himself.

He begins to walk about, giving some indication of how it should be done. BEATRICE's *smile has vanished.*

BEATRICE. Don't think I've enjoyed wearing the breeches . . . to use that horrid phrase . . . all through my married life. But someone had to plan and make decisions and do accounts. We weren't sparrows or lilies of the field. . . . [*She becomes conscious of his strutting and smiles rather mischievously.*] Ah . . . if I'd married you, Booth!

BOOTH's *face grows beatific.*

MAJOR BOOTH VOYSEY. Well, I own to thinking that I am a masterful man . . . that it's the duty of every man to be so. [*He adds forgivingly.*] Poor old Hugh!

BEATRICE [*unable to resist temptation*]. If I'd tried to leave you, Booth, you'd have whipped me . . . wouldn't you?

MAJOR BOOTH VOYSEY [*ecstatically complacent*]. Ha . . . Well . . .!

BEATRICE. Do say yes. Think how it will frighten Emily.

The Major strokes his moustache and is most friendly.

MAJOR BOOTH VOYSEY. Hugh's been a worry to me all my life. And now . . . as head of the family . . . well, I suppose I'd better go and give the dear chap a quiet talking to. I see your point of view, Beatrice.

BEATRICE. Why disturb him at his book?

MAJOR BOOTH *leaves them, squaring his shoulders as becomes a lord of creation. The two sisters-in-law go on with their work silently for a moment; then* BEATRICE *adds* . . .

BEATRICE. Do you find Booth difficult to manage, Emily?

EMILY [*putting down her knitting to consider the matter*]. No. It's best to let him talk himself out. When he has done that he'll often come to me for advice. But I like him to get his own way as much as possible . . . or think he's getting it. Otherwise he becomes so depressed.

BEATRICE. [*quietly amused*]. Edward shouldn't be listening to this. [*Then to him.*] Your presence profanes these Mysteries.

EDWARD. I won't tell . . . and I'm a bachelor.

EMILY [*solemnly, as she takes up her knitting again*]. Do you really mean to leave Hugh?

BEATRICE [*slightly impatient*]. Emily, I've said so.

They are joined by ALICE MAITLAND, *who comes in gaily.*

ALICE. What's Booth shouting about in the billiard-room?

EMILY [*pained*]. Oh . . . on Christmas Eve, too!

BEATRICE. Don't you take any interest in my matrimonial affairs?

MRS. VOYSEY *shuts up the Nineteenth Century and removes her spectacles.*

MRS. VOYSEY. That's a very interesting article. The Chinese Empire must be in a shocking state. Is it ten o'clock yet?

EDWARD. Past.

MRS. VOYSEY [*as* EDWARD *is behind her*]. Can anyone see the clock?

ALICE. It's past ten, Auntie.

MRS. VOYSEY. Then I think I'll go to my room.

EMILY. Shall I come and look after you, Mother?

MRS. VOYSEY. If you'd find Honor for me, Emily.

EMILY *goes in search of the harmless, necessary* HONOR, *and* MRS. VOYSEY *begins her nightly chant of departure.*

MRS. VOYSEY. Good-night, Alice. Good-night, Edward.

EDWARD. Good-night, Mother.

MRS. VOYSEY [*with sudden severity*]. I'm not pleased with you, Beatrice.

BEATRICE. I'm sorry, Mother.

But without waiting to be answered the old lady has sailed out of the room. BEATRICE, EDWARD *and* ALICE, *now left together, are attuned to each other enough to be able to talk with ease.*

BEATRICE. But there's something in what Hugh says about this family. Had your great-grandfather a comfortable income, Edward?

EDWARD. I think so. It was his father made the money . . . in trade.

BEATRICE. Which has been filtering away ever since. But fairly profitably, surely . . . to the rest of the world. You'd a great-aunt who was quite a botanist and an uncle who edited Catullus, hadn't you?

EDWARD. Yes.

She is beginning to work out this theme.

BEATRICE. Well, that didn't pay them. Then there was the uncle killed in the Soudan. A captain's pension and no more wouldn't have been much for a widow and four children. . . .

ALICE. Five.

BEATRICE. Was it? Dear me . . . how prolific we were! And though I chaff Booth . . . I've seen him with his regiment giving weedy young slackers chest and biceps and making them "decent chaps." It takes a few generations, you know, to breed men who'll feel that it pays to do that for its own sake . . . and who'll be proud to do it. Oh, I can find a lot to say for the Upper Middle Class.

EDWARD. The family's petering out as its income does. D'you notice that? Six of us. But there are only Booth's two children.

BEATRICE. It's more than the shrinking income that's doing it . . . more even than Hugh's "worship of comfort." Some fresh impulse to assert itself . . . I expect that is what a class needs to keep it socially alive. Well . . . your father developed one.

EDWARD. Not a very happy one!

BEATRICE. It might have been . . . if he'd had the good sense to borrow the money for his financial operations just a little less casually.

EDWARD. D'you know what I think I've found out about him now?

BEATRICE. Something interesting, I'm sure.

EDWARD. He did save my grandfather and the firm from a smash. That was true. A pretty capable piece of heroism! Then . . . six years after . . . he started on his own account . . . cheating again. I suppose he found himself in a corner.

BEATRICE [psychologically fascinated]. Not a bit of it! He did it deliberately. One day when he was feeling extra fit he must have said to himself: Why not? . . . well, here goes! You never understood your father. I do . . . it's my business to.

EDWARD. He was an old scoundrel, Beatrice, and it's sophistry to pretend otherwise.

BEATRICE. But he was a bit of genius too. You can't be expected to appreciate that. It's tiresome work, I know . . . tidying up after these little Napoleons. He really did make money, didn't he, besides stealing it?

EDWARD. Lord, yes! And I daresay more than he stole. An honest two thousand a year from the firm. He had another thousand . . . and he spent about ten. He must have found the difference somewhere.

BEATRICE. There you are, then. And we all loved him. You did, too, Alice.

ALICE. I adored him.

EDWARD. He was a scoundrel and a thief.

ALICE. I always knew he was a scoundrel of some sort. I thought he probably had another family somewhere.

BEATRICE. Oh . . . what fun! Had he, Edward?

EDWARD. I fancy not.

BEATRICE. No, he wasn't that sort . . . and it spoils the picture to overcrowd it.

EDWARD. Pleasant to be able to sit back and survey the business so coolly.

BEATRICE. Somebody has to . . . some time or other . . . try to find a meaning in this and everything that happens . . . or we should run mad under what seems the wicked folly of it all. But it's only the flippant and callous little bit of me which writes my flippant and callous little books that sits back so coolly, Edward. And even that bit . . . when you're not looking . . . stands up to make you a pretty low bow. Aren't matters any better . . . aren't you nearly through?

EDWARD. Yes, they are better.

BEATRICE. I'm glad. Have you ever been sorry that you didn't do the obviously wise thing . . . uncover the crime and let the law take its course?

EDWARD. Often.

BEATRICE. Why did you take up the challenge single-handed . . . lawlessly . . . now that perhaps you can look back and tell?

EDWARD *rather unwillingly, rather shyly, confesses . . .*

EDWARD. I think that I wanted . . . quite selfishly . . . a little vaingloriously, I daresay . . . to prove what my honesty was worth . . . what I was worth. And I was up against it. [*After which comes, perhaps, a more inward truth.*] And then, you know, I loved the Pater.

BEATRICE [*touched*]. In spite of all?

EDWARD. Oh, yes. And I felt that if the worst of what he'd recklessly done was put right . . . it might be the better for him somehow.

BEATRICE, *who has no such superstitious beliefs, lets this sink in on her nevertheless.*

BEATRICE. Silence in the Court.

Another moment, and she collects her sewing, gets up and goes.

ALICE *has had all the while a keen eye on* EDWARD.

ALICE. But something has happened since dinner.

EDWARD. Could you see that?

ALICE. Tell me.

12

EDWARD [*as one throwing off a burden*]. The smash has come . . . and it's not my fault. Old George Booth . . .

ALICE. I knew he'd been here.

EDWARD. He found out . . . I had to tell him. You can imagine him. I told him to take what was left of his money and prosecute. Well . . . he'll take what he can get and he won't prosecute. For he wants to bleed me, sovereign by sovereign as I earn sovereign by sovereign, till he has got the rest. And he has told the Vicar . . . who has told his wife . . . who has told the choir boys by this time I daresay. So it's a smash. And I thank God for it.

ALICE [*quiet but intent*]. And what'll happen now?

EDWARD. One can't be sure. Gaol, possibly. I'll be struck off the Rolls anyhow. No more Lincoln's Inn for me.

ALICE. And what then?

EDWARD. I don't know . . . and I don't care.

ALICE [*still quieter*]. But I do.

EDWARD. Oh, I shan't shoot myself. I've never cared enough about my life to take the trouble to end it. But I'm damned tired, Alice. I think I could sleep for a week. I hope they won't undo what I've done, though. They won't find it very easy to . . . that's one thing. And I shan't help them. Well, there it is. Nobody else knows yet. I like you to be the first to know. That's all. A Merry Christmas. Good-night.

As he takes no more notice of her, ALICE *gets up and goes to the door. There she pauses, and turns; and then she comes back to him.*

ALICE. I'm supposed to be off to Egypt on the twenty-eighth for three months. No. I'm not ill. But, as I've never yet had anything to do except look after myself, the doctor thinks Egypt might be . . . most beneficial.

EDWARD. Well, you may find me still at large when you come back.

ALICE. Oh, I'm not going . . . now.

EDWARD [*sharply*]. Why not? Good God . . . don't make it worse for me. To have you about while I'm being put through this . . . have you reading the reports the next morning . . . coming into Court perhaps to look pityingly at me! Go away . . . and stay away. That's all I ask.

ALICE [*unperturbed*]. At the best, I suppose, you'll be left pretty hard up for the time being.

EDWARD. If His Majesty doesn't find me a new suit, they'll leave me the clothes on my back.

ALICE. What a good thing I've my eight hundred a year!

EDWARD [*with a gasp and a swallow*]. And what exactly do you mean by that?

ALICE. Could they take my money as well . . . if we were married already? I've never been clear about married women's property. But you know. It's your business to. Could they?

EDWARD [*choking now*]. Are you . . . are you . . .?

ALICE. Because if they could it would be only sensible to wait a little. But if not . . .

EDWARD *hardens himself.*

EDWARD. Look here, now. Through these two damnable years there's only one thing I've been thanking God for . . . that you never did say yes to me.

ALICE [*chaffing him tenderly*]. Four times and a half you proposed. The first time on a walk we took down in Devon . . . when you cut a stick of willow and showed me how to make a whistle from it. I have that still . . . and there are four and a half notches in it. The half was only a hint you dropped. But I could have caught you on it if I'd wanted to.

EDWARD. Well . . . you didn't.

ALICE. No. But I kept the stick.

EDWARD. If you didn't care enough for me to marry me then . . .

ALICE. Well . . . I didn't.

EDWARD. You don't suppose that now your eight hundred a year . . .

ALICE. Are you still in love with me, Edward?

EDWARD *sets his teeth against temptation.*

EDWARD. The answer must be no.

She smiles.

ALICE. You're lying.

EDWARD. Can't we stop this? I've had about as much as I can stand.

ALICE. Don't be so difficult. If I ask you to marry me, you'll refuse. And then what can I do? I can't coquet and be alluring. I don't know how.

EDWARD [*trying to joke his way out*]. Something to be thankful for!

ALICE. But, my dear . . . I love you. I didn't before. I thought you were only a well-principled prig. I was wrong. You're a man . . . and I love you with all my heart and soul. Oh . . . please . . . please ask me to be your wife.

EDWARD [*for he resists happiness no more*]. If I've luck . . . if they let me go free . . .

ALICE. No . . . now . . . now . . . while you're in trouble. I won't take you later . . . when the worst is over. I'm dashed if I do. I'll marry you to-morrow.

EDWARD [objecting but helplessly]. That's Christmas Day.

ALICE. And Boxing Day's next. Well, the old wretch of a Vicar can marry us on Saturday.

EDWARD [giving his conscience one more hysterical chance]. I haven't asked you yet.

ALICE. I don't believe, you know, that they will put you in prison. It would be so extraordinarily senseless.

EDWARD. But now the scandal's out, we must go smash in any case.

ALICE. You couldn't call them all together . . . get them round a table and explain? They won't all be like Mr. Booth and the Vicar. Couldn't we bargain with them to let us go on?
     The "we" and the "us" come naturally.

EDWARD. But . . . heavens above . . . I don't want to go on. You don't know what the life has been.

ALICE. Yes, I do. I see when I look at you. But it was partly the fear, wasn't it . . . or the hope . . . that this would happen. Once it's all open and above-board . . .! Besides . . . you've had no other life. Now there's to be ours. That'll make a difference.

EDWARD [considering the matter]. They just might agree . . . to syndicate themselves . . . and to keep me slaving at it.

ALICE. You could make them.

EDWARD. I! I believe my father could have . . . if that way out had taken his fancy.

ALICE [her pride in him surging up]. My dear . . . don't you know yourself yet . . . as I now know you, thank God? You're ten times the man he ever was. What was he after all but a fraud?

EDWARD [soberly]. Well . . . I'll try.

ALICE [gentle and grave]. I'm sure you should. [For a moment they sit quietly there, thinking of the future, uncertain of everything but one thing.] The others must have gone up to bed. This is no way for an Upper Middle Class Lady to behave . . . sitting up hob-nobbing with you. Good-night.

EDWARD. Good-night. God bless you.
     She is going again, but again she stops, and says half-humorously.

ALICE. But even now you haven't asked me.

EDWARD [simply]. Will you marry me?

ALICE [as simply in return]. Yes. Yes, please. [Then, moving nearer to him.] Kiss me.

EDWARD [*half-humorously too*]. I was going to.

And he does, with a passion that has reverence in it too.

ALICE. Oh, my dear. My very dear. Till to-morrow then.

EDWARD. Till to-morrow.

She leaves him sitting there; a man conscious of new strength.

ROCOCO

A play in one act

ROCOCO

ROCOCO

*Do you know how ugly the drawing-room of an English vicarage can be?
Yes, I am aware of all that there should be about it; the old-world
grace and charm of Jane-Austenism. One should sit upon Chippen-
dale and glimpse the grey Norman church-tower through the
casement. But what of the pious foundations of a more industrial
age, churches built in mid-nineteenth century and rather scamped
in the building, dedicated to the Glory of God and the soul's health
of some sweating and sweated urban district? The Bishop would
have a vicarage added, grumbled the church-donor. Well, then,
consider his comfort a little, but to the glory of the Vicar nothing
need be done. And nothing was. The architect (this an added
labour of but little love to him) would give an ecclesiastical touch
to the front porch, a pointed top to the front door, add some stained
glass to the staircase window. But a mean house, a stuffy house,
and the Vicar must indeed have fresh air in his soul if mean and
stuffy doctrine was not to be generated there.*

*The drawing-room would be the best room, and not a bad room in its way,
if it weren't that its proportions were vile, as though it felt it
wanted to be larger than it was, and if the window and the fireplace and the door didn't seem to be quarrelling as to which should
be the most conspicuous. The fireplace wins.*

*This particular one in this particular drawing-room is of yellow wood,
stained and grained. It reaches not quite to the ceiling. It has a
West Front air, if looking-glass may stand for windows; it is
fretted, moreover, here and there, with little trefoil holes. It bears
a full assault of the Vicar's wife's ideas of how to make the place
"look nice." There is the clock, of course, which won't keep time;
there are the vases which won't hold water; framed photographs,
as many as can be crowded on the shelves; in every other crevice,
knick-knacks. Then, if you stand, as the Vicar often stands, at
this point of vantage you are conscious of the wall-paper of amber
and blue with a frieze above it measuring off yard by yard a sort
of desert scene; a mountain, a lake, three palm-trees, two camels;
and again; and again; until by the corner a camel and a palm-tree*

*are cut out. On the walls there are pictures, of course. Two of
them convey to you in a vague and water-colour sort of way that
and English countryside is pretty. There is "Christ among the
Doctors," with a presentation brass plate on its frame; there is
"Simply to Thy Cross I Cling." And there is an illuminated
testimonial to the Vicar, a mark of affection and esteem from the
flock he ministered to as senior curate.*

*The furniture is either very heavy, stuffed, sprung, and tapestry-covered,
or very light. There are quite a number of small tables (occasional-
tables they are called), which should have four legs but have only
three. There are several chairs, too, on which it would be unwise
to sit down.*

*In the centre of the room, beneath the hanging, pink-shaded, electric
chandelier, is a mahogany monument, a large round table of the
"pedestal" variety, and on it tower to a climax the vicarage
symbols of gentility and culture. In the centre of this table,
beneath a glass shade, an elaborate reproduction of some sixteenth-
century pietà (a little High Church, it is thought; but Art, for
some reason, runs that way). It stands on a Chinese silk mat, sent
home by some exiled uncle. It is symmetrically surrounded by
gift-books, a photograph album, a tray of painted Indian figures
(very jolly! another gift from the exiled uncle), and a whale's
tooth. The whole affair is draped with a red embroidered cloth.*

*The window of the room, with so many sorts of curtains and blinds to it
that one would think the Vicar hatched conspiracies here by night,
admits but a blurring light, which the carpet (Brussels) reflects,
toned to an ugly yellow.*

*You really would not expect such a thing to be happening in such a place,
but this carpet is at the moment the base of an apparently mortal
struggle. The Vicar is undermost; his baldish head, when he tries
to raise it, falls back and bumps. Kneeling on him, throttling his
collar, is a hefty young man conscientiously out of temper, with
scarlet face glowing against carroty hair. His name is Reginald
and he is (one regrets to add) the Vicar's nephew, though it be only
by marriage. The Vicar's wife, fragile and fifty, is making
pathetic attempts to pull him off.*

"Have you had enough?" asks Reginald and grips the Vicar hard.

"Oh, Reginald . . . be good," is all the Vicar's wife's appeal.

*Not two yards off a minor battle rages. Mrs. Reginald, coming up to
reinforce, was intercepted by Miss Underwood, the Vicar's sister,
on the same errand, the elder lady now has the younger pinned by*

*the elbows and she emphasizes this very handsome control of the
situation by teeth-rattling shakes.*

"Cat . . . cat . . . cat!" *gasps* Mrs. Reginald, *who is plump and flaxen
and easily disarranged.*

Miss Underwood *only shakes her again.* "I'll teach you manners, Miss."

"Oh, Reginald . . . do drop him," *moans poor* Mrs. Underwood. *For
this is really very bad for the Vicar.*

"Stick a pin into him, Mary," *advises her sister-in-law. Whereat* Mrs.
Reginald *yelps in her iron grasp.*

"Don't you dare . . . it's poisonous," *and then,* "Oh . . . if you weren't
an old woman I'd have boxed your ears."

Three violent shakes. "Would you? Would you? Would you?"

"I haven't got a pin, Carinthia," *says* Mrs. Underwood. *She has
conscientiously searched.*

"Pull his hair, then," *commands* Carinthia.

At intervals, like a signal gun, Reginald *repeats his query:* "Have you
had enough?" *And the Vicar, though it is evident that he has,
still, with some unsurrendering school-days' echo answering in his
mind, will only gasp,* "Most undignified . . . clergyman of the
Church of England . . . your host, sir . . . ashamed of you . . .
let me up at once."

Mrs. Underwood *has failed at the hair; she flaps her hands in despair.*
"It's too short, Carinthia," *she moans.*

Mrs. Reginald *begins to sob pitifully. It is very painful to be tightly held
by the elbows from behind. So* Miss Underwood, *with the neatest
of twists and pushes, lodges her in a chair, and thus released
herself, folds her arms and surveys the situation.* "Box my ears,
would you?" *is her postscript.*

MRS. REGINALD. Well . . . you boxed father's.

MISS UNDERWOOD. Where is your wretched father-in-law?
Her hawklike eye surveys the room for this unknown in vain.

REGINALD [*the proper interval having apparently elapsed*]. Have
you had enough?
Dignified he cannot look, thus outstretched. THE VICAR, *therefore,
assumes a mixed expression of saintliness and obstinacy, his next
best resource. His poor wife moans again. . . .*

MRS. UNDERWOOD. Oh, please, Reginald . . . the floor's so hard
for him!

REGINALD [*a little anxious to have done with it himself*]. Have you
had enough?

THE VICAR [*quite supine*]. Do you consider this conduct becoming a gentleman?

MRS. UNDERWOOD. And . . . Simon! . . . if the servants have heard . . . they must have heard! . . . what will they think?

No, even this heart-breaking appeal falls flat.

REGINALD. Say you've had enough and I'll let you up.

THE VICAR [*reduced to casuistry*]. It's not at all the sort of thing I ought to say.

MRS. UNDERWOOD [*so helpless*]. Oh . . . I think you might say it, Simon, just for once.

MISS UNDERWOOD [*grim with the pride of her own victory*]. Say nothing of the sort, Simon!

> THE VICAR *has a burst of exasperation; for after all he is on the floor and being knelt on.*

THE VICAR. Confound it all, then, Carinthia, why don't you do something?

> CARINTHIA *casts a tactical eye over* REGINALD. THE VICAR *adds in parentheses . . . a human touch! . . .*

THE VICAR. Don't kneel there, you young fool, you'll break my watch!

MISS UNDERWOOD. Wait till I get my breath.

> *But this prospect raises in* MRS. UNDERWOOD *a perfect dithyramb of dispair.*

MRS. UNDERWOOD. Oh, please, Carinthia. . . . No . . . don't start again. Such a scandal! I wonder everything's not broken. [*So coaxingly to* REGINALD.] Shall I say it for him?

MRS. REGINALD [*fat little bantam, as she smooths her feathers in the armchair*]. You make him say it, Reggie.

> *But now the servants are on poor* MRS. UNDERWOOD's *brain. Almost down to her knees she goes.*

MRS. UNDERWOOD. They'll be coming up to see what the noise is. Oh . . . Simon!

> *It does strike* THE VICAR *that this would occasion considerable scandal in the parish. There are so few good excuses for being found lying on the carpet, your nephew kneeling threateningly on the top of you. So he makes up his mind to it and enunciates with musical charm; it might be a benediction. . . .*

THE VICAR. I have had enough.

REGINALD [*in some relief*]. That's all right.

> *He rises from the prostrate church militant; he even helps it rise. This pleasant family party then look at each other, and, truth to tell, they are all a little ashamed.*

MRS. UNDERWOOD [*walking round the re-erected pillar of righteous-ness*]. Oh, how dusty you are!

MISS UNDERWOOD. Yes! [*The normal self uprising.*] Room's not been swept this morning.

THE VICAR, *dusted, feels that a reign of moral law can now be resumed. He draws himself up to fully five foot six.*

THE VICAR. Now, sir, you will please apologize.

REGINALD [*looking very muscular*]. I shall not.

THE VICAR *drops the subject.* MRS. REGINALD *mutters and crows from the armchair.*

MRS. REGINALD. Ha . . . who began it? Black and blue I am! Miss Underwood can apologize . . . your precious sister can apologize.

MISS UNDERWOOD [*crushing if inconsequent*]. You're running to fat, Gladys. Where's my embroidery?

MRS. UNDERWOOD. I put it safe, Carinthia. [*She discloses it and then begins to pat and smooth the dishevelled room.*] Among relations too! One expects to quarrel sometimes . . . it can't be helped. But not fighting! Oh, I never did . . . I feel so ashamed!

MISS UNDERWOOD [*Britannia-like*]. Nonsense, Mary.

MRS. REGINALD. Nobody touched you, Aunt Mary.

THE VICAR [*after his eyes have wandered vaguely round*]. Where's your father, Reginald?

REGINALD [*quite uninterested. He is straightening his own tie and collar*]. I don't know.

In the little silence that follows there comes a voice from under the mahogany monument. It is a voice at once dignified and pained, and the property of REGINALD's *father, whose name is* MORTIMER UGLOW. *And it says* . . .

THE VOICE. I am here.

MRS. UNDERWOOD [*who may be forgiven nerves*]. Oh, how uncanny!

REGINALD [*still at his tie*]. Well, you can come out, father, it's quite safe.

THE VOICE [*most unexpectedly*]. I shall not. [*And then more unexpectedly still.*] You can all leave the room.

THE VICAR [*who is generally resentful*]. Leave the room! Whose room is it, mine or yours? Come out, Mortimer, and don't be a fool.

But there is only silence. Why will not MR. UGLOW *come out? Must he be ratted for? Then* MRS. UNDERWOOD *sees why. She points to an object on the floor.*

MRS. UNDERWOOD. Simon!

THE VICAR. What is it?

Again, and this time as if to indicate some mystery, MRS. UNDERWOOD *points.* THE VICAR *picks up the object, some disjection of the fight he thinks, and waves it mildly.*

THE VICAR. Well, where does it go? I wonder everything in the room's not been upset!

MRS. UNDERWOOD. No, Simon, it's not a mat, it's his . . .

She concludes with an undeniable gesture, even a smile. THE VICAR, *sniffing a little, hands over the trophy.*

REGINALD [*as he views it*]. Oh, of course.

MRS. REGINALD. Reggie, am I tidy at the back?

He tidies her at the back; a meticulous matter of hooks and eyes and, oh, his fingers are so big. MRS. UNDERWOOD *has taken a little hand-painted mirror from the mantelpiece, and this and the thing in question she places just without the screen of the falling tablecloth much as a devotee might place an offering at a shrine. But in* MISS UNDERWOOD *dwells no respect for persons.*

MISS UNDERWOOD. Now, sir, for Heaven's sake put on your wig and come out.

There emerges a hand that trembles with wrath; it retrieves the offerings; there follow bumpings into the tablecloth as of a head and elbows.

THE VICAR. I must go and brush myself.

MRS. UNDERWOOD. Simon, d'you think you could tell the maids that something fell over . . . they are such tattlers. It wouldn't be untrue. [*It wouldn't!*]

THE VICAR. I should scorn to do so, Mary. If they ask me, I must make the best explanation I can.

THE VICAR swims out. MR. MORTIMER UGLOW, *his wig assumed and hardly awry at all, emerges from beneath the table. He is a vindictive-looking little man.*

MRS. UNDERWOOD. You're not hurt, Mortimer, are you?

MR. UGLOW's only wound is in the dignity. That he cures by taking the situation oratorically in hand.

MR. UGLOW. If we are to continue this family discussion and if Miss Underwood, whom it does not in the least concern, has not the decency to leave the room and if you, Mary, cannot request your sister-in-law to leave it, I must at least demand that she does not speak to me again.

Whoever else might be impressed, MISS UNDERWOOD *is not. She does not even glance up from her embroidery.*

MISS UNDERWOOD. A good thing for you I hadn't my thimble
on when I did it.

MRS. UNDERWOOD. Carinthia, I don't think you should have
boxed Mortimer's ears . . . you know him so slightly.

MISS UNDERWOOD. He called me a Futile Female. I considered
it a suitable reply.

The echo of that epigram brings compensation to MR. UGLOW.
He puffs his chest.

MR. UGLOW. Your wife rallied to me, Reginald. I am much
obliged to her . . . which is more than can be said of you.

REGINALD. Well, you can't hit a woman.

MR. UGLOW [*bitingly*]. And she knows it.

MISS UNDERWOOD. Pf!

*The sound conveys that she would tackle a regiment of men with
her umbrella: and she would.*

REGINALD [*apoplectic, but he has worked down to the waist*]. There's
a hook gone.

MRS. REGINALD. I thought so! Lace torn?

REGINALD. It doesn't show much. But I tackled Uncle Simon
the minute he touched Gladys . . . that got my blood up all right.
Don't you worry. We won.

This callously sporting summary is too much for MRS. UNDER-
WOOD: *she dissolves!*

MRS. UNDERWOOD. Oh, that such a thing should ever have
happened in our house! . . . in my drawing-room!! . . . real
blows!!! . . .

MRS. REGINALD. Don't cry, Aunt Mary . . . it wasn't your fault.

THE VICAR *returns, his hair and his countenance smoother. He
adds his patting consolations to his poor wife's comfort.*

MRS. UNDERWOOD. And I was kicked on the shin.

MRS. REGINALD. Say you're sorry, Reggie.

THE VICAR. My dear Mary . . . don't cry.

MRS. UNDERWOOD [*clasping her beloved's arm*]. Simon did it . . .
Reggie was throttling him black . . . he couldn't help it.

THE VICAR. I suggest that we show a more or less Christian
spirit in letting bygones be bygones and endeavour to resume the
discussion at the point where it ceased to be an amicable one.
[*His wife, her clasp on his coat, through her drying tears has found more
trouble.*] Yes, there is a slight rent . . . never mind.

*The family party now settles itself into what may have been more
or less the situations from which they were roused to physical combat.*
MR. UGLOW *secures a central place. There is silence for a moment.*

MR. UGLOW. My sister-in-law Jane had no right to bequeath the vase . . . it was not hers to bequeath.

> *That is the gage of battle. A legacy! What English family has not at some time shattered its mutual regard upon this siren rock? One notices now that these good people are all in deep mourning, on which the dust of combat shows up the more distinctly, as it should.*

MRS. UNDERWOOD. Oh, Mortimer, think if you'd been able to come to the funeral and this had all happened then . . . it might have done!

MISS UNDERWOOD. But it didn't, Mary . . . control yourself.

MR. UGLOW. My brother George wrote to me on his death-bed . . . [*And then fiercely to* THE VICAR, *as if this concerned his calling.*] . . . on his death-bed, sir. I have the letter here. . . .

THE VICAR. Yes, we've heard it.

REGINALD. And you sent them a copy.

> MR. UGLOW's *hand always seems to tremble; this time it is with excitement as he has pulled the letter from his pocket-book.*

MR. UGLOW. Quiet, Reginald! Hear it again and pay attention. [*They settle to a strained boredom.*] "The Rococo Vase presented to me by the Emperor of Germany". . . Now there he's wrong. [*The sound of his own reading has uplifted him*: *he condescends to them.*] They're German Emperors, not Emperors of Germany. But George was an inaccurate fellow. Reggie has the same trick . . . it's in the family. I haven't it.

> *He is returning to the letter. But* THE VICAR *interposes, lamblike, ominous though.*

THE VICAR. I have not suggested on Mary's behalf . . . I wish you would remember, Mortimer, that the position I take up in this matter I take up purely on my wife's behalf. What have I to gain?

REGINALD [*clodhopping*]. Well, you're her husband, aren't you? She'll leave things to you. And she's older than you are.

THE VICAR. Reginald, you are most indelicate. [*And then, really thinking it is true* . . .] I have forborne to demand an apology from you. . . .

REGINALD. Because you wouldn't get it.

MRS. UNDERWOOD [*genuinely and generously accommodating*]. Oh, I don't want the vase . . . I don't want anything!

THE VICAR [*he is gradually mounting the pulpit*]. Don't think of the vase, Mary. Think of the principle involved.

MRS. UNDERWOOD. And you may die first, Simon. You're not

strong, though you look it . . . all the colds you get . . . and
nothing's ever the matter with me.

MR. UGLOW [*ignored . . . ignored!*]. Mary, how much longer am
I to wait to read this letter?

THE VICAR [*ominously, ironically lamblike now*]. Quite so. Your
brother is waiting patiently . . . and politely. Come, come; a
Christian and a businesslike spirit!

> MR. UGLOW's *breath has been taken to resume the reading of the
> letter when on him . . . worse, on that tender top-knot of his . . .
> he finds* MISS UNDERWOOD's *hawklike eye. Its look passes through
> him, piercing Infinity as she says . . .*

MISS UNDERWOOD. Why not a skull-cap . . . a sanitary skull-cap?

MR. UGLOW [*with a minatory though fearful gasp*]. What's that?

THE VICAR. Nothing, Mortimer.

REGINALD. Some people look for trouble!

MISS UNDERWOOD [*addressing the Infinite still*]. And those that it
fits can wear it.

THE VICAR [*a little fearful himself. He is terrified of his sister, that's
the truth; and well he may be*]. Let's have the letter, Mortimer.

MISS UNDERWOOD. Or at least a little gum . . . a little glue . . .
a little stickphast for decency's sake.

> *She swings it to a beautiful rhythm. No, on the whole* MR.
> UGLOW *will not join issue.*

MR. UGLOW. I trust that my dignity requires no vindication.
Never mind . . . I say nothing. [*And with a forgiving air he returns
at last to the letter.*] "The Rococo Vase presented to me by the
Emperor of Germany". . . or German Emperor.

THE VICAR. Agreed. Don't cry, Mary. Well, here's a clean one.
[*Benevolently he hands her a handkerchief.*]

MR. UGLOW. "On the occasion of my accompanying the
mission."

MISS UNDERWOOD. Mission!

> *The word has touched a spot.*

THE VICAR. Not a r e a l mission, Carinthia.

MR. UGLOW. A perfectly real mission. A mission from the
Chamber of Commerce at . . . Don't go on as if the world were
made up of low-church parsons and . . . and . . . their sisters!

> *As a convinced secularist behold him a perfect fighting cock.*

REGINALD [*bored; oh, so bored!*]. Do get ahead, father.

MR. UGLOW [*with a flourish*]. "Mission et cetera." Here we are.
"My dear wife must have the enjoyment". . . [*Again he condescends to them.*] Why he called her his dear wife I don't know. They

13

hated each other like poison. But that was George all over . . . soft . . . never would face the truth. It's a family trait. You show signs of it, Mary.

THE VICAR [*soft and low*]. He was on his death-bed.

REGINALD. Get on . . . father.

MR. UGLOW. "My wife". . . She wasn't his dear wife. What's the good of pretending it? . . . "must have the enjoyment of it while she lives. At her death I desire it to be an heirloom for the family." [*And he makes the last sentence tell, every word.*] There you are!

THE VICAR [*lamblike ominous, ironic, persistent*]. You sit looking at Mary. His sister and yours. Is she a member of the family or not?

MR. UGLOW [*cocksure*]. Boys before girls . . . men before women. Don't argue that . . . it's the law. Titles and heirlooms . . . all the same thing.

MRS. UNDERWOOD [*worm-womanlike, turning ever so little*]. Mortimer, it isn't as if we weren't giving you all the family things . . . the miniature and the bust of John Bright and grandmother's china and the big Shakespeare.

MR. UGLOW. Giving them, Mary, giving them?

THE VICAR. Surrendering them willingly, Mortimer.They have ornamented our house for years.

MRS. REGINALD. It isn't as if you hadn't done pretty well out of Aunt Jane while she was alive!

THE VICAR. Oh, delicacy, Gladys! And some regard for the truth!

MRS. REGINALD [*no nonsense about her*]. No, if we're talking business let's talk business. Her fifty pounds a year more than paid you for keeping her, didn't it? Did it or didn't it?

REGINALD [*gloomily*]. She never eat anything that I could see.

THE VICAR. She had a delicate appetite. It needed teasing . . . I mean coaxing. Oh, dear, this is most unpleasant!

REGINALD. Fifty pound a year is nearly a pound a week, you know.

THE VICAR. What about her clothes . . . what about her little holidays . . . what about the doctor . . . what about her temper to the last? [*He summons the classics to clear this sordid air.*] Oh . . . "De mortuis nil nisi bonum."

MRS. UNDERWOOD. She was a great trouble with her meals, Reginald.

MR. UGLOW [*letting rip*]. She was a horrible woman. I disliked

her more than any woman I've ever met. She brought George
to bankruptcy. When he was trying to arrange with his creditors
and she came into the room, her face would sour them . . . I tell
you, sour them.

MRS. REGINALD [*she sums it up*]. Well, Uncle Simon's a clergyman and can put up with unpleasant people. It suited them well
enough to have her. You had the room, Aunt Mary, you can't
deny that. And anyway she's dead now . . . poor Aunt Jane!
[*She throws this conventional verbal bone to Cerberus.*] And what with
the things she has left you . . .! What's to be done with her
clothes?

> GLADYS *and* MRS. UNDERWOOD *suddenly face each other like
> two ladylike ghouls.*

MRS. UNDERWOOD. Well, you remember the mauve silk . . .

THE VICAR. Mary, pray allow me. [*Somehow his delicacy is
shocked.*] The Poor.

MRS. REGINALD [*in violent protest*]. Not the mauve silk! Nor her
black lace shawl!

MISS UNDERWOOD [*shooting it out*]. They will make soup.

> *It makes* MR. UGLOW *jump, physically and mentally too.*

MR. UGLOW. What!

MISS UNDERWOOD. The proceeds of their sale will make much
needed soup . . . and blankets. [*Again her gaze transfixes that wig
and she addresses Eternity.*] No brain under it! . . . No wonder it's
loose! No brain.

> MR. UGLOW *just manages to ignore this.*

REGINALD. Where is the beastly vase? I don't know that I
want to inherit it.

MR. UGLOW. Yes, may I ask for the second or third time
to-day? . . .

MISS UNDERWOOD. The third.

MR. UGLOW [*he screws a baleful glance at her*]. May I ask for the
second or third time . . .

REGINALD. It is the third time, father.

MR. UGLOW [*his own son, too!*]. Reginald, you have no tact.
May I ask why the vase is not to be seen?

MISS UNDERWOOD [*sharply*]. It's put away.

MRS. REGINALD [*as sharp as she. Never any nonsense about* GLADYS].
Why?

MR. UGLOW. Gladys . . . ignore that, please. Mary?

MRS. UNDERWOOD. Yes, Mortimer.

MR. UGLOW. It has been chipped.

THE VICAR. It has not been chipped.

MR. UGLOW. If it has been chipped . . .

THE VICAR. I say it has not been chipped.

MR. UGLOW. If it had been chipped, sir . . . I should have held you responsible! Produce it.

He is indeed very much of a man. A little more and he'll slap his chest. But THE VICAR, *lamblike, etc. . . . we can now add dangerous. . . .*

THE VICAR. Oh, no, we must not be ordered to produce it.

MR. UGLOW [*trumpet-toned*]. Produce it, Simon.

THE VICAR. Neither must we be shouted at.

MISS UNDERWOOD . . . or bawled at. Bald at! Ha, ha!

And she taps her grey-haired parting with a thimbled finger to emphasize the pun. MR. UGLOW *rises, too intent on his next impressive stroke even to notice it, or seem to.*

MR. UGLOW. Simon, if you do not instantly produce the vase I shall refuse to treat this any longer in a friendly way. I shall place the matter in the hands of my solicitors.

This, in any family—is it not the final threat? MRS. UNDERWOOD *is genuinely shocked.*

MRS. UNDERWOOD. Oh, Simon!

THE VICAR. As a matter of principle, Mary. . . .

REGINALD [*impartially*]. What rot!

MRS. UNDERWOOD. It was put away, I think, so that the sight of it might not rouse discussion . . . wasn't it, Simon?

REGINALD. Well, we've had the discussion. Now get it out.

THE VICAR [*lamblike . . . etc.; add obstinate now*]. It is my principle not to submit to dictation. If I were asked politely to produce it. . . .

REGINALD. Ask him politely, father.

MR. UGLOW [*why shouldn't he have principles, too?*]. I don't think I can. To ask politely might be an admission of some right of his to detain the property. This matter will go further. I shall commit myself in nothing without legal advice.

MRS. REGINALD. You get it out, Aunt Mary.

MRS. UNDERWOOD [*almost thankful to be helpless in the matter*]. I can't. I don't know where it is.

MR. UGLOW [*all the instinct for law in him blazing*]. You don't . . .! This is important. He has no right to keep it from you, Mary. I venture to think. . . .

THE VICAR. Husband and wife are one, Mortimer.

MR. UGLOW. Not in law. Don't you cram your religion down

my throat. Not in law any longer. We've improved all that. The Married Woman's Property Act! I venture to think. . . .

> MISS UNDERWOOD *has disappeared. Her comment is to slam the door.*

MRS. UNDERWOOD. I think perhaps Carinthia has gone for it, Mortimer.

MR. UGLOW [*the case given him, he asks for costs, as it were*]. Then I object. . . . I object most strongly to this woman knowing the whereabouts of a vase which you, Mary . . .

THE VICAR [*a little of the mere layman peeping now*]. Mortimer, do not refer to my sister as "this woman."

MR. UGLOW. Then treat m y sister with the respect that is due to her, Simon.

> *They are face to face.*

THE VICAR. I hope I do, Mortimer.

MR. UGLOW. And will you request Miss Underwood not to return to this room with or without the vase?

THE VICAR. Why should I?

MR. UGLOW. What has she to do with a family matter of mine? I make no comment, Mary, upon the way you allow yourself to be ousted from authority in your own house. It is not my place to comment upon it, and I make none. I make no reference to the insults . . . the unwomanly insults that have been hurled at me by this Futile Female . . .

REGINALD [*a remembered schoolmaster joke. He feels not unlike one as he watches his two elders squared to each other*]. "Apt alliteration's artful aid". . . what?

MR. UGLOW. Don't interrupt.

MRS. REGINALD. You're getting excited again, father.

MR. UGLOW. I am not.

MRS. REGINALD. Father!

> *There is one sure way to touch* MR. UGLOW. *She takes it. She points to his wig.*

MR. UGLOW. What? Well . . . where's a glass . . . where's a glass?

> *He goes to the mantelpiece mirror. His sister follows him.*

MRS. UNDERWOOD. We talked it over this morning, Mortimer, and we agreed that I am of a yielding disposition and I said I should feel much safer if I did not even know where it was while you were in the house.

MR. UGLOW [*with very appropriate bitterness*]. And I your loving brother!

THE VICAR [*not to be outdone by* REGINALD *in quotations*]. "A little more than kin and less than kind."

MR. UGLOW [*his wig is straight*]. How dare you, Simon? A little more than ten minutes ago and I was struck . . . here in your house. How dare you quote poetry at me?

THE VICAR *feels he must pronounce on this.*

THE VICAR. I regret that Carinthia has a masterful nature. She is apt to take the law into her own hands. And I fear there is something about you, Mortimer, that invites violence. I can usually tell when she is going to be unruly; there's a peculiar twitching of her hands. If you had not been aggravating us all with your so-called arguments, I should have noticed it in time and . . . taken steps.

MRS. UNDERWOOD. We're really very sorry, Mortimer. We can always . . . take steps. But . . . dear me! . . . I was never so surprised in my life. You all seemed to go mad at once. It makes me hot now to think of it.

The truth about CARINTHIA *is that she is sometimes thought to be a little off her head. It's a form of genius.*

THE VICAR. I shall have a headache to-morrow. . . my sermon day.

MR. UGLOW *now begins to glow with a sense of coming victory. And he's not bad-natured, give him what he wants.*

MR. UGLOW. Oh, no, you won't. More frightened than hurt! These things happen . . . the normal gross-feeding man sees red, you know, sees red. Reggie as a small boy . . . quite uncontrollable!

REGINALD. Well, I like that! You howled out for help.

THE VICAR [*lamblike and only lamblike*]. I am willing to obliterate the memory.

MRS. REGINALD. I'm sure I'm black and blue . . . and more torn than I can see.

MR. UGLOW. But what can you do when a woman forgets herself? I simply stepped aside . . . I happen to value my dignity.

The door opens. MISS UNDERWOOD *with the vase. She deposits it on the mahogany table. It is two feet in height. It is lavishly blotched with gold and white and red. It has curves and crinkles. Its handles are bossy. My God, it is a vase!!!*

MISS UNDERWOOD. There it is.

MR. UGLOW [*with a victor's dignity*]. Thank you, Miss Underwood. [*He puts up gold-rimmed glasses*]. Ah . . . pure Rococo!

REGINALD. The Vi-Cocoa vase!

MR. UGLOW. That's not funny, Reginald.

REGINALD. Well . . . I think it is.

The trophy before him, MR. UGLOW *mellows.*

MR. UGLOW. Mary, you've often heard George tell us. The Emperor welcoming 'em . . . fine old fellow . . . speech in German . . . none of them understood it. Then at the end . . . "Gentlemen, I raise my glass. Hock . . . hock . . . hock!"

REGINALD [*who knows a German accent when he hears it*]. A little more spit in it.

MR. UGLOW. Reginald, you're very vulgar.

REGINALD. Is that Potsdam?

The monstrosity has coloured views on it, one back, one front.

MR. UGLOW. Yes . . . home of Friedrich der Grosse! [*he calls it grocer*]. A great nation. We can learn a lot from 'em!

This was before the war. What he says of them now is unprintable.

REGINALD. Yes. I suppose it's a jolly handsome piece of goods. Cost a lot.

MR. UGLOW. Royal factory . . . built to imitate Sèvres!

Apparently he would contemplate it for hours. But THE VICAR, *lamblike, etc. . . . . Add insinuating now.*

THE VICAR. Well, Mortimer, here is the vase. Now where are we?

MRS. REGINALD [*really protesting for the first time*]. Oh . . . are we going to begin all over again? Why don't you sell it and share up?

MRS. UNDERWOOD. Gladys, I don't think that would be quite nice.

MRS. REGINALD. I can't see why not.

MR. UGLOW. Sell an heirloom! . . . it can't be done.

REGINALD. Oh, yes, it can. You and I together . . . cut off the entail . . . that's what it's called. It'd fetch twenty pounds at Christie's.

MR. UGLOW [*the sight of it has exalted him beyond reason*]. More . . . more! First-class Rococo. I shouldn't dream of it.

MISS UNDERWOOD *has resumed her embroidery. She pulls a determined needle as she says . . .*

MISS UNDERWOOD. I think Mary would have a share in the proceeds, wouldn't she?

MR. UGLOW. I think not.

THE VICAR. Why not, Mortimer?

MR. UGLOW [*with fine detachment*]. Well, it's a point of law. I'm not quite sure . . . but let's consider it in equity [*not that he knows what on earth he means!*]. If I died . . . and Reginald died childless and Mary survived us . . . and it came to her? Then there would be our cousins the Bamfords as next inheritors. Could she by arrangement with them sell and . . .?

MRS. UNDERWOOD. I shouldn't like to sell it. It would seem like a slight on George . . . because he went bankrupt perhaps. And Jane always had it in her bedroom.

MISS UNDERWOOD [*thimbling the determined needle through*]. Most unsuitable for a bedroom.

MRS. UNDERWOOD [*anxious to please*]. Didn't you suggest, Simon, that I might undertake not to leave it out of the family?

THE VICAR [*covering a weak spot*]. In private conversation with you, Mary. . . .

MR. UGLOW [*most high and mighty, oh most!*]. I don't accept the suggestion. I don't accept it at all.

THE VICAR [*and now taking the legal line in his turn*]. Let me point out to you, Mortimer, that there is nothing to prevent Mary's selling the vase for her own exclusive benefit.

MR. UGLOW [*his guard down*]. Simon!

THE VICAR [*satisfied to have touched him*]. Once again, I merely insist upon a point of principle.

MR. UGLOW [*but now flourishing a verbal sword*]. And I insist . . . let everybody understand it . . . I insist that all thought of selling an heirloom is given up! Reginald . . . Gladys, you are letting me be exceedingly upset.

REGINALD. Well . . . shall I walk off with it? They couldn't stop me.

> *He lifts it up; and this simplest of solutions strikes them all stupent; except* MISS UNDERWOOD, *who glances under her bushy eyebrows.*

MISS UNDERWOOD. You'll drop it if you're not careful.

MRS. UNDERWOOD. Oh, Reggie, you couldn't carry that to the station . . . everyone would stare at you.

THE VICAR. I hope you would not be guilty of such an un-principled act.

MRS. REGINALD. I won't have it at home, Reg, so I tell you. One of the servants'd be sure to . . .! [*She sighs desperately.*] Why not sell the thing?

MR. UGLOW. Gladys, be silent.

REGINALD [*as he puts the vase down, a little nearer the edge of the table*]. It is a weight.

> *So they have argued high and argued low and also argued round about it; they have argued in a full circle. And now there is a deadly calm.* MR. UGLOW *breaks it; his voice trembles a little, as does his hand with its signet ring rattling on the table.*

MR. UGLOW. Then we are just where we started half an hour ago . . . are we, Simon?

THE VICAR [*lamblike in excelsis*]. Precisely, Mortimer.

MR. UGLOW. I'm sorry. I'm very sorry. [*He gazes at them with cool ferocity.*] Now let us all keep our tempers.

THE VICAR. I hope I shall have no occasion to lose mine.

MR. UGLOW. Nor I mine.

He seems not to move a muscle, but in some mysterious way his wig shifts: a sure sign.

MRS. UNDERWOOD. Oh, Mortimer, you're going to get excited.

MR. UGLOW. I think not, Mary. I trust not.

REGINALD [*proffering real temptation*]. Father . . . come away and write a letter about it.

MR. UGLOW [*as his wrath swells*]. If I write a letter . . . if my solicitors have to write a letter . . . there are people here who will regret this day.

MRS. UNDERWOOD [*trembling at the coming storm*]. Simon, I'd much sooner he took it . . . I'd much rather he took everything Jane left me.

MR. UGLOW. Jane did not leave it to you, Mary.

MRS. UNDERWOOD. Oh, Mortimer, she did t r y to leave it to me.

MR. UGLOW [*running up the scale of indignation*]. She may have tried . . . but she did not succeed . . . because she could not . . . because she had no right to do so. [*And reaching the summit.*] I am not in the least excited.

Suddenly MISS UNDERWOOD *takes a shrewd hand in the game.*

MISS UNDERWOOD. Have you been to your lawyer?

MR. UGLOW [*swivelling round*]. What's that?

MRS. REGINALD. Have you asked your lawyer?

He has not.

MR. UGLOW. Gladys, I will not answer her. I refuse to answer the . . . the . . . the female. [*But he has funked the "futile".*]

MRS. REGINALD [*soothing him*]. All right, father.

MISS UNDERWOOD. He hasn't because he knows what his lawyer would say. Rot's what his lawyer would say!

MR. UGLOW [*calling on the gods to protect this woman from him*]. Heaven knows I wish to discuss this calmly!

REGINALD. Aunt Mary, might I smoke?

MISS UNDERWOOD. Not in the drawing-room.

MRS. UNDERWOOD. No . . . not in the drawing-room, please, Reginald.

MR. UGLOW. You're not to go away, Reginald.

REGINALD. Oh, well . . . hurry up.

MR. UGLOW *looks at* THE VICAR. THE VICAR *is actually*

smiling. Can this mean defeat for the house of Uglow? Never.

MR. UGLOW. Do I understand that on your wife's behalf you entirely refuse to own the validity of my brother George's letter ... where is it? ... I read you the passage written on his death-bed.

THE VICAR [*measured and comforted. Victory gleams for him now*]. Why did he not mention the vase in his will?

MR. UGLOW. There were a great many things he did not mention in his will.

THE VICAR. Was his widow aware of the letter?

MR. UGLOW. You know she was.

THE VICAR. Why did she not carry out what you think to have been her husband's intention?

MR. UGLOW. Because she was a beast of a woman.

MR. UGLOW *is getting the worst of it; his temper is slipping.*

MRS. UNDERWOOD. Mortimer, what language about the newly dead!

THE VICAR. An heirloom in the family?

MR. UGLOW. Quite so.

THE VICAR. On what grounds do you maintain that George's intentions are not carried out when it is left to my wife?

And indeed MR. UGLOW *is "against the ropes," so to speak.*

MISS UNDERWOOD. The man hasn't a wig to stand on... I mean a leg.

MR. UGLOW [*pale with fury, hoarse with it, even pathetic in it*]. Don't you speak to me ... I request you not to speak to me.

REGINALD *and* GLADYS *quite seriously think this is bad for him.*

REGINALD. Look here, father, Aunt Mary will undertake not to let it go out of the family. Leave it at that.

MRS. REGINALD. We don't want the thing, father ... the drawing-room's full already.

MR. UGLOW [*the pathos in him growing; he might flood the best Brussels with tears at any moment*]. It's not the vase. It's no longer the vase. It's the principle.

MRS. UNDERWOOD. Oh, don't, Mortimer ... don't be like Simon. That's why I mustn't give in. It'll make it much more difficult if you start thinking of it like that.

MISS UNDERWOOD [*pulling and pushing that embroidery needle more grimly than ever*]. It's a principle in our family not to be bullied.

MRS. REGINALD [*in almost a vulgar tone, really*]. If she'd go and mind her own family's business!

THE VICAR *knows that he has his* UGLOWS *on the run. Suavely he presses the advantage.*

THE VICAR. I am sorry to repeat myself, Mortimer, but the vase was left to Jane absolutely. It has been specifically left to Mary. She is under no obligation to keep it in the family.

MR. UGLOW [*control breaking*]. You'll get it, will you . . . you and your precious female sister?

THE VICAR [*quieter and quieter; that superior quietude*]. Oh, this is so unpleasant.

MR. UGLOW [*control broken*]. Never! Never!! . . . not if I beggar myself in law-suits.

MISS UNDERWOOD [*a sudden and vicious jab*]. Who wants the hideous thing?

MR. UGLOW [*broken all of him . . . in sheer hysterics . . . tears starting from his eyes*]. Hideous! You hear her? They'd sell it for what it would fetch. My brother George's Rococo vase! An objet d'art et vertu . . . an heirloom . . . a family record of public service! Have you no feelings, Mary?

MRS. UNDERWOOD [*dissolved*]. Oh, I'm very unhappy.

Again are MR. UGLOW *and* THE VICAR *breast to breast.*

THE VICAR. Don't make your sister cry, sir.

MR. UGLOW. Make your sister hold her tongue, sir. She has no right in this discussion at all. Am I to be provoked and badgered by a Futile Female?

THE VICAR *and* MR. UGLOW *are intent on each other, the others are intent on them. No one notices that* MISS UNDERWOOD's *embroidery is very decidedly laid down and that her fingers begin to twitch.*

THE VICAR. How dare you suppose, Mortimer, that Mary and I would not respect the wishes of the dead?

MR. UGLOW. It's nothing to do with you, either.

MISS UNDERWOOD *has risen from her chair. This* GLADYS *does notice.*

MRS. REGINALD. I say . . . Uncle Simon.

THE VICAR. What is it?

REGINALD. Look here, Uncle Simon, let Aunt Mary write a letter undertaking . . . there's no need for all this row. . . .

MRS. UNDERWOOD. I will! I'll undertake anything!

THE VICAR [*the Church on its militant dignity now*]. Keep calm, Mary. I am being much provoked, too. Keep calm.

MR. UGLOW [*stamping it out*]. He won't let her . . . he and his sister . . . he won't give way in anything. Why should I be reasonable?

REGINALD. If she will undertake it, will you . . .?

MRS. REGINALD. Oh, Aunt Mary, stop her!

In the precisest manner possible judging her distance with care, aiming well and true, MISS UNDERWOOD *has, for the second time to-day, soundly boxed* MR. UGLOW's *ear. He yells.*

MR. UGLOW. I say . . . I'm hurt.

REGINALD. Look here now . . . not again!

THE VICAR [*he gets flustered. No wonder*]. Carinthia! I should have taken steps! It is almost excusable.

MR. UGLOW. I'm seriously hurt.

MRS. REGINALD. You ought to be ashamed of yourself.

MISS UNDERWOOD. Did you feel the thimble?

MRS. UNDERWOOD. Oh, Carinthia, this is dreadful!

MR. UGLOW. I wish to preserve my dignity.

He backs out of her reach that he may the better do so.

MISS UNDERWOOD. You wig's crooked.

MRS. REGINALD [*rousing: though her well-pinched arms have lively recollections of half an hour ago*]. Don't you insult my father.

MISS UNDERWOOD. Shall I put it straight? It'll be off again.

She advances, her eyes gleaming. To do . . . Heaven knows what!

MR. UGLOW [*still backing*]. Go away.

REGINALD [*who really doesn't fancy tackling the lady either*]. Why don't you keep her in hand?

MR. UGLOW [*backed as far as he can, and in terror*]. Simon, you're a cad and your sister's a mad cad. Take her away.

But this THE VICAR *will not endure. He has been called a cad, and that no English gentleman will stand, and a clergyman is a gentleman, sir. In ringing tones and with his finest gesture you hear him. "Get out of my house!"* MR. UGLOW *doubtless could reply more fittingly were it not that* MISS UNDERWOOD *still approaches. He is feebly forcible merely. "Don't you order me about," he quavers. What is he but a fascinated rabbit before the terrible woman? The gentlemanly* VICAR *advances—"Get out before I put you out," he vociferates—Englishman to the backbone. But that is* REGINALD's *waited-for excuse. "Oh, no, you don't," he says and bears down on* THE VICAR. MRS. UNDERWOOD *yelps in soft but agonized apprehension: "Oh, Simon, be careful."* MR. UGLOW *has his hands up, not indeed in token of surrender—though surrender to the virago poised at him he would—but to shield his precious wig.*

"Mind my head, do," he yells; *he will have it that it is his head.* "Come away from my father," *calls out* MRS. REGINALD, *stoutly clasping* MISS UNDERWOOD *from behind round that iron-corseted waist.*

MISS UNDERWOOD *swivels round.* "*Don't you touch me, Miss,*" *she snaps.* But GLADYS *has weight and the two are toppling groundward while* REGINALD, *one hand on* THE VICAR, *one grabbing at* MISS UNDERWOOD, *to protect his wife* ["*Stop it, do!*" *he shouts*], *is outbalanced. And* THE VICAR *making still determinedly for* MR. UGLOW, *and* MR. UGLOW, *his wig securer, preparing to defy* THE VICAR, *the mêlée is joined once more. Only* MRS. UNDERWOOD *is so far safe.*

The fighters breathe hard and sway. They sway against the great mahogany table. The Rococo Vase totters; it falls; it is smashed to pieces. By a supreme effort the immediate authors of its destuction —linked together—contrive not to sit down among them. MRS. UNDERWOOD *is heard to breathe,* "*Oh . . . thank goodness!*"